BUILDING BETTER PARTNERSHIPS

The final Report of the
Commission on Public Private
Partnerships

30-32 Southampton St
London WC2E 7RA
Tel: 020 7470 6100
Fax: 020 7470 6111
postmaster@ippr.org.uk
www.ippr.org
Registered charity 800065

The Institute for Public Policy Research is an independent charity whose purpose is to contribute to public understanding of social, economic and political questions through research, discussion and publication. It was established in 1988 by leading figures in the academic, business and trade-union communities to provide an alternative to the free market think tanks.

IPPR's research agenda reflects the challenges facing Britain and Europe. Current programmes cover the areas of economic and industrial policy, Europe, governmental reform, human rights, defence, social policy, the environment and media issues.

Besides its programme of research and publication, IPPR also provides a forum for political and trade union leaders, academic experts and those from business, finance, government and the media, to meet and discuss issues of common concern.

Production & design by **EMPHASIS**
ISBN 1 86030 158 4
© IPPR 2001

Contents

List of tables, figures, case studies and appendices

Tables

Figures

Case studies

Appendices

Responses to the Report

This report has performed an important public service in taking us further than any effort yet in showing how to reduce the bone-headed ideology in public private partnerships and insert desperately needed practicality. Despite its progress, I would argue that we need to go much further if real accountability is to be achieved in PPPs and in ensuring they offer genuine value for money.

Will Hutton, Chief Executive, Industrial Society

This report is an important contribution to the difficult debate about public private partnerships. While the TUC would not agree with all its conclusions, I welcome its recognition that employees - particularly those taken on after transfer - have often lost out. In particular the news that such a broadly based team have been able to sign up to the need to give more protection to employees who lose out can only boost the campaign for a new fair wages resolution.

John Monks, General Secretary, TUC

The CBI welcomes this Report. Above all, it makes a strong case for diversity in how public services are provided. This is the only way to deliver the improvements in public services and infrastructure demanded by the public and the business community. The Report draws on the success of public private partnerships to date. And it balances encouragement with challenges for all those in the public, private and voluntary sectors working towards an extensive and diverse use of PPPs.

Digby Jones, Director General, CBI

The arguments of the IPPR's public private partnership commission are a breath of fresh air. By recognising it's the quality of outcomes that matters to public service users and divorcing that issue from the public v private sector debate, the IPPR's thinking could be the catalyst that allows public services to be truly customer-centred.

Anna Bradley, Director, National Consumer Council

Acknowledgements

A piece of work such as this draws on the input of numerous people and organisations. Without the generous financial support of KPMG, BT, The Serco Institute, Nomura and Norwich Union Public Private Partnership Fund, the work would literally never have got off the ground. Many of the detailed issues arising during the Commission's inquiry were examined by four Working Groups. These involved a number of experts who were not Commissioners, all of whom gave up a considerable amount of time to contribute to the discussions: our thanks go to Andrew Gamble, Tania Burchardt, Richard Nicholls, Shriti Vadera, John Hawksworth, Jeremy Colman, Dan Corry, Terry Powley, John Tizard, Peter Fanning, Alan Pike, Richard Footitt, Steve Jacobs and Andrea Westall. We have benefited hugely from these groups – the ideas that they generated and expertise that they supplied.

At the IPPR, we would like to thank Will Paxton and Richard Brooks for their excellent research assistance and Sue Regan for her encouragement and valuable comments on drafts. Many others have given support, expert advice and contributed to putting together events and publications. We would particularly like to thank: Joe Hallgarten, Tony Grayling, Liz Kendall, Laura Edwards, Robin Clarke, Lisa Harker, Helena Scott, Jess Tyrell, Esther McCarthy, Julie Foley and Sarah Spencer. We have also been greatly helped by a number of interns during the course of the project: thanks to Oliver Pearce, Christian Thams, Simon Bell, Nathan Yeowell and Helen Evans.

A number of other people have been particularly supportive of our work. Andrew Gamble read and commented on the whole draft report; Tania Burchardt was an invaluable source of information for the data in Chapter 3; Nick Sharman, Margie Jaffe, Ian Harden, Carey Oppenheim, Harry Bush, David Kent and Amanda McIntyre answered many queries, provided information or read draft Chapters.

We are also very grateful to all of the authors of the Commission's publications (listed at the back of this Report), all respondents who submitted written and oral evidence to the Commission (also listed), and to all those who spoke at our conferences and seminars. We are particularly grateful to UNISON for supporting a seminar on employee protection.

It should be pointed out that though we have benefited a great deal from the above people, the views expressed in this Report are solely those of the Commissioners.

The Commissioners and the Secretariat

Commissioners

Martin Taylor (Chair)
Chairman, WHSmith and International Advisor, Goldman Sachs

Kate Barker
Chief Economic Adviser, Confederation of British Industry (CBI)

Bill Callaghan
Chair, Health & Safety Commission

David Denison
Industry Consultant, ICL

Sarah Ebanja
Director, Local Govt and Europe Division, Government Office for London (seconded from London Borough of Hackney)

Ruth Kelly
MP for Bolton West

Julian Le Grand
Richard Titmuss Professor of Social Policy at the London School of Economics and the Centre for the Analysis of Social Exclusion

Chris Nicholson
Partner, KPMG

Claire Perry
Project Director, United Kingdom Central Council for Nursing, Midwifery and Health Visiting (UKCC)

Amanda Root
Senior Research Fellow, Local Government Centre, Warwick Business School

Victor Smart

Gerry Stoker
Professor of Politics, Manchester University and Chair, New Local Government Network

Matthew Taylor
Director, Institute for Public Policy Research

Lady Winifred Tumim OBE
Chair, National Council of Voluntary Organisations

The Secretariat

Gavin Kelly (Secretary)
Peter Robinson
Ella Joseph
Rachel Lissauer
Paul Thompson

Foreword

The IPPR's Commission on Public Private Partnerships began work in the autumn of 1999. At that time the subject of PPPs evoked little interest beyond two small groups, equally enthusiastic, of devotees and detractors, although it was widely accorded some kind of abstract importance by others interested in micro-economic policy.

Eighteen months later, with the temperature rising in the NHS, endless circling in the Air Traffic Control debate, and rumblings on the London Underground which grow at once louder and less coherent, the subject is at centre stage. Unfortunately, greater relevance has not been accompanied by greater clarity, since the debate is still dominated by prejudice supported by selective anecdote.

On one side are those who recognise no organisational form other than the limited company. For them it is self-evident that financial incentives alone can cut paths through the tangled jungles of the public sector. On the other side are those who believe that public ownership and management represent a civilised ideal which only falls short of perfection in practice through want of money. For them, a surgeon who makes a catastrophic blunder in an NHS hospital is constrained by shortage of funds; the same surgeon suffering the same misfortune in a private hospital is blinded by lust for profit. (We heard little of incompetence as a source of error, although in other areas of endeavour it appears to be widespread. On the public/private battleground, even mistakes are politically motivated.)

These are not caricatures, I'm afraid: the Commission heard much evidence of both kinds. But they help to explain why the publication of this Report may be timely. A group of people of widely differing political views have done their best to look at the subject dispassionately, to draw up a balance-sheet of experience to date and to make some recommendations. For some members of the Commission these do not go far enough. They would have liked to see a proposal, for example, for the transfer of a district general hospital to private management. Others are held back from such a step by the thinness of the evidence base for successful PPPs and by their concerns about the treatment of labour on transfer. Whilst not every Commissioner agrees with every recommendation in this Report all agree with the key arguments put forward, that the present dividing line between the private and public domains is essentially arbitrary, that diversity of provision should be encouraged, and that competition between rival providers should be fair and open.

It is not the purpose of an introduction such as this to summarise the contents of the Report. That leaves me free to indulge myself by giving some personal observations on the subject that has occupied a part of the Commissioners' lives over a fair period of time. I do not associate my colleagues with the views that follow, although none is far from the spirit of our Report.

- The rebuilding of Britain's public service infrastructure is one of the major tasks facing government in this country. Progress to date has been lamentable, because of a noxious blend of financial constraints, managerial weakness and organisational timidity.

- Financial constraint – for the moment at least – is no longer an excuse. But in the absence of organisational reform and managerial improvement, very large sums of money may be ineffectively spent.

- The private sector has been involved in this task as a means of diversifying sources of capital. This is curious, since the crucial ingredient that the private sector possesses and the public sector needs is management. Money is a secondary issue, and in any case (as Chapter 4 demonstrates) the Government keeps a liability for future payments in all arrangements short of full privatisation.

- Although full privatisations of genuine enterprises have frequently been successful, the creation and subsequent privatisation of pseudo-enterprises carved out from activities that essentially require subsidy does not work and transferring run-down assets from the public to the private sector is unlikely to produce good results.

- The distinguishing feature of the private sector is not profit but competition. It follows that arrangements with private firms that reduce the level of competition are unlikely to be fruitful from the public's point of view. It is the failure to address this point properly which allows the argument 'It is immoral to profit from...[here the reader may add any sensitive activity]' to retain its resonance in the public mind.

- I am sceptical of the doctrine of the public sector ethos, which attributes nobility of motives to those who work in the public sector and to them alone. But I do recognise two phenomena – a lack of rapaciousness in the public sector and an idealistic aspiration to high service standards that may be found within a wide range of organisations, public, private or voluntary. In any case, purity of motive does not compensate for inadequacy of outcome.

- That said, if the private sector is to play a greater role in public sector activities, it cannot do this on the basis of the very high returns earned on the highly leveraged structures erected by the venture capital industry. These may make sense in some project finance applications where there are high risks in the early stages; they cannot form the general model for outsourced public services. (But they do explain in part the private sector's fondness for structures involving finance – and of course Britain is a country where the only form of engineering that flourishes is financial.)

- Slogans are dangerous. PPPs live in the world of Liberté, Egalité, Fraternité – where the contradictions between the first and the second conspire to make the third unattainable. This can be the source of a lot of trouble. In the NHS, the slogan is free, universal and comprehensive, and 'comprehensiveness' has exploded in scope since the foundation of the service. Here the forces generated by the internal contradictions are resolved by waiting lists. Managing the waiting lists without admitting the contradictions is the purest form of treating the symptom not the cause – an unrespectable error in a medical organisation. It is clearly in the wider popular interest to use the capability (in the widest sense) of the private sector to reform and rebuild the NHS rather than to supplant and destroy it. Nevertheless, a short time ago, the Secretary of State for Health said he would be 'astonished' if the private sector played a larger part in the NHS. We should welcome the prospect that he looks set to be astonished, and soon.

I would like to thank most warmly my fellow commissioners, many of whom have given time well beyond what was asked or could reasonably have been expected of them. Finally, our debt to the staff of the IPPR – tireless, cheerful and immensely hard-working – is enormous. Deftly suspended between the private and public sectors, they cast discerning and affectionate eyes on both. Gavin Kelly has been a magnificent Secretary to the Commission, Matthew Taylor has found time amongst his other duties to be an excellent and committed Commissioner and Peter Robinson has acted as an unfailing source of advice. Paul Thompson, Rachel Lissauer and Ella Joseph have played roles in thinking, drafting and organising, not just of the report itself but of the many seminars and publications that have occurred along the way, in a manner both delightful and indispensable.

Martin Taylor
Chair, Commission on Public Private Partnerships

Executive summary

I: PRINCIPLES

Chapter 1: The new partnership agenda

This Report argues that getting public private partnerships (PPPs) right is vital if the quality of the UK's public services is to meet the expectations of the British public over the next decade. Delivering this will require significant changes in the direction of policy as many PPPs have performed poorly over recent years.

Our starting point is that this should be a golden age for the champions of public service. For the first time in several decades we have a Government that has asked to be judged by its ability to improve the quality of collectively funded services. This provides an opportunity that has to be seized. If in five years time, after a sustained period of increased funding, citizens feel that those services are still failing to deliver there could be a major political backlash. Those opposed to the principle of collective provision would find it easier to argue that public services are an anachronism; blunt, inefficient, restrictive of choice. If the case for universal public services cannot be won now it could soon be lost forever.

To date there have been few even-handed studies into the contribution that partnerships between public, private and voluntary sectors can make to our public services: prejudice and anecdote have tended to dominate analysis and evidence. We aim to cut through the arguments on the rights and wrongs of PPPs and set out a reform programme aimed at ensuring that in the future PPPs are used at the right times and to maximum effect.

Being open minded about the contribution that partnerships could make to public services means challenging two intransigent perspectives on public-private relations. On the one hand we totally reject the *privatisers'* vision of public services: their aim is always and everywhere to increase the role of the private sector in the provision *and* funding of public services. Their desired outcome is smaller government and residualised public services. On the other, we distance ourselves from a *public monopoly* perspective which holds that as a matter of principle public services should always and everywhere be provided by the public sector.

Both approaches view PPPs as a form of privatisation by stealth. We take a different view. For too long there has a been lack of *diversity* in the way in which public services are provided and projects are procured. Government has tended to rely on too limited a pool of service providers and too restrictive an approach towards undertaking large capital projects. This has resulted in public services missing out on the skills, creativity, and areas of expertise that reside in a wide range of private and voluntary organisations. This means less choice for public authorities, less innovation than may otherwise be the case, and less scope for learning within public service organisations.

The real challenge we face is to manage a diverse public service sector effectively so that it enhances social equity by improving the quality of, and commitment to, publicly funded services. Our approach can be summed up in four steps.

- *Reassert the case for publicly funded universal services.* The reason we are interested in PPPs is because we want to explore all possible avenues for increasing the quality and responsiveness of publicly funded services. Services that are universal and free at the point of use form a central part of our commitment to social justice, economic efficiency and democratic accountability.

- *Distinguish clearly between the funding and provision of public services.* It is helpful to distinguish between public authorities responsible for commissioning services and those organisations which deliver them. We need to examine where and when it makes sense to allow purchasers to work with providers who come from the private or voluntary sectors.

- *Be open minded about public authorities entering into partnerships.* Weak arguments are sometimes used for imposing blanket restrictions on the types of services that public authorities can deliver through partnership. These need to be reassessed. As the practice of partnership becomes more widespread we will see the emergence of a growing public service sector made up of a mixture of public, private and voluntary sector organisations. If this development is properly managed it should be seen as an opportunity not a threat.

- *Have clear criteria for assessing whether PPPs are the right approach.* Our first criterion is guaranteeing social equity and ensuring that public services respond to the needs of all citizens. The second is that partnerships offer value-for-money in the delivery of efficient, high quality and responsive services – if the quality of a service deteriorates then a partnership has failed. The third criterion is that clear forms of accountability and redress should apply across the public service sector. If PPPs do not meet these criteria they should not be adopted.

Chapter 2: Foundations for partnership

One of the reasons why debates on PPPs tend to generate more heat than light is because there is little agreement as to what constitutes a partnership or the types of problem that they might help solve. Public managers do not have a clear account of how partnerships can help to improve the quality of services. We argue that PPPs are a risk-sharing relationship based upon an agreed aspiration between the public and private (including voluntary) sectors to bring about a desired public policy outcome.

More often than not this takes the form of a long-term and flexible relationship, usually underpinned by contract, for the delivery of a publicly funded service. Greater freedom to enter into PPPs should run alongside the decentralisation of decision-making authority to public managers.

There are several rationales for considering the use of this type of arrangement:

- improving service quality through greater diversity and contestability

- focusing on outcomes

- getting more from public assets over their life cycle

- accessing private sector management skills and expertise

- engaging citizens and civic groups in the governance, and monitoring

Making a success of partnerships is difficult. We argue that if PPPs are to make a significant improvement to the quality of public services over the medium term then a number of conditions need to be in place:

- adequate funding for public services

- a consistent rationale for using PPPs

- a strong public sector partner

- responsible private and third-sector providers willing to embrace high standards of transparency and accountability

- legitimacy among the general public and the public services workforce. If partnerships are to endure, citizens and employees need to feel they have a stake in them

- an evidence-based approach to policy. A commitment is necessary to pilot, monitor, and systematically evaluate a spectrum of partnership arrangements. Depending on the evidence that emerges PPPs could be rolled out or rolled back.

II: ECONOMICS

Chapter 3: How significant are PPPs?

Keeping a sense of perspective on discussions of partnership requires an awareness of the significance of PPP arrangements within today's public services. The overall picture is one of the continuing dominance of services that are publicly funded and publicly provided. The Private Finance Initiative still plays a fairly modest role in relation to overall levels of investment, accounting for nine per cent of total publicly sponsored gross capital spending between 1997 and 2000. It is also important to distinguish between the types of role that government asks the private and voluntary sector to play. A spectrum of different approaches exist:

- *Public Sector Default.* The public sector provides all services.

- *Private Sector Rescue.* The public sector provides all services, except if public providers are seen as under-performing in which case the private sector acts as provider of last resort.

- *Level Playing Field.* There is equal treatment between different organisations seeking to deliver public services – the decision as to who provides the service is taken solely on a judgement of which provider will provide the best service.

- *Public Sector Rescue.* The private sector provides all services, except if private providers are seen as failing when the public sector would act as provider of last resort .

- *Private Sector Default.* The private sector provides all services on contract to public purchasers/commissioners.

In prisons there appears to be a 'private sector default' position in relation to the building and operation of new prisons. In social services there appears to be a 'level playing field' between different types of provider. In clinical health services there is almost a 'public sector default' position. It remains unclear why one approach applies in one sector but not in another.

Chapter 4: The lessons of the Private Finance Initiative

The economic arguments for PPP and in particular for PFI have been confused from the start. Two rationales have been offered: one serious, one spurious. The potentially serious argument is that in the right circumstances PPPs can offer significant value-for-money gains and generate improvements in service quality. At the moment the evidence on value-for-money is variable across sectors, PFI seems to be offering significant gains in roads and prisons but not in hospitals and schools. The spurious argument is that using private finance to pay for capital investment allows government to undertake more projects than would otherwise be the case. All PFI projects are publicly funded and incur future liabilities for the exchequer.

We see the lessons of PFI as follows:

- The framework for public finances should be revised so that privately financed public investment is taken into account in deciding the 'sustainability' of the public finances.

- Government departments should be set an overall capital spending budget that encompasses both traditionally financed public spending and the capital value of PFI spending.

- Public authorities need to have a clear policy planning framework which integrates all forms of investment and service provision.

- PFI projects should not go ahead because a public authority believes there is no alternative.

- The accounting treatment of a PPP/PFI project should be settled *after* a decision to go ahead on value-for-money grounds has been made.

- All PPP/PFI proposals need to be subjected to a sensitivity analysis to see whether different assumptions, for example, about different forms of risk allocation, would significantly alter the value-for-money assessment.

- Consideration should be given to reducing the discount rate used by the Treasury from six to five per cent.

- Government should experiment with a range of procurement models for capital projects. A new mono-culture of procurement based on the current PFI model should be avoided.

- All contracts should have explicit provisions for sharing super-profits arising from re-financing deals.

Chapter 5: PPPs and public enterprise

Over recent years the most contentious debates on PPPs have concerned government proposals for revenue-generating public enterprises such as London Underground and National Air Traffic Systems (NATS). The arguments over the use of the proposed PPP models resemble those for the use of the PFI approach in public services. The extra costs of private finance have to be outweighed by the benefits resulting from the skills and risk-transfer that comes from working in partnership with the private sector.

There are significant problems with the proposed PPPs for these two public enterprises, though some of the criticisms made of them are wide of the mark. The key issue in relation to London Underground is ensuring the integration of investment and maintenance with operations rather than whether or not bonds are used to finance investment. In relation to NATS, other more attractive structures were available but not considered.

In general there should be a wider diversity of models of public enterprise. In some instances there are arguments in favour of transferring the ownership of public enterprise to a not-for-profit trust, particularly where there is a natural monopoly and where safety is a key feature. Such a trust should still be able to raise private capital and contract for private management.

The financial framework for public enterprises also needs to be reformed to ensure that PPPs are used as a way of securing value-for-money rather than evading financial controls.

- Public enterprises that demonstrate they could fund investment through revenue streams should have direct access to capital markets outside normal Treasury financial controls.

- The option of some public enterprises 'opting out' of Treasury financial controls also needs to be considered. This would require an effective form of 'public sector bankruptcy' to be introduced so long as failing management teams could be replaced without threatening continuity of provision.

III: PRACTICE

Chapter 6: Where is partnership appropriate?

If partnership is to make a significant contribution to improving public services then new models of partnership need to be developed. Currently, PPPs often provide what are called 'ancillary' rather than 'core' elements of a service. Distinguishing between core and ancillary services is highly problematic: it can lead to fragmentation, awkward interfaces within an organisation, reduced innovation, and undermine those employees classified as 'ancillary'. In some instances the private sector is allowed to provide core services if, and only if, public sector agencies are found to have seriously under-performed. We argue that there needs to be a new approach to identifying the types of services that can be included within PPPs.

- Broad categorisations such as 'core' and 'ancillary' should not be used to distinguish between services which can and cannot be provided through partnerships.

- The private/voluntary sector should not be restricted to providing services only after a public sector agency is deemed to have 'failed'.

- Successful public authorities should not be excluded from helping improve (or takeover) a service from an under-performing public sector authority.

We also favour a flexible approach which allows individual public authorities to make a case-by-case assessment of the package of services that they want to incorporate within a PPP. In making these decisions the assumption should be that public purchasers will involve citizens and service users in the process of selecting providers. On this basis, public authorities should be entitled to enter into partnerships with public service providers (regardless of whether they come from the public, private or voluntary sector) who are best placed to deliver publicly agreed outcomes. The use of new forms of partnership needs to be carefully piloted and evaluated before they are used more widely.

Chapter 7: PPPs and key public services

There is scope for policy-makers to encourage greater diversity in provision across the health, education and local government sectors. In some areas, there are solid grounds for moving to a position where all purchasers select the most appropriate provider regardless of whether they are based in the public, private or voluntary sector. In other areas, such as clinical services in health, a more cautious approach is necessary as the arguments are less clear cut and the evidence is more contested. In all areas an evidence-based approach needs to be adopted. If evaluations show that PPPs are not performing satisfactorily, the policy must be revised accordingly.

Health

The relationship between private and public sectors in health has often been restrictive, relying on short-term contracting and the provision of buildings through the PFI. The challenge is to create genuine partnerships with opportunities for innovation.

- As Primary Care Groups/Trusts become more established and Care Trusts emerge, consideration needs to be given to the application of the Best Value regime to primary health and community services.

- Advice and expertise on procurement strategies should be contracted separately from the direct provision of the primary care infrastructure and primary care services.

- In relation to intermediate care a number of pilot sites should be used to establish long-term partnering arrangements between public, private and voluntary sectors.

- New medical units (for example Diagnostic and Treatment Centres) should be procured and operated using a range of partnering approaches – including PFI and non-PFI models. These partnerships should be designed to allow for a degree of contestability in the provision of core services.

- Restrictions on the inclusion of clinical and support-clinical services within PFI hospital projects should be removed. Purchasing authorities should consider whether the inclusion of these services would improve service quality and value-for-money. Such a move must not be imposed by central government.

Local government

In many local government services the use of different types of service provider is already firmly established. The challenge here is to make a reality of diversity and to avoid a new mono-culture of provision from emerging.

- All Best Value authorities should publish an annual 'diversity statement' that would specify the volume of services provided in-house, externally, and through partnership arrangements. Local authorities that systematically under-perform could be set a 'diversity target' by the Audit Commission if it is felt that this underperformance can be attributed to a lack of diversity in service provision.

- The rise of large-scale partnership agreements with a single provider – or 'one-company towns' – sits uneasily with the principle of diversity. Authorities (together with DETR) need to establish how large partnering agreements can accommodate sub-contracting to smaller local firms and social enterprises.

- A prudential framework for local authority capital spending should be instituted as a matter of priority. PFI projects and joint venture companies should be treated in the same way as conventionally financed projects.

- Authorities who have performed well in their Best Value inspections should be allowed greater freedom to trade, within prudential limits, with other public bodies.

Education

Diversity has been introduced with some success in relation to the provision of Local Education Authorities (LEA) services but has not been widely applied in relation to school management. LEAs are good examples of where an effective relationship exists between a purchaser and service provider. The complex relationship between governing bodies, senior school managers and LEAs is more problematic and represents an obstacle to greater diversity in school management.

- Partnerships for the delivery of LEA core services should not be seen as an emergency measure, but as a part of the wider Best Value process. All LEAs should consider the role that partnerships might play in increasing educational attainment. Restrictions on the use of partnerships with LEAs except in cases of under-performance should be removed. Government should make it clear that partnerships are not the only way of improving performance.

- The Government should make it clear that partnerships for LEA services in no way alters an LEA's statutory responsibilities.

- Greater diversity in school management will require a clarification of the relationship between LEAs, school governing bodies and school managers.

- The model of enabling independent providers to establish Voluntary or Foundation Schools under contract with an LEA compromises the independent role of the governing body and should not be the way forward if private and voluntary providers are to be involved in school management. Instead, where they consider this to be in the interests of the school, governing bodies should be provided with the support and resources necessary to enter into partnerships with private or voluntary sector educational providers.

Chapter 8: Making the public sector a better partner

If partnership is to play a major role in the modernisation of public services then government needs to become a more effective partner. At the moment it suffers from a severe shortage of skills and those it has are often under-utilised. It finds it hard to learn from past mistakes, it is poor at picking quality partners, and it is fiendishly difficult to get different bits of the public sector to work together to purchase services. Change is needed on all these fronts.

- Across the public sector the status and career structures of procurement officers need to be enhanced.

- Public agencies should be able to bid to become accredited commissioning experts.

- Flexibility needs to be built into PPP contracts if they are to promote continuous improvement and value-for-money over time.

- Outcome-based contracting should become a regular feature of PPPs, linking an element of contractual payments to the tangible benefits brought to service users.

- User satisfaction should be used regularly to determine a portion of the payment made to providers.

- Gain-sharing provisions should always be a feature of partnerships where achieving revenue-generation or cost reduction relies on active co-operation from the public sector and/or there is a high degree of uncertainty about the quality of the information available.

- The Government Offices for the Regions should be provided with a pump-priming fund to reward joint commissioning by groups of local authorities

In addition to this government must play a pivotal role in promoting good employment practices across the public service sector: public money should not support poor employers. A motivated workforce is critical in delivering high quality services to the public.

- Public authorities need to be aware that they are under no duty to select least-cost bidders – indeed this may fail to achieve best value.

- Purchasers should always be allowed to make issues such as health and safety, equality, and training a feature of PPP contracts if they so wish. There should be a greater willingness to select providers with good track records on employment issues.

- Revised TUPE regulations should be implemented by autumn 2001.

- The evidence base on the impact of PPPs on the workforce needs to be improved.

- If the evidence demonstrates that PPPs have an adverse impact on the pay and conditions of new employees then there should be moves to strengthen the regulatory framework through a voluntary code and/or legislation.

IV: ACCOUNTABILITY

Chapter 9: Communities and partnership

Public service providers should be accountable and responsive to local citizens and communities. Policy-makers and local public managers need to explore new and innovative ways of engaging local people in the design and governance of their public services and spaces. There are several ways in which policy and practice need to be reformed to ensure that partnerships are based on community consent.

- The Cabinet Office and the Office of Government Commerce should provide joint guidance on how to conduct community consultation in PPP projects.

- In areas of service delivery which impinge directly on citizen's everyday lives (for example, housing or schools), particular effort should be made to involve users substantively in the selection of service providers.

- Pilots for neighbourhood level 'community trusts' should be established which allow local people to take a strategic view of the fit between existing public sector assets and neighbourhood needs.

- There should be a moratorium on new funding streams for local partnership initiatives for at least three years in order to allow for evaluation of current schemes.

- There should always be clarity about what it is that the private sector is expected to contribute to local partnerships. Generally the role of the private sector will focus on management and commercial skills rather than the provision of funding.

For too long proposals for enhancing community involvement in public services have lacked bite. If PPPs are really to help transform public service delivery it is essential that the vision of communities as the agents of partnership moves from lofty aspiration to concrete reality.

Chapter 10: Making partnerships accountable

The traditional model of accountability assumed that public services were delivered through the public sector. PPPs stretch this traditional approach in a number of ways but they also offer a device through which clarity can be brought to the role of purchasers and providers, transparency can be ensured, and the responsiveness of service providers to users enhanced. The involvement of private and voluntary providers in public services need not and should not lead to a dilution of public accountability. Ensuring that this is the case necessitates a range of reforms.

- Private and voluntary providers must accept that higher standards of disclosure and transparency apply in the public service sector than in the rest of the economy.

- Performance data on services provided through partnerships should always be made publicly available.

- The mandatory framework for disclosing information that currently exists in the NHS should be extended to all PFI projects.

- The National Audit Office should have statutory powers to access information on private providers relating to public contracts above a certain size.

- The responsibility held by different bodies in a partnership should always be made explicit in the contract. Public authorities should remain responsible for ensuring that citizens will not suffer as a result of contractual deficiencies.

- The status and areas of competence of decision-making bodies set up within PPP contracts (such as 'partnership boards') should always be made explicit.

- Contracts need to set out clearly the actions that public purchasers can take to enforce agreed terms – this is particularly relevant when there is more than one public body involved in purchasing services.

- The public body that will be held to account legally and politically for managing a contract should always be the body that establishes that contract in the first place.

- The application of judicial review to service providers who are not in the public sector needs to be clarified. The test for whether public law should be applied should be the nature of the function being performed by a public service organisation rather than its legal structure.

- All PPP contracts should clearly set out the grievance procedures through which individual citizens have redress.

Thus the shift towards pluralism in procurement and/or provision which PPPs represent can go hand in hand with more effective forms of accountability.

V: CONCLUSION

Chapter 11: Partnership 2010

If PPPs are to be a significant feature of the public service landscape in 2010 then much has to change. The association between private or voluntary provision of public services and cost-cutting will have ended. Partnerships will no longer be seen as privatisation by stealth. Public mangers will have the experience and confidence to allow more innovative partnership models to emerge and will be able to work alongside a diverse menu of leading edge public, private and voluntary organisations. Employees will be confident about how they will be treated by private providers and citizens will see partnership as an opportunity rather than an obstacle to participation in decision-making.

Is this destination ever likely to be reached? Many would say not. It will require a commitment to sustainable increases in public funding, a political desire to make the case for partnership, a willingness to admit the flaws of some recent models of PPPs and a determination to make a reality of the rhetoric of evidence based policy. It will also require action to be taken now. High quality and popular universal public services need to be a defining feature of Britain in 2010: the sooner we get partnerships right, the more likely this is to be the case.

I: Principles

1. The new partnership agenda

The people of Britain demand better public services. They continue to believe in the traditional virtues of free, universal and comprehensive core services. However, as modern citizens they also want services that are of a high quality, that are built around their needs and lifestyles and over which they have a real say as users and citizens. They demand these services because they and their families benefit from them now and throughout their lives, but also because they embody a national commitment to fairness and the good society. After four years of progressive government that has begun to commit significantly more resources to the public services, the public's commitment to the further improvement of these services has if anything grown stronger.

This should be a golden age for the champions of public service; those who believe that Britain could and should aspire to provision that rivals that available in other successful European societies. However, we have been here before. The bold plans of those who created the modern welfare state in the post-war period subsided into the 25 years of retrenchment and flawed reform that followed during the Thatcher years. The fundamental aspirations and the moral compass of citizens has not changed but their faith in the capacity of public services to deliver has become fragile. If, in the future, after a sustained period of increased funding by a Government unquestionably committed to the success of public services, citizens feel that those services are still failing to deliver there could be a political backlash. A resurgent right could start to win the argument that universal public services are an anachronism; blunt, inefficient and restrictive of choice. If the case for universal public services cannot be won now it may soon be lost forever.

To win this fight the case for public services needs to be made in terms of values and outcomes rather than particular forms of service delivery. The founding principles of the National Health Service – the public service to which British citizens are most attached – were that it should be free, universal and comprehensive, not that it should be provided through a particular structure, process or set of employees. The enduring goals of public policy must be distinguished from the particular means through which they are pursued at different times and in different circumstances.

This, of course, was a key point in the debate surrounding the rewriting of Clause IV of the Labour Party's constitution, signifying the final acceptance that forms of ownership were only a means to achieve socialist objectives and not the main objective itself. However, despite the outcome of that debate there is still a lack of intellectual and political confidence on the centre-left in embracing a new account of the relationship between social ends, public spending, public services and private, public and voluntary enterprise. A recent authoritative, and generally positive, account of Labour's first term reflects the view of many commentators in arguing that it is the

Government's willingness to experiment with private provision of public services that is its greatest failure (Toynbee and Walker, 2001). The case has yet to be won for partnership as a legitimate means of delivering high quality public services.

The establishment in autumn 1999 of IPPR's Commission on Public Private Partnerships (PPPs) was driven by the need for a more robust account of the potential role of private and voluntary organisations – together with the wider community – within public services. We agreed that the centre-left was correct to replace public ownership with equality and fairness as the goals of progressive politics. We also acknowledged that in many areas the new Government had made reforms that removed barriers to better partnerships between the public, private and voluntary sectors. However, it seemed that between the general principle and the detailed policy there was a gap where a systematic and forward-looking account of the potential and limits of partnership should be.

It is this gap that still feeds public concern and even cynicism about partnership. It is this gap that explains the widely differing and sometimes contradictory approaches to partnership being pursued in different parts and at different levels of government. It is this gap which limits the learning that can take place about what partnerships can and cannot deliver. And it is this gap that inhibits our capacity to think openly and radically about how new forms of partnership could help us remodel public services to meet the needs of the 21st century. It is this gap in our understanding, our analysis and our vision that this Report attempts to fill.

The Report is split into four Parts. The first (Chapters 1 and 2) provides an overview of our core argument and sets out the conditions that need to be in place if partnerships are to play a major role in improving public services. The second (Chapters 3 to 5) clarifies the extent to which partnership arrangements are already in existence within different parts of the UK's public services, and then analyses the strengths and weaknesses of the economic arguments surrounding the use of PFI and PPPs more broadly. The third Part of the Report considers the rules that currently determine the types of services that can and cannot be incorporated within PPP projects. It then examines the partnership arrangements (and corresponding reforms) that could emerge in the health, local government and education sectors; and explores the ways in which government will have to adapt if it is to able to manage this new agenda. The final Part of the Report (Chapters 9 and 10) sets out the arguments for much greater citizen and community participation in partnerships, and assesses the challenges of ensuring that PPPs are compatible with public accountability. The Report ends with a brief sketch of how we would like partnerships to have evolved by 2010 (Chapter 11).

Even though many of the arguments made in this Report are generic in nature and apply across all sectors, there are several noteworthy areas of the public services that we have omitted to consider, not least the defence and IT sectors. This is not because we see them as unimportant. It is simply that we could not undertake an exhaustive study of all service areas and we therefore wanted to concentrate on the sectors – education, health, local government, housing, prisons – where we thought there was most potential for learning lessons from which wider conclusions could be drawn.

The shifting politics of public and private

The 1997 Labour Government was elected to power on a pledge to put partnership at the heart of its strategy for modernising public services.[1] It would harness the energies and skills of the private and voluntary sectors in order to deliver public services. But the case for partnership went beyond a desire to be pragmatic. Demonstrating a full-hearted commitment to the future of public services while at the same time striving to recast the relationship between public and private sectors was proclaimed as a leitmotif of the Government's 'new politics'.

This stance seemed to fit well with popular opinion. The British public is arguably far more interested in the quality of public services than with who is providing them. It also seemed to run with the grain of international experience that demonstrates that a range of countries with standards of public services to which we can only aspire have long utilised partnerships in a variety of service areas.[2]

Embracing partnership within public services seems a world apart, however, from the mindset of the last Labour administration in the second half of the 1970s, at which point the role of the public sector in directly producing goods and services had been steadily increasing since the Second World War. The UK government owned and operated the key utilities; ran a broad sweep of public enterprises producing coal, steel, cars and ships; owned one of the world's largest oil companies, and controlled all bus and rail services. On top of this it directly managed the country's health system while local authorities had a virtual monopoly on the provision of the nation's schooling, social services, street and refuse collection, and also owned and managed over a third of the country's housing stock (Corry *et al*, 1997). The main policy debate in relation to the public/private divide among leading left intellectuals focused on whether the Labour government should aim to bring the largest hundred companies into public ownership. The notion of a diversity of suppliers in the provision of public services was anathema for the left. For many it still is.

In the two intervening decades the British state has been radically restructured. There has been a massive reduction in the scope of public enterprise; a significant, if highly uneven and often bitterly contested, shift towards greater private and voluntary sector involvement in the delivery of some public services; and a transformation in systems of public management. These shifts in the role and scope of government made it inevitable that in 1997 the newly elected Labour Government, with its cautious attitude to public ownership and pro-business image, would be willing to embrace a more constructive approach towards partnerships between the public and private sectors in delivering public services.

Four years on, however, much of the early shine has come off the politics of partnership. This is not to say that a number of positive measures were not adopted by the 1997-2001 administration or that the Government was not willing to challenge long-standing ideological prejudices about involving the private and voluntary sectors. In fact, it did both. A wide array of detailed reforms and guidelines have facilitated the use of Public Private Partnerships (PPPs) and overcome many of the obstacles that had hindered the use of the Private Finance Initiative (PFI) between 1992 and 1997. These include the ending of the obligation for universal testing of capital projects, the enhancement of employee protection, the standardisation of PFI contracts and reassuring investors about the legal security of PPP projects. Without these steps, any increase in partnership activity simply would not have occurred and the private sector's interest would have melted away. At the same time, the Prime Minister and many of his colleagues repeatedly made it clear that they have no ideological qualms about the private and voluntary sectors being involved in core areas of the public services such as health and education.

So what is the problem?

This twin agenda of sweeping away the ideological baggage that hindered thinking on partnership, and detailed measures aimed at easing the administration of PPPs, has been helpful but is ultimately inadequate. There remains a large and seemingly growing gap between ideological rhetoric and implementation, which the invocation of the language of 'what works' does not fill. This gap has been created by the absence of a strategic account and philosophical rationale for PPPs. The absence of such an account is in part responsible for the persistence of negative images about PPPs. It has also given rise to a number of policy mistakes.

- *The rationale for PPPs appears confused.* Too often the justifications used by different government departments for the use of partnership arrangements have been muddled and contradictory. This has fed scepticism about the real purpose of involving the private and voluntary sectors and exposed the lack of an underlying account of what it is policy-makers think PPPs offer public services.

- *Unrealistic expectations have been created.* There has been a tendency to spray the demand for 'private-sector involvement' across most new government initiatives without proper consideration of what the different partners would have to offer. This has fuelled partnership fatigue rather than unleashing new energy and innovation.

- *PPPs are sometimes 'the only game in town'.* Much of the antagonism towards PPPs is the result of widespread and at times justified suspicion that PPPs are still being used simply to get public investment 'off-balance sheet.' Worse still, the desire to press ahead with PPPs for these reasons has sometimes led to short-cuts being taken in relation to accountability and value-for-money procedures.

- *The impression has been given that partnership is a punishment for failure.* The idea that the private sector should be used as a punishment with which to threaten 'failing' public bodies (for example, Local Education Authorities, schools and prisons) has created a jaundiced view of the very notion of partnership.

- *The record of the PFI has been patchy.* The early evidence from PFI projects suggests that although they may not be performing as poorly as some of the critics suggest, many offer at best marginal value-for-money gains without delivering the promised innovations in the design and organisation of services.

- *The model for PPPs has often been too rigid.* In a number of high-profile instances the Government has made an almost ideological commitment to very particular forms of PPP, refusing to consider the case for alternative models. The symbolic importance attached to the success of particular PPP projects has hindered sensible policy-making and has aroused public mistrust.

- *The PFI threatens to create a new mono-culture.* The political determination to make a success of particular models of PPP, such as PFI, risks diverting attention away from finding other successful forms of service delivery and procurement. Policy should actively foster a diversity of approaches to provision rather than creating a new 'mono-culture'.

- *PPPs raise the spectre of privatisation.* The link made by Government between PPPs and the part-privatisation of some public enterprises has also served to fuel suspicion among commentators that partnership and privatisation are one and the same thing, and that partnership is a step towards full privatisation.

These problems reflect the lack of a clear narrative about partnerships: what the rationale of partnerships should be, when they should be used, and what different partners stand to gain. However, they also reveal that the rhetoric of partnership has far outpaced understanding of what PPPs should and should not do. Addressing this shortfall is a necessity if PPPs are to play a significant role in achieving our aspirations for public services and the creation of a dynamic public service sector.

It would be easy but wrong to place all the blame for this strategic confusion on ministers or civil servants. They operate in an environment where there is a continual need to find new ways of improving performance, addressing social problems and responding to political pressures. They could hardly put all decisions on hold while waiting for the evidence on past PPPs to come in. Nevertheless there is now an urgent need to reflect on the criteria which should inform the use of PPPs.

Providing clarity as to how PPPs should fit into the wider context of Government policy will require credible research and analysis. At the moment evidence on PPPs is woefully inadequate. The strong tradition of analytical inquiry into the types of services that should be funded through taxation, together with the best way of raising these taxes (Fabian Society, 2000; Burchardt and Hills, 1996), has not been extended into an equally robust examination of the efficacy of different methods of *delivering* public services. As a result strong assertions made by those with an interest in different models of delivery are rarely backed up by anything more than anecdote. It is perhaps not surprising therefore that many on the centre-left have a clearer idea of which services government should pay for than which services it should deliver.

However, the problems that the Government faces in articulating its own account of partnership go beyond a paucity of evidence. The Hatfield train crash in autumn 2000 represented the nadir of the privatising agenda of the Thatcher years – a moment which spurred popular demands for an end to the 20 year 'jihad' against the public sector, public investment, and public enterprise (Hutton, 2000).

For many this sentiment against privatisation reinforces a profound scepticism about the capacity of government ever to harness private interests for public purposes. Though the ill-advised privatisation of the railways bears little relation to most of the PPPs considered in this Report, many of the criticisms it has attracted echo those made in relation to partnership. These include: the charge that the private sector will always seek to cut costs rather than raise quality and improve safety; the chaos that can arise through the involvement of multiple sub-contractors within a complex service system; the proliferation of bodies responsible for providing and regulating services which fragments and ultimately makes a mockery of accountability. To the extent that these types of concerns are also raised about PPPs we tackle them in this Report.

Avoiding the blind alleys

The lack of a clear narrative on partnership, together with the mixed record of some PPPs and the fall-out from rail privatisation, has been of great comfort to different camps at either end of the political spectrum. They cling to polarised accounts of the relationship between the public and the private sectors that have for too long been allowed to set the terms of debate within the UK. These two extremes either regard the private as good and the public as bad or vice-versa. They therefore place intrinsic value on services being provided exclusively by either the public or private sector. In our view, these approaches lead us up blind alleys for the delivery of public services.

First, we outline the arguments of the private sector privatisers and then the public sector monopolists, then we give our own alternative.

The privatisers: private good, public bad

For neo-liberals the encouragement of the private sector in the funding and provision of public services are seen as twin, and mutually reinforcing, objectives of policy. There are different strands to the argument offered by privatisers. What they all have in common, however, is hostility to publicly funded universal services.

- Firstly, privatisers argue that rising affluence means public services are doomed. Right-wing commentators argue that any attempt to reform public services (including the use of PPPs) is a desperate effort to paper over the structural problem of continuing to fund public services that are free to all at the point of use. As prosperity grows and incomes continue to rise it is argued that the near universal nature of core public services will gradually fall away. That only 19 per cent of the British public would not use private education or private health if they had sufficient income provides some support for this pessimistic view (*Observer*, 2001). However, if the earth is moving in this direction, it is moving very slowly. Reliance on private health insurance and private education has barely increased over recent decades despite real increases in the standard of living (Brooks, 2000).

- Secondly, privatisers believe that even if it were theoretically possible to maintain universal public services of such a quality that the private option became unattractive this would not be desirable. Self-provision rather than 'dependency' on the state is a moral virtue: for true believers this applies as much in relation to public services as it does to social security. It is not just that self-provision is a pre-requisite for the rugged individualism that they favour, they also believe that the tax-implications of collectively funded services necessarily entail a restriction on individual choice. The trade-off is simple: more publicly funded provision means less individual freedom. From this vantage point, the only genuine route to improving services is to privatise public assets, encourage new market entrants and, if necessary, protect the public interest through regulation and a minimal safety-net. Despite the major transfer of public enterprise into private hands during the 1980s and 1990s the failure of Conservative administrations to increase significantly private funding in areas such as health and education was a source of disappointment to neo-liberal intellectuals. Many of them look forward to the days when the right will again renew the programme of reining back public provision (Heffer, 2001).

If universal public services free at the point of use are to be reduced to a residual safety net in the UK it is unlikely to be as a result of a full-scale privatisation of the NHS or state schools by Act of Parliament. Far more likely is a slow withering away as incentives are introduced for individuals to make personal contributions to 'top-up' a base-line of state provision (Green, 2000), thus gradually turning public provision into a rump service only relied upon by those on low and moderate incomes.

- Thirdly, despite their enthusiasm for restricting the scope of public provision, privatisers do concede that in some instances public funding will have to remain in place. In these instances it is argued that the role of policy should be to allow individuals to behave as if they were operating in a market (for example through the use of vouchers). Wherever possible there is a desire to restrict the role of public agencies in making collective decisions on behalf of citizens.

- Fourthly, privatisers assume that where public purchasing does take place the private sector should be the 'default' mode of provision for public services. Privatisers speak glowingly of zealots such as Stephen Goldsmith – Mayor of Indianapolis – who argues that in the future cities could be run by little more than a mayor, police chief, planning director, and a small (but busy) contracts team (Savas, 2000). The attraction of this approach flows inexorably from the neo-liberals' in-built scepticism about the ability of the public sector to be efficient, reform itself or act entrepreneurially. For them, the lack of sharp performance incentives inherent in public ownership makes the notion of 'public enterprise' a contradiction in terms. The twin agenda of privatisation wherever possible and outsourcing everywhere else remains the 'one-best' strategy for the efficient production of public services. Privatisers are not interested in creating a 'level playing field', addressing the restrictions which impede public sector innovation, or building joint ventures between public and private sectors which allow the tax-payer to benefit from the commercial exploitation of public sector assets. Government is always the problem not the solution.

- Fifthly, relationships between service-providers and purchasers tend to be adversarial and short-term. There is little support for the view that it is the role of public authorities to cultivate and manage a diverse set of public, private and non-profit service providers, or to build up collaborative and high-trust relationships with partners. Privatisers anticipate that this would only result in corruption or impediments to free enterprise.

- Sixthly, privatisers maintain that public action crowds out private altruism. It is only after the state has withdrawn from both the funding and provision of public services (and welfare more generally) that civil society in the form of voluntary, community and religious groups will flourish. Public funding of services, together with the attendant demands for accountability, ensures that the dead hand of government will stifle the efforts of civil society. Conversely, public services are not highly valued for any contribution they make to social cohesion or helping to maintain and renew civil society. For privatisers the very concepts of the public domain and social solidarity are contested: individuals will value all services purely in terms of the utility they derive from them; moreover the state has no role in seeking to foster voluntary association or social capital.

- Finally, privatisers subscribe to a highly restricted account of the scope of politics and public action. The role of government should be to set the rules within which individuals can successfully conduct social and economic exchange. It is not to articulate a wider public interest and to take public action in pursuit of it. Conversely, the reason why notions such as the 'enabling' state retain such currency on the centre-left (Brown, 2001) is precisely because it is felt that there is an ambitious role for government to play over and above the production of services: planning for local needs; supporting associational groups; co-ordinating change involving different agencies; and representing different interests (Stoker, 2000). For those on the right reducing the role of government as a producer is a means of eroding the public domain, reining back state-capacity, and minimising the reach of elected representatives.

The monopolists: public good, private bad

The historical counterpoint to the privatisers' position has been the defence of all things public. The view that as a matter of *principle* public services should always and everywhere be provided by public sector employees is one that still commands a great deal of emotional and intellectual support on the left. The public domain is conceived as a realm that must remain entirely separate from the market and uncontaminated by it. There is considerable suspicion of any proposal that questions this. The difference between the view taken in this Report and this 'public sector monopoly' position is substantial but it is a difference based around means rather than ends. In contrast our difference with the privatisers is that we have a fundamentally different conception of the good society and the role of government in creating it.

Three overlapping sets of arguments are used by those on the left who are opposed in principle to partnerships:

- Firstly, monopolists argue that any private involvement in the delivery of public services is intrinsically undesirable. This is because at the heart of private sector involvement in public services is the basic motivation of commercial enterprise.

Organisations driven by the profit motive will always be self-interested, peopled by 'knaves' in the language of David Hume (Le Grand, 1998) whereas organisations in the public sector are driven by altruism and a concern for the public good and therefore peopled by 'knights'.[3] This is not necessarily because of any personal moral deficiencies on the part of private sector managers or staff – rather it is the environment they operate within. Shareholder pressure to maximise profits will permeate down into workplace practices and result in constant efforts to cut costs and to restrict the nature of services offered to citizens, particularly those least able to object. This is a continuous rather than a one-off pressure; throughout the life of a public contract the private sector will seek to reduce costs in order to increase returns.

As a result private sector involvement will necessarily undermine public service values, distort the nature of the service provided, and erode social equity. Those who pretend otherwise are simply misunderstanding the way business operates and has to operate. Public discontent with the public services which private companies provide is the unavoidable outcome. Given this chain of reasoning partnership arrangements are easily represented as little more than a staging-post on the route to full-scale privatisation (Whitfield, 2001). Partnership is privatisation by stealth. In addition, it is argued that the introduction of the profit motive will undermine efforts to secure value-for-money. The public sector's ability to raise cheap finance and avoid paying dividends will more than compensate for any increases in efficiency generated by private management. This logic leads to the conclusion that the only route through which private partners can provide services at lower cost is through cuts in the terms and conditions of employees.

• Secondly, monopolists stress the unique advantage of the public sector as the exclusive provider of services. People enter public service to help and serve others. Public sector management systems should seek to cultivate rather than corrode this ethos. Employment terms and conditions, particularly for lower paid employees, should surpass those in the private sector. Comparatively flat pay scales, together with the avoidance of performance related pay, should help to maintain a collegiate approach to problem solving and a service-based ethos. In short, the introduction of all market-based incentives should be avoided. Partnerships run the risk of turning public sector knights into knaves.

• Thirdly, monopolists argue that retaining a public sector monopoly on service delivery increases both flexibility and accountability. Instead of having to engage in contractual negotiations in order to alter the specification of services, those provided internally can be changed by executive decision. Moreover, if the public sector is the sole service provider, then lines of democratic accountability in terms of responsibility, transparency and responsiveness are said to be more direct and complete. Under partnership public managers (and their political masters) can only be held to account for the contractual terms to which they agreed. With in-house provision citizens can hold managers responsible, so the argument goes, for the actual quality of services experienced. Direct provision also provides an opportunity for democratic involvement in shaping service priorities. In contrast, private companies will have little interest in consulting citizens. From this point of view, as the scope of PPPs expands the public realm of civic values shrinks.

These arguments either alone or in combination lead to an outright opposition to experiments with partnership. They suggest that any problems within current public services or procurement models are not related to a lack of management skills, blunt incentives, or a lack of diversity or innovation among providers. Rather, any shortcomings are put down to a shortage of funds and the growing use of market-type mechanisms. The introduction of partnership arrangements, it is argued, will only accentuate these problems. A more moderate version of this position recognises that, in addition to improved funding, there is a need for a continuing process of public sector reform if the public services are to be revitalised but sees no need for the public sector to work in closer partnership with the private or voluntary sectors. The public sector may, where appropriate, want to draw upon private sector techniques and skills – but only in order to solve its problems in-house. If PPPs are to be used at all they should be strictly restricted to the provision of capital projects. Involvement of the private sector in direct service provision remains out of bounds.

Summary

The two 'blind alleys' set out above reflect the tramlines in which political debate on public-private relations in the UK have long been stuck. On one side those arguing for higher levels of spending on services make the case for the public sector retaining a monopoly on the provision of all services. On the other, privatisers seek to undermine the public sector – both in relation to *funding* and *provision* – wherever possible. The approach taken in this Report departs from both of these analyses.

The partnership approach: our argument in four steps

The approach adopted by this Report rejects the defeatist strand of thought which maintains that all new forms of private involvement in the delivery of public services should be put on hold because the risks are too great and the politics too hot. To recoil from the excesses of the privatisation era into the false comfort of 'the public sector always knows best' would be to return to the position that made it so easy for the privatisers' arguments to attain such an ascendancy in the first place. Equally, however, we need to guard against the opposite view – one which almost became a cross-party consensus during the late 1990s – that the only way to run a new public service is to place it in the hands of a plc. It must be possible to argue for public sector solutions to many of the challenges of the public services whilst also recognising the potential contribution of partnership. The centre-left needs to regain confidence in its ability to put forward a distinctive vision for the public services, one that is based on finding new ways of helping the public sector to be enterprising and to deliver the quality of services that people want.

Step 1: Remaking the case for public funding of services

Despite the degree of ideological fluidity that is said to characterise modern politics there are still clear dividing lines on some issues. In Britain the sharpest divide of all continues to be the level of spending on public services, and in particular, the strength of the commitment to maintain universal services funded by general taxation in key areas such as education and health.[4] For all its ambiguity about many elements of traditional social democracy, a second-term Labour Government will want to be remembered for delivering a step-change in the funding and quality of public services – and in doing so succeeding in sustaining a universal basis for public service provision.

   A long line of centre-left thought has made the case for an extensive menu of goods and services to be made available to citizens on non-market criteria; a case based on arguments about social justice, efficiency and democracy. These arguments need to be remade.

Social Justice

Universal public services are at the heart of strategies for social justice. Since the Second World War, a guaranteed entitlement to the key services has been recognised by social democratic and liberal thought as a vital pre-condition for social citizenship and the possibility of individual fulfilment (Marshall, 1950). Without this common baseline of security the language of equality of opportunity and worth rings hollow. The fact that for much of the post-war period welfare services have been of greater benefit to the middle classes than to lower income groups (Le Grand, 1982) does not alter the fact that disadvantaged groups are, and will remain, particularly reliant upon collectively funded services for their day to day well-being. Pooling risks collectively rather than bearing them individually helps ensure that the disadvantages that low income groups face are not further compounded by restricted access to vital services (Walzer, 1983). If services such as health were to be provided through private insurance then large numbers of disadvantaged individuals would remain unprotected. Given the levels of income inequality which currently disfigure British society such an approach would lead to further polarisation between the life-chances of the rich and the poor.

Market failure and economic efficiency

A second argument for public services derives from considerations of market failure. First, there is a range of classic public goods that need to be publicly funded if they are to be provided at all or at anything like a reasonable standard.[5] The conventional list of these services includes the military, policing, parks and street-lighting. Second, and perhaps more significantly, there is a broad spectrum of 'merit' goods and services that would tend to be under-provided if it was left to the market to supply them. The most widely cited examples tend to be health, education, and public transport. Finally, in a range of areas serious informational and incentive problems inhibit the creation of effective markets (for example, for insurance against unemployment and disability). In these instances the pooling of social risk has a powerful economic logic. Without public action in the form of the provision of tax-funded benefits or compulsory insurance many individuals will be left exposed to economic risks beyond their control.

Democracy and the public domain

A third argument is that public funding of a broad range of services also widens the possible scope of politics and public deliberation. Public services remain a crucial site at which individuals from different backgrounds can 'rub shoulders' and come together in order to make collective decisions. They therefore form part of the public domain in which individuals function as equal citizens rather than self-interested market agents.

The possibility of direct involvement in running and governing local services also serves to enliven otherwise anaemic accounts of representative democracy in which the role of the citizen is simply to cast a vote in elections. Government funding of these services provides public authorities and leaders with the leverage to ensure that public service organisations seek to harness citizen participation in decision-making and work with the grain of civil society.

Step 2: Distinguishing funding from provision

There are a host of reasons why discussions of PPPs tend to generate more heat than light: the arcane terminology, the limited evidence-base, the sometimes technically challenging nature of the issues, and the ideological baggage. However, the over-riding source of confusion concerns the distinction between *funding* and *providing* public services. The former refers to whom it is that pays for these services, the latter signifies who it is that actually delivers these services to citizens. Throughout this Report the overwhelming focus is on whether or not PPPs should be used to deliver public services which are publicly funded through the tax system.[6]

As will be discussed in Chapter 2, one of the most significant features of public sector reform over the last twenty years has been the growing separation of those responsible for the commissioning of public services from those whose role it is to deliver them. Up until now both the commissioner and the deliverer of services – sometimes referred to as the *purchaser* and *provider* – have more often than not remained within the public sector. Nonetheless, this division of responsibilities, which has been mirrored in many countries around the world, provides an institutional architecture which enables the purchaser of a service to survey the organisations (or groups of them) who are best placed to meet their requirements. Examining where and when it makes sense for this purchaser-provider split to straddle the public/private divide takes us to the next step of the argument adopted in this Report.

Step 3: Be open minded about the case for partnership and diversity

The third step is to establish why public authorities should be given the *option* of purchasing services from non-public bodies. In many areas of the public services a range of service providers from different sectors have long been in existence. Blanket opposition to non-public providers flies in the face of the established experience of public service provision by different types of providers within the UK. It also ignores the international lessons that suggest the role that diversity of provision can play in helping generate high quality public services. Though by comparative standards the UK's public sector has been unusually dominant in service provision it is a gross simplification to think that the delivery of public services in the UK has ever been an island of public sector purity.

Many of the companies engaged in PFI deals lived off public contracts long before the phrase PPP had ever been coined. Moreover, the public face of the NHS comes in the form of GPs who are independent contractors with as much in common with self-employed small business people as with salaried employees of the NHS. In local government, health, social and community care, the prison service, defence, the employment service, careers service, education, and social housing, a multitude of relationships with the private and voluntary sectors are already in existence. Partnership is not new. However, our argument does not just rely on the fact that PPPs are not as much of a departure as some make out. Outright opposition to partnership and diversity in public services is unappealing for political, ideological, analytical and policy reasons.

Politically, the case for progressives considering the use of partnerships appears strong, though it is by no means uncontroversial. The fundamental starting-point is that the political fortunes of the centre-left are inextricably linked to convincing the electorate that public services are improving. Whereas the right can thrive by persuading people to exit from public services altogether, this is simply not an option for social democrats. This reinforces the case for the centre-left being open minded about examining the role of the private and voluntary sectors in delivering public services. Against this, there is a view that, even if partnerships make sense in narrow efficiency terms, they should still be avoided because of the supposedly regressive political dynamic they help create. Less direct public provision, the argument goes, will necessarily lead to a more privatised society, the erosion of non-market values, and, eventually, a reduced willingness on the part of citizens to fund public services.

At the extreme this argument may have something in it. If government loses too much visibility then citizens may eventually become less inclined to support publicly funded programmes. Government needs to be branded on public service success stories in order to remind people what their taxes achieve. However, this argument cuts both ways. One of the easiest ways of haemorrhaging support for tax-funded services is if the public loses confidence in government's capacity to deliver service improvements. This is not an abstract possibility. Studies of voting behaviour have repeatedly shown that the public would support a higher tax burden if they had greater confidence in government to improve the quality of services.

Moreover, in some though by no means all parts of the public services the image of the public sector is more of a hindrance than a help to those seeking to make the case for collective provision. This is not to say that PPPs will be an elixir, transforming the public's confidence in the capacity of government – some of the most eye-catching examples of government failure over recent years have involved partnership arrangements. However, there is plenty of scope for government to draw on the best elements of a diverse *public service sector* – consisting of a variety of public, private and voluntary organisations – whilst still maintaining its own visibility. Greater pluralism in provision could also provide something of a buffer against the possibility of a renewed assault from those who seek to residualise public services. Partnerships may help forge new coalitions of support for adequate public spending between private and voluntary providers and the commissioners of public services.

We also reject the *ideological* argument that utilising different types of providers *necessarily* destroys the scope for citizen participation, democratic accountability, and the maintenance of civic values. At one level the weakness of this claim can be amply demonstrated by pointing to the large swathes of the public sector which have systematically resisted calls for greater openness, accountability and responsiveness to citizens. However, the argument runs deeper than this. The idea that the public domain can be neatly equated with the public sector is hugely constraining and ignores the wider role of government in shaping relationships throughout civil society (Gamble, 2000). For this reason some on the left have long argued that the move away from a monolithic state provider, if appropriately managed, has the potential to help renew the bond between citizens and their services and thereby improve their quality.[7]

The need to cut through the *analytical* fog which hangs over existing accounts of the appropriate dividing lines between public, private and voluntary sectors is a theme running through this Report (see Chapter 2 and 6). At this stage we need only to flag up two points. First, as will already be obvious to many observers of public policy, there is no coherent rationale for the different types of services that can be provided through partnerships in different parts of the public services. Second, we need to acknowledge and learn from the strong theoretical and empirical arguments which show how and why public ownership, public sector delivery of services and public enterprise, can be and often are, economically efficient (Helm, 1989; Holtham, 1998). At no point should it simply be assumed that the private sector is *inherently* more efficient than the public (or vice-versa).

This lack of a clear analysis of partnership is not just a matter of concern for the intellectual purist, it also hinders practical *policy-making*. Our argument is that a clear and consistent account of when and how to use different PPPs would be of great value to public managers. The strategies applied to public management by the new right (privatise and marketise) and the traditional left (spend more and centralise) need to be answered by a more flexible and diverse 'tool-kit' approach that includes the option of using different kinds of service delivery including a variety of forms of partnership.

Even though we think that some of the criticisms made of partnerships from first principles are spurious we do not argue that PPPs are always and everywhere a good thing. Far from it. This Report emphatically does not seek to defend or endorse all the approaches to PPPs that have been adopted over recent years. Nor will it argue that partnerships are the right approach for all areas of the public services. There are circumstances in which the underlying nature of the service obviates against having a multitude of providers or where the sum of the problems that can arise from having different types of providers – such as awkward organisational interfaces – outweigh any potential gains. Even in sectors where there is a strong case for PPPs, there are key conditions that need to be in place if partnerships are to work.

No-one should think that building effective partnerships is easy. In all of the areas where diversity has been introduced there have been teething problems. In some instances the quality of service provided through PPP has been lamentable and the taxpayer has received a poor deal. Anyone who claims that in every instance the quality of service produced through a PPP supersedes what came before is seriously misinterpreting or ignoring the available evidence. We take the evidence that we have seen of the apparent shortcomings of both PPPs *and* direct provision seriously. It suggests the need to ensure that genuine alternatives to PPPs remain in place and are perceived to be viable alternatives by public managers. It also suggests the need to reform the types of PPPs that are used in order to secure greater innovation and value-for-money.

And yet, despite all these concerns and caveats, we find little reason for anticipating that a return to a 'one size fits all' model of public sector provision in any of the sectors that we have considered would benefit citizens. Preventing public managers from commissioning services in partnership with the private and voluntary sectors will not help improve public services. On balance, and so long as it is properly managed, we think that the uneven shift towards greater diversity in service provision has the potential to generate favourable outcomes – and we are not alone in holding this view. It is worth noting that few serious commentators are calling for the nationalisation of service provision in areas where a plurality of providers already exists. Diversity looks set to become more prevalent: the new generation of public service organisations and programmes that have emerged since 1997 – the New Deals, Sure Start, Employment Zones, the Children's Fund, National Grid for Learning, Learning and Skills Councils – all involve working in partnership. This seems to have strengthened, rather than undermined, the capacity of government to achieve policy outcomes.

Where these changes will take us is not yet clear. The 'industrial organisation', as economists term it, of the emerging public service sector will vary from area to area. In some service sectors, such as social services, it will be made up of a dispersed set of autonomous organisations, resembling a 'flotilla of dinghies' (6 and Kendall, 1997). In other areas, such as prisons, the traditional public provider will remain the dominant force but a small collection of relatively large consortia will continue to keep it on its toes. In all areas the era of the monolithic public provider operating in isolation from the private and voluntary sectors seems to be passing. Diversity has crept into the UK's public services, often on terms that the left is uncomfortable with. It now seems set to stay. The challenge we face is to learn how to harness diversity in order to improve our public services.

Step 4: Establishing the criteria for assessing partnerships

So far we have emphasised the case for tax-based funding of services, highlighted the distinction between funding and provision and made clear that the choice of PPPs should be available in all service areas. Our argument has been that the concept of partnership between the sectors is not flawed, but often the practice has been. The fourth step of our argument is to be clear about the criteria used to assess whether individual PPP proposals should proceed. We do this in the full knowledge that care needs to be taken to compare the expected performance of PPPs with a realistic account of the outcomes that public sector provision would produce.

Protecting social equity

Public services represent the collective desire of society to respond to the social needs of citizens. Access to these services should not, by definition, be determined by ability to pay, social status, or the preferences of the service provider. The prioritisation of investment projects must be determined by the public interest rather than whether or not they are 'PPP-friendly'. The nature of services must be determined by the relevant public authority. Partnerships must not be used as a way to introduce charges or fees or reduce the comprehensiveness of services. If it were the case that the use of PPPs militated against this focus on social need and the public interest then we would oppose them regardless of whether or not they met other criteria such as value-for-money.

Value-for-money and quality

If a project is not expected to deliver value-for-money then it should not proceed. Making a reality of this statement requires two things. Firstly, there needs to be a shared understanding of what the term value-for-money actually means. It does not focus only on cost-effectiveness in the delivery of public services. The concept of value-for-money gives equal weight to quality considerations: it is the optimum combination of cost and quality in meeting the needs of service users (discussed in Chapter 4). Achieving value-for-money should be about identifying the most cost-effective way of securing a high quality service – if the quality of a service deteriorates then a partnership has failed. The second requirement is that there needs to be a credible and transparent procedure for determining whether or not value-for-money is being attained.

Clear political accountability and transparency

The type of partnerships highlighted in this Report involve spending public funds, providing key services and setting policy priorities. As a result they impact directly on the rights and interests of citizens and communities. Clear forms of accountability and redress are a pre-condition for the legitimacy of partnerships. Moreover, appropriate accountability mechanisms need to reflect the varying interests that individuals have as citizens, service users and taxpayers. It is also vital that high and common standards of accountability apply across the public service sector – levels of access to information and redress should not vary according to whether or not public services are delivered via the public or private sectors.

Conclusion

While some at opposite ends of the political spectrum take comfort in the fact that their strategies for reforming public services can be expressed in very simple terms, we think that the pragmatic centre-left should forsake simplistic solutions. Instead it should develop a pluralist model of public management that does full justice to the complexity of delivering the best possible public services. Partnership will play an important role in this.

Underpinning this will be the recognition that the increasing role of partnership arrangements has created a considerable grey area in which traditionally troublesome questions of ownership lose some of their edge. This fits with the view, long espoused in British politics by centre-left reformers, that the whole significance of public ownership is overblown. Formal ownership arrangements matter far less than the quality of the services.

This does not mean that we endorse the view adopted by some that PPPs herald an entirely new era of public administration, in which the role of the role of government is confined to that of purchaser and regulator. However, we do recognise that the question of who should own the underlying assets used in public services is increasingly a second order issue. This is not a coded way of saying that there is no role for public ownership. Often this will provide the best and most pragmatic solution. It does, however, suggest that the main focus for the centre-left should be in linking the case for high and sustainable levels of public spending to step-changes in service quality and responsiveness. This means clarifying the potential role of a diverse range of partnerships in improving value-for-money, securing greater social equity, increasing the scope for community and user participation and guaranteeing that all public service providers are responsive to the changing needs of the citizens who rely on them. These are the themes of the rest of this Report.

Endnotes

1   'Let me say at the outset that partnerships between the public and the private sector are a cornerstone of the Government's modernisation programme for Britain. They are central to our drive to modernise our key public services. Such partnerships are here and they are here to stay' (Milburn, 1999).

2   International experience demonstrates the extent to which diversity in the provision of core public services is already an established fact of life. A defining characteristic of health care in Canada, for example, is that it is publicly funded but delivered by private, not-for-profit organisations (World Health Organisation, 1996). Numerous OECD countries, including Belgium, France, Germany, Austria, Japan and Luxembourg can be characterised as having social insurance based funding of healthcare, with a mix of public and private

providers. Similarly a mixed economy of provision exists in a number of EU education systems.

3   'In contriving any system of government, and fixing the several checks and controls of the constitution, every man ought to be supposed a knave and to have no other end, in all his actions, than private interest. By this interest, we must govern him and, by means of it, notwithstanding his insatiable avarice and ambition, co-operate to the public good'

4   This claim that there is still a deep left-right split on spending on public services does not go uncontested, especially since New Labour accepted planned Conservative spending limits for its first two years in government after 1997, and the Conservatives similarly pledged to accept much of Labour's higher planned spending levels announced in the Comprehensive Spending Review of 2000. But this Review did mark an important watershed, and in the 2001 Parliament the divide between the parties is likely to become still clearer.

5   These goods are, in the jargon of economists, 'non-rivalrous, non-divisible and non-rejectable' (one person's consumption does not diminish another's).

6   There are several exceptions to this and these will be clearly sign-posted, for example, the discussions of public enterprise in Chapter 5.

7   See for example Donnison, 1984; Hirst, 1994; Rustin *et al*, 1997. The real cause of the progressive left, as these authors make clear, should be in ensuring that all service providers open up their governance structures to public scrutiny and deliberation and that government does not move from favouring in-house monopoly to a cosy relationship with a few favoured private providers.

2. Foundations for partnership

Improving public services based upon either of the polar positions – privatisation or a public sector monopoly – is unlikely to bring about the improvements that we want to see. But why should PPPs make a difference? What are the types of partnership on offer and what might public managers achieve through partnerships that they would find it difficult to deliver on their own? This Chapter explores these issues. It sets out why in principle PPPs have a contribution to make and provides a foundation for the more detailed arguments which follow. It has four main components. First, it provides a context for the discussion of PPPs by sketching out stylised models of management in public services (later we return to the issue of how partnerships fit into these categorisations). Second, it examines what the term PPP actually means, the range of approaches to partnership, and the extent to which PPPs actually represent a new way of thinking about the governance of public services. Third, it outlines the type of contribution that, in principle at least, partnerships could make within public services. Fourth, it explores the conditions that need to be in place if partnerships are to play a substantive role in improving services.

Models of public management

In traditional thinking, there have been four different models of governance and organisation for delivering public services. These are all highly stylised, and most actual systems of public service delivery in practice contain elements of more than one of them. However, it is possible to characterise actual systems, in different service areas, according to the dominant model employed.

Command and control

The first, variously described as 'command and control' or 'managerial hierarchy', relies upon a state-funded administrative bureaucracy to organise and deliver services. The state owns all the relevant facilities and employs, directly or indirectly, all staff. Resources are allocated according to managerial fiat. Service delivery occurs through administrative processes, through the instructions given by superiors to those lower down in the hierarchy. Individuals are assumed to be motivated to follow those instructions by both positive and negative incentives: positive rewards include salary rises and promotions; possible penalties include salary cuts and threats to job security. Whether positive or negative, the incentives are fundamentally self-interested: those working within the hierarchy of the public sector are assumed to be 'knaves', working for themselves rather than the public good (Le Grand, 1998). Those at the head of the hierarchy, on the other hand, are assumed to be issuing their instructions, not so as to further their own interests, but in order to promote the public interest: not 'knaves' but 'knights'. Pre-1979, nationalised industries providing public utilities (electricity, gas, water, railways) were predominantly command and control in organisational form. This model can serve the public interest effectively, but only under highly specific conditions. The top of the hierarchy must have the public interest at the centre of their concerns and be able to express that interest as a simple objective that can be communicated readily to all those involved in the delivery of services. The hierarchy must be able effectively to monitor their subordinates' actions; to be clear whether their instructions have or have not been followed. Finally, achievement of the objective should not depend on subordinates exercising initiative or discretion.

Networks and trust

The second model of governance depends on trust and networks as means of service delivery. This is a version of what has been described as a 'clan' culture (Ouchi, 1980). As with command and control, the state provides the funds, employs staff directly or indirectly and owns all facilities. However, service delivery on the ground is undertaken by qualified professionals who are allowed a great deal of freedom in making the relevant decisions. Resource allocation at higher levels is undertaken by collaborative networks, with all interested parties working together to achieve a mutually acceptable outcome. Unlike command and control, the individuals working in the public sector are assumed to be motivated by a public service or a professional ethos at all levels; their principal concern is assumed to be with the needs and wants of the clients they are serving and all their resource and service allocation decisions are made with those needs and wants in mind. All involved are assumed to be knights, not knaves.

Trust and network systems can operate effectively if the individuals who work within the public sector, and hence the institutions which they staff, can be safely relied upon to serve the public interest with each profession regulating itself. However, if those individuals have a different conception of the public interest from that of the public and/or its representatives – then trust and network systems can prove very troublesome. Perhaps the principal difficulty with this model is that there are few mechanisms for bringing individuals not pursuing the public interest into line, or incentives to encourage them to improve performance. One of the few means available is moral persuasion: trying to persuade the defaulters to mend their ways by appealing to their sense of public duty. This can be done either internally or in public, as, with the current vogue for naming-and-shaming. The pre-1991 National Health Service was an example of this kind of model, relying upon politicians and civil servants to allocate resources at a macro level and giving medical professionals almost complete clinical freedom to make ground-level decisions as to what treatment patients should receive.

Purchase and provide

Under the third model, often called the 'new public management', the state relies upon a range of techniques and market-based mechanisms to improve the performance of public agencies. One of the best known variants of this model (the one focused on here) uses quasi-markets for delivering public services. This involves a separation of the purchasers and providers of public services, and competition between the latter for service delivery.[1] The state funds the purchase of services, usually allocating resources to centralised purchasing agencies. Provision is undertaken by providers competing with one another for contracts for service delivery from purchasers. In the stylised model providers are assumed to be motivated primarily by the interests of the organisation for which they work, purchasers by the needs and wants of the people on whose behalf they are purchasing. Economic theory suggests a number of conditions need to be met if quasi-markets are to work in the public interest. However, experience of quasi-markets in action, in Britain and abroad, suggests that often these conditions do not exist (Le Grand and Bartlett, 1993):

- A competitive market for providers is needed, though in reality this is often limited.

- Purchasers must genuinely want quality and be able to gauge it. Otherwise, self-interested providers may engage in what has been termed 'opportunistic' behaviour (Williamson, 1985). That is, they will reduce costs by sacrificing quality.

- Purchasers and providers need to have the right motivations and incentive structures.

- There should be limited opportunity for providers to select users otherwise they may choose to offer services to only selected groups of citizens (known as the problem of 'cream-skimming').

Privatise and regulate

The fourth model is where both provision and funding are undertaken privately, but the state acts as a regulator. All facilities are privately owned by providers, who sell their services to consumers. Consumers purchase these services out of their own resources. Resource allocation decisions are taken by individual providers and purchasers, with the market acting as an invisible hand supposedly bringing them into accord with each other and with the public interest. However, for a variety of reasons, including natural monopoly and poorly informed consumers, the market fails at this task and the highly visible hand of the state regulator is needed, determining the structure of the market and the price, quantity, and quality of the services provided. The providers are assumed to be motivated by self-interest (knaves) and the regulators by the public interest (knights).

The privatisation/regulation model can work, sometimes delivering significant service improvements, but again only under very specific conditions. The regulating authority must have enough information properly to do its job; and it must not be 'captured' by the industry that it is regulating, though in practice both of these conditions are often difficult to fulfil.[2] But the principal condition for this model to be suitable for public service delivery is that it is applied to a service where public funding is not critical to secure the public interest. This may be true for utilities such as telecommunications and gas but, as we have already made clear, this is not the case for the key public services with which we are primarily concerned. Hence the privatise and regulate model is not of relevance to most of our discussion on partnership.

Public Private Partnerships

All these stylised models have problems in delivering public services. Do they exhaust the range of possible governance models, or is there an alternative, a variant on one or more of the models, that could reap the benefits of some of these models without incurring all the costs? We think there is. Some of the emerging models of partnership constitute a potentially innovative hybrid of existing approaches to public management. They primarily draw on the insights of the new public management, though too often they are not sensitive to some of the telling critiques made of this approach. However, before taking this discussion forward we need first to take a step back in order to clarify what we do and do not mean by the term 'public private partnership'. Then we shall be in a better position to assess the extent to which PPPs represent something new.

The starting point for an analysis of partnership must be clarity over the phrase PPP. 'Public' 'private' and 'partnership' are three of the most slippery terms in the modern political dictionary. Putting them together is almost an invitation to muddled thinking and confusion. Avoiding this requires a proper understanding of each of the component elements.

What do we mean by 'public'?

The 'public' part of a PPP is generally easy to identify, typically constituting a recognised public sector authority such as a local council, next-step agency, hospital trust or central government department. In some instances, however, the definition of the public sector agency is less clear cut.[3] Organisations formally constituted as private bodies, such as housing associations, may be so dependent upon public funding and regulation, that they exist in a no-man's land between the two sectors. Moreover the expansion of joint venture organisations straddling the public and private sectors will itself challenge the traditional ways in which the public-private interface has been managed.

There is also the possibility that in some service areas the 'public' element of PPPs could refer as much to groups of citizens as it does to legally recognised public sector agencies. Conventional PPPs are deals done between public sector purchasers and private providers. Service users and local citizens are solely the consumers rather than the commissioners or monitors of these public services. Often this approach makes sense. However, in an increasing number of areas there are demands for the ultimate beneficiaries of services to have a say in how services are set up and who provides them. The challenge of designing appropriate and tractable forms of user and community involvement applies to all types of service provision, but raises particular issues for the design of PPPs (discussed in Chapter 9).

What do we mean by 'private'?

Throughout this Report the term PPPs will be used in a broad sense, encompassing relationships between government and both the private and the voluntary and charitable sectors. Often, however, we explicitly distinguish between the voluntary (not-for-profit) and private (for-profit) sector,[4] a divide that for some people is every bit as important as that between the public and private sectors. It is also important to bear in mind the incredible variety of firms that exists *within* the for-profit sector. Discussions of PPPs tend to focus on a small number of large, high-profile facilities management, building and IT companies. If partnerships are truly to bring change to the public services then these established players will need to be complemented by more innovative combinations of voluntary organisations, social enterprises and smaller firms. One of the themes running through this Report is that public authorities need to learn how to encourage greater diversity in the provision of public services. This argument applies as much within the 'for-profit' and 'not-for-profit' sectors as it does between them.

What do we mean by 'partnership'?

Inevitably a term that has been associated with so many different types of initiative will arouse suspicion. While we accept that there is not, and probably never will be, a universally accepted definition of partnership, we need to set out how the term is used in this Report. Some people are content to label any contact between government and business or civil society a partnership, others seek to reserve the term for relationships fulfilling a multitude of criteria.

Generally it is far easier to say what a partnership is not rather than what it is. A relationship that is entirely regulatory in nature is unlikely to constitute a risk-sharing partnership (for example, between a regulator and a utility company). Nor would the payment of a subsidy to a firm. A short-term contract for the provision of a good or service is not a partnership – otherwise 'every time the public sector orders a round of sandwiches from a caterer we have created a new partnership'.[5] If the entire basis of the relationship can be specified in a contract it is unlikely to constitute a meaningful partnership.

A relatively straightforward working definition would go along the following lines: 'a PPP is a risk-sharing relationship between the public and private sectors based upon a shared aspiration to bring about a desired public policy outcome'. This is a broad account that says little about the qualitative nature of the relationship between the parties involved, or the process through which partnerships are formed or sustained. It does not, for instance, demand ingredients such as 'high-trust relationships'. Nor does it require that the partners share an 'identity of interests' – some types of partnership come into being precisely to contain and manage the conflicting interests of different groups. Moreover, the private sector will often have an interest in making a profit; whereas the public sector (typically) will not. However, this working definition does require the relationship to be structured in such a way that ensures that there is a shared aspiration to bring about an agreed outcome.

The emphasis on shared risk in this definition is based on the view that PPPs entail a degree of mutual dependence – whether they work or fail should depend upon the actions of both sides to the agreement. The form of this shared risk will vary. It may be financial, such as contractual incentives or penalties linking payment to performance, or it may involve less tangible (but still important) reputational risk.

The other key feature of this definition is the suggestion that the partnership's purpose is to deliver a publicly agreed 'outcome' rather than a 'public service' *per se*. This casts the net more widely than those definitions of partnership that have focused entirely on public services. This is an important distinction: we want to consider not only partnerships which exist to deliver specific goods and services (cleaning, security), but also 'strategic' partnerships that exist to bring about more general policy outcomes (for example, local economic regeneration) which cannot be characterised as the delivery of a particular service.

The following are examples of public-private relationships – often referred to as PPPs – some of which will give stronger expression to joint-risk sharing than others:

- *Private Finance Initiative.* This is generally where a private consortium contracts to design, build, finance and operate an asset-based service. The public sector client pays a fee over the life of the contract to the private consortium that is in part contingent upon services meeting specified standards.

- *Long-term service provision contracts.* These are long-term public-private agreements for the provision of a service or a group of services. PPPs of this type often include contracts for the management of public assets and include the provision of other services where no 'new build' of public assets is required.

- *Joint ventures.* Here a distinct legal form is given to the partnership arrangement usually involving the public and private bodies assuming some form of equity stake in the PPP. Joint ventures benefit from not relying on arms length relationships between the public and private sectors – the organisational form of joint ventures gives tangible expression to the commitment to work in partnership. However, they can prove to be unstable in the face of changing circumstances and also raise difficult issues concerning accountability and risk-transfer.

- *Wider markets.* There is also a growing use of partnership arrangements whereby the private sector enters into an agreement to exploit public sector assets commercially and share the proceeds with the relevant public agency.

- *Strategic partnerships.* These come in a number of forms. One variety involves groups of organisations coming together to put forward a bid to receive funds, for example for regeneration purposes (such as Single Regeneration Budget). The partnership organisation may then determine how these funds are to be spent. Other types of regeneration partnership will be more 'bottom-up' in nature, arising spontaneously rather than in response to central initiatives. Strategic partnerships are also created for the purpose of policy formulation and the setting of local priorities. They can take the form of either legal organisations or decision-making forums in which the public and private sectors work together to agree a plan for a local area.

The single most important component of a true partnership is probably the element hardest to measure, impose from the outside, or capture in a neat definition. This is the need for goodwill, flexibility and a degree of trust on both sides of the agreement. The view that 'partnership is more a state of mind than a legal formulation' is one that we have heard repeatedly. This focus on the extra-legal elements of partnership does not imply that there is no role for formal contracting within PPPs. On the contrary, most successful partnerships require the clarity that an underlying contact or formal agreement can bring. However, there must be something more to the relationship than a contract. Often shared risk (and the need for sharing rewards) arises precisely because it is impossible to write contracts that cover all the contingencies that arise when providing complex services. As suggested above, if it is possible for the *entire* basis of a relationship to be articulated in a contract, then it is unlikely to be a meaningful partnership.

PPPs: what can they help government to achieve?

One reason the term partnership excites passion and confusion in equal measures is the range of views about the rationale for introducing PPPs. Partnership can be a means or an end; a way of engendering collaboration or competition; and a method of delivering services or a new form of political governance. Given this spectrum of possibilities it is not surprising that there is no one rationale for adopting a 'partnership approach' towards the delivery or governance of public services. There are a number of inter-related 'problems' for which a PPP may be a solution. Here we set out the main rationales given for the types of partnership examined in this Report: outcome-oriented government; service improvement through diversity and contestability in public services; resolution of complex incentive problems within large projects; citizen participation; and better use of public assets.

Outcome-oriented government

A major potential benefit of PPPs is that they can help government to focus more clearly on the services people want, rather than simply on managing existing forms of service delivery. Partnerships help shift the focus from the inputs into service delivery to a concern with social *outcomes*. Discussions of public management tend to distinguish between the *inputs* into public services (hours of teaching); the outputs that are the product of public agencies (number of children undertaking a course); and the *outcomes* that are desired by wider community (educational attainment).

Boldly stated the ambition to focus on outcomes can appear glib. Yet the underlying philosophy of public managers (whether politicians or officials) should be to ensure that public services are designed so as to have a maximum effect on bringing about desirable outcomes. Providing services *per se* is not an end in itself. The question that has to be answered is what contributions a particular service makes to achieving an outcome. Consulting with users, developing quality audits and other mechanisms for improving the responsiveness of public services help to ensure a focus on end results. A constant readiness to think again about what is being achieved is also necessary.

Outcome orientation within public services is said to be aided by separating the commissioning role from the providing role. Commissioners are not then distracted from strategic planning, consulting, specifying and monitoring roles by having to manage a service delivery organisation. Public managers often comment that attempting to specify the nature of a planned service formally is a challenging experience – forcing out in the open issues which would otherwise remain hidden. This is an indication that the commissioning process can prove a highly effective way of concentrating minds on how to shape services to improve outcomes. A number of potentially radical implications follow from this view:

- Starting with the outcomes expected by service users rather than the existing shape of public sector agencies creates space for *new ideas about the role of government* in seeking to improve citizens' well-being. The whole configuration of a service – whether or not a particular service should exist, the relevant agency (or partnerships of agencies) responsible for commissioning services, the role of citizens in shaping them and the nature of the organisation providing them – is assessed and evaluated in relation to the agreed outcomes.

- A focus on outputs or outcomes should increase the *scope for innovation* in the management and delivery of public services. Traditional systems of public management, auditing and public accountability have focused on the inputs used in the production of public services. Likewise, public service career paths and reward systems have often favoured those who prioritise the observance of due process and minimise the chance of making mistakes. Entrepreneurship and innovation have not been accorded a similar status. A focus on outcomes should foster these attributes by allowing managers of services the maximum degree of flexibility in working out how to achieve agreed targets.

- Potential *service providers* are assessed on their ability to help bring about service outcomes (rather than on their legal structure or their public, private or voluntary sector status). This implies that there are few reasons in principle to exclude voluntary or private service providers from sensitive areas of the public services *if they can help achieve desired outcomes*. Inevitably this line of argument rubs up against the still strongly held belief that large swathes of frontline public services should be 'no-go' areas for anyone other than the public sector. Our view is clear on this. We believe that the arguments used to maintain these 'no-go' areas are often flawed (as Chapter 6 argues, they are often arbitrary, based upon defending organisational rather than citizen interests, and sit uneasily with long-standing practice within parts of the public services). But we are equally clear that government should base its decisions on evidence rather than a pre-disposition towards using partnership agreements as a way of delivering public services. A willingness to utilise partnerships must not result in a 'private good, public bad' approach to policy.

However, it is easy to overstate the link between PPPs and outcome-orientation. There are many ways of encouraging public sector providers to focus on outcomes. Indeed central government often imposes red tape and process requirements on public sector service providers which makes it hard for them to do this. Accountability procedures often focus on inputs. If outcome-orientation is desirable, then it should apply to in-house provision just as much as to services delivered through partnership.

Quality though diversity and contestability in public services

A different approach to partnership emphasises its role in providing government with a wider menu of options for procuring capital projects and delivering services. Its starting point is that – as well as suffering from too little investment – public services have had too little *diversity* in provision over recent decades.

One central argument for encouraging diversity is lack of knowledge about the forms of procurement that deliver value-for-money and a high quality of service. For example, traditional models of capital procurement have long been criticised for offering questionable value-for-money. However, the lack of diversity in the system and bias against experimenting with new ways of managing capital projects has ensured a slow response to this under-performance. In many areas systems of procurement have been allowed to ossify due to a lack of exposure to new thinking. As Chapter 4 makes clear, the onset of the PFI had the benefit of generating a shake-up in approaches to procurement. The risk now is that in some sectors a narrow model of PFI has itself become the new orthodoxy.

The same arguments in favour of diversity also apply to the provision of mainstream services – though here they are likely to generate more controversy. In too many parts of the public services there has been a limited pool of potential providers, too little exposure to new ways of working, and too many restrictions on the type of organisations that can work with the public sector in delivering quality services. In the right circumstances, a wider array of providers is likely to trigger more innovation, more learning, a better fit between services and local preferences and a better basis for comparison and benchmarking.

Allowing for diversity could go hand in hand with efforts to make public services (or components of them) more *contestable*: that is, creating the possibility that new providers can be brought in to replace those who are not performing adequately in running a service. Contestability differs from the forced use of competition within public services (for example, the former Compulsory Competitive Tendering regime in local government) in a key respect. Compulsory competition insists on regular market testing of services (usually favouring the cheapest bidder) which inhibits the development of collaborative relationships and creates an adversarial relationship between purchasers and providers. In contrast contestability provides the purchaser with the *option* of going to an alternative provider if they feel that this will provide citizens with a better service. Whether or not this choice is exercised is not determined according to a rigid formula. It is determined by public managers on the ground.

There will always be restrictions on the extent to which this approach can take hold in the public sector: poorly performing businesses will go bankrupt in a way that government agencies will not and should not. But the issue remains of whether it would be desirable to introduce *a degree* of contestability within services, or the management of services. Our view is that there are areas in which contestability should be a lever available to public managers involved in commissioning sevices.

Contestability has been applied in different ways around the world.[6] It often involves providers agreeing long-term contracts with public purchasers on the basis that the contract remains in place if the quality of the service is maintained and improved at a reasonable rate. The key point about contestability is the *latent* but real possibility that services can be switched to other organisations, acting as a continual incentive for providers to consider how they can improve their performance. This can have real impact. Citizens within a locality benefit if a failing provider is evicted and a contract transferred to a new provider; citizens elsewhere can also benefit from the knock-on effect that this has on providers in their locality.[7]

In principle contestability offers the potential for clear gains. However, it does not necessarily make a case for using PPPs:

- It does not in itself require public-private contracting. It is perfectly possible to create a degree of contestability *within* the public sector (for example, 'fresh start' schools in education). Much of the evidence confirms that the largest gains derive from contestability *per se*, regardless of whether or not there is a public-private element to it (Szymanski and Williams, 1993). This chimes with the point made in Chapter 1 that the private sector is not inherently more efficient than the public. However, before this type of argument is used to exclude private or voluntary providers from delivering public services we need to be clear about whether or not this would be in the interests of citizens.

- The problems and costs of making contestable systems work should not be underestimated. Past experience suggests that inappropriate contestability can generate large transaction costs for unclear benefits. The lessons from the 'quasi-market' experience in the UK and abroad need to be learnt. Contestability can also lead to fragmentation and division across provider organisations. As a result citizens can experience a disjointed service. Similarly, service organisations which are potential competitors may be reluctant to work together, share best-practice, or adopt integrated information systems.

- A related concern is the apparent tension between the benefits of creating long-term collaborative relationships between purchasers and providers and the ever-present possibility that a purchaser may choose to switch to a new provider. This tension is real but by no means unique to the public sector. Many commercial firms build-up long-run relationships with suppliers, based upon flexibility and mutual accommodation, at the same time as being aware that these relationships will not endure if suppliers seriously under-perform. There is often a 'stickiness' in these relationships even though contracts do get switched from time to time: long-term collaboration can co-exist alongside a degree of contestability (Deakin and Michie, 1997).

ll these issues must inform discussions about whether it is desirable to introduce a degree of contestability within particular areas of the public services. Even if it is, this still leaves open what we mean by the term 'degree'. The *dosage* of contestability required within a service to generate pressures for improved performance is a critical issue. In the past policy has tended to swing between polar positions, either favouring monopoly public provision or the (attempted) creation of a fully private market. As Chapter 1 pointed out, different public service structures are likely to evolve in different service areas. However, it is worth emphasising that often it only takes a relatively small dose of contestability to generate a significant response from incumbent providers.

Finally, if a degree of contestability between public and private sectors is deemed to be desirable within an area of the public services, this needs to be reflected in wider regulatory frameworks. At the least it requires some form of 'level playing field' between sectors, implying a willingness to address arbitrary regulatory and accounting provisions favouring private, public, or voluntary sectors. Equally significant, the creation of a level playing field also means being prepared to challenge the cultural barriers that impede the selection of 'best' partners regardless of their sector.

Currently factors impeding creation of a level playing field, and introduction of a degree of contestability, work in both directions. Many public managers feel they have no choice but to use private finance (and service providers) if they want to get the go-ahead for a new project (the subject of Chapter 4). Similarly, restrictions on public agencies' ability to raise capital, take financial risks, or to trade with other public bodies have greatly inhibited public enterprise (Chapters 6 and 7). Restrictions on public enterprise need to be rooted out and removed. On the other hand, even in the areas where private and voluntary organisations are not restricted from providing public services we have heard evidence from a range of organisations who feel that they are at a serious disadvantage in tendering for public contracts if there is also an in-house bid. The question of how to create a level playing field is a theme throughout this Report.

Resolving incentive problems

Perhaps the argument most often made for using PPPs in large-scale projects is the powerful incentive they provide to private partners to deliver capital projects on time and to budget and then to ensure that underlying assets are properly maintained over their life-cycle. The fact that the private sector puts its own capital at risk, receives payments linked to performance, and has to compete with other consortia (and a public sector comparator), is claimed to produce a clear drive for cost-effectiveness and innovation compared to conventional public sector procurement. However, too sharp a distinction between models of procurement should not be drawn: there is a continuum of possible partnership arrangements that exist between current models of PFI and traditional procurement. The most suitable form of procurement will be contingent on the nature of the risks involved in the project (Chapter 4). The PPP deals that work well give the right incentives to both sides; allowing the private sector to innovate to deliver value-for-money while the public sector pre-commits to funding proper capital maintenance.

Accessing new skills

The move towards a more diverse public service sector opens up possibilities for drawing on the skills of leading edge private and voluntary organisations. Most notably the public sector can import generic contract management, risk analysis, and financial planning skills that it sometimes lacks. It can also draw on specialisms that exist in a range of policy areas from special needs education to re-skilling the long-term unemployed.

Citizen participation and civic governance

It has already been indicated that it is a mistake to think partnership is just about service provision – it is also about creating new forms of civic governance. A partnership can be a forum providing new opportunities for community, voluntary, and business groups to play a role in formulating responses and setting priorities in relation to local needs. In the past partnerships have been thought of in relation to local regeneration strategies that have arisen out of initiatives such as the Single Regeneration Budget. Ensuring the effective involvement of local communities in these projects is an important end in itself. A central question relating to PPPs in the future is how far this imperative for community involvement will spread into more mainstream forms of service provision.

The last few years have provided plenty of attempts. Education Action Zones have tried to give the local community and business groups a stake in local educational strategies. The Government's proposals for Local Strategic Partnerships could see a range of public, private and voluntary groups involved in shaping patterns of public service provision across local authorities. Chapter 9 illustrates the growing range of areas where public authorities could help cultivate the idea that civil society should be a producer and commissioner – not just a consumer – of public services. This point needs to be considered alongside the above discussion on contestability. Should the decision to select or switch service providers in a locality reside solely with public authorities or might there be a way of including service users in this process? To date there has been little creative policy analysis about the role citizens/users could play in the contestability process.[8] Traditional price-based competition managed by public sector purchasers has been the basis for allocating contracts. Democratising the process of contestability is, however, an idea gathering momentum in sectors such as housing and education.

Better use of public sector assets and skills

Partnerships can also be a way of helping the public sector to make the most of its existing assets. The public sector has within its control a huge store of assets whose commercial and social value has remained untapped for too long. Traditional forms of public sector accounting have provided few incentives and plenty of barriers to making better use of them. At one level agreements with commercial partners are a means for public agencies to generate revenue from under-utilised *physical* assets (for example, developing derelict land, or laying cable underneath the hard-shoulder on motorways or canal-sides). Increasingly, however, the same argument applies to the *intellectual* capital that exists within the public sector. High profile examples of this include efforts to harness the enormous technical expertise that exists within many government departments and agencies. A less developed strand of thought concerns the extent to which joint ventures between successful public sector providers and specialist private firms (for example, Local Education Authorities and educational organisations) could be used to help other public bodies. It is also the case that many public institutions own a 'brand' which is itself commercially valuable (for example, the BBC). Using these types of partnership as a spur to public enterprise raises a host of further issues including the application of the fiscal rules relating to public enterprise (Chapter 5) and the rules governing joint ventures and public sector trading (Chapter 7).

Pre-conditions for success

While the rationales for PPPs require clarification, it is also vital to identify the political and institutional factors that need to be in place if a partnership approach is to work and endure throughout the public services. In this section we focus on these overarching 'macro' factors, leaving aside for now the detailed 'micro' considerations which are critical in determining the success of any one PPP.

A commitment to adequate funding for public services

Chapter 1 made clear that those who support high public spending on services have traditionally backed public sector monopoly provision. Occasionally this political alignment has been challenged – but usually for the wrong reasons. In times of fiscal hardship some on the pragmatic left in the UK and elsewhere have been willing to make the case for contracting-out or PFI on the basis that this will (respectively) shave some of the costs of service provision or provide off-balance-sheet investment. Inevitably, support for PPPs based on these arguments falls away when resources become more plentiful. The argument made throughout this Report is that this is precisely the wrong type of approach to take to PPPs. Partnerships born out of fiscal austerity are much more likely to end in failure. Their focus tends to be exclusively on price rather than quality. Similarly, the rush to get investment projects off-balance sheet can lead to poor projects being undertaken due to an unbalanced approach to risk-transfer (discussed in Chapter 4).

Indeed we find the opposite line of argument more convincing. A sustained period of high spending on public services can give rise to a lack of pressure for cost-effectiveness and innovation. Diversity in service provision and models of procurement provides a safeguard against this. The stronger the case for higher levels of spending on public services, the greater the need to think about how value-for-money including continual improvements in quality can be secured.

A consistent approach

At the moment there are a range of approaches towards the use of the private and voluntary sector in public services – these are laid out in Chapter 3. In some services it is felt that there should be no non-public sector involvement at all. In other areas government has made a positive virtue of encouraging pluralism in provision. It is often unclear, however, why any given approach is deemed suitable for one service area but not others.

Does it matter if there are contrasting approaches towards the use of PPPs across service areas? There are, after all, different types of market failure and varying degrees of private sector capacity in different service areas that might explain these variations. What is striking is the extent to which these market-failure and capacity arguments fail to provide a rationale for the patterns of private and voluntary provision of public services that have emerged in the UK. Indeed, as Chapter 3 shows, often it is in precisely the areas where the problems of contracting for services could be expected to be most acute (psychiatric care, prisons), and existing private sector capacity is most limited, that some of the most significant increases in partnership activity have occurred.

This scatter-gun approach towards the role of partnership appears inchoate and opportunistic rather than coherent and principled. It leaves policy-makers open to the charge that they appear to favour the use of PPPs as a remedy for short-term political problems rather than as a long-term solution to the requirements of public services. So a key condition for building support for a partnership-based approach to public services is a clear and consistent account of when and why PPPs have a role to play.

A strong public sector: skills, strategy, and structure

Making a success of partnerships also demands a new breed of public manager. The skills required for successful commissioning of services are very different to those necessary for running traditional public bureaucracies. At the moment public managers are by and large trained for the latter rather than the former. Consequently, in many service areas a gap has emerged between government's appetite for partnerships and its capacity to manage them. Indeed, one of the ironies of political debate on PPPs is that this under-investment in public sector capacities has led to some poorly specified and managed contracts which themselves have given rise to some of the most prominent examples of so-called 'government failure'.[9]

This lack of capacity to manage partnerships may seem an unlikely problem for government to suffer from. The public sector is by far the biggest purchaser of goods and services. It should have huge bargaining power and a reservoir of expertise to draw upon. However, the public sector is a large spender made up of many small purchasers. Often public agencies will have far less experience of negotiating partnering agreements than the organisations they are contracting with, as well as restricted access to specialist advice. Without a co-ordinated approach each small purchasing unit – a hospital trust, or district authority – is likely to remain at a considerable disadvantage in the negotiation and management of a partnership. As Chapter 8 argues, rectifying this will involve improving skills, sharing templates of successful contracts, pooling information on the performance of different providers and fostering vibrant supplier markets in order to increase choice and avoid dependency on particular providers. It will also mean retaining and circulating aspirational public managers with expertise in commissioning a variety of projects and an ability to engage with leading-edge service providers. The surest way for PPPs to fail is if they become a safe backwater for the least dynamic elements of both public and private sectors.

It is not just the skill-gap within public authorities that needs to be addressed, it is also the capacity of different public agencies and authorities to work together on partnerships. Over recent years a lack of a clear delineation of responsibility between different public agencies involved in PPPs has contributed to a number of poorly put-together projects. Other potentially innovative PPPs do not proceed because joined-up public sector working is so hard to bring about. There is an irony in all this. In the early years of the 1997-2001 Blair administration it was often said that public service reform should focus on 'standards not structures'. This sounded like a neat way of focusing on what matters most to citizens. However, it also diverted attention from the underlying truth that 'structures' matter – and they tend to matter more in partnership arrangements.

The lessons set out throughout Part III of this Report are clear. Introducing PPPs in areas where there is a lack of public sector management skills, unclear responsibilities between different parts of the public sector, or an unwillingness on the behalf of public agencies to work jointly can be a recipe for under-performance and sometimes chaos. Careful thought therefore needs to be given to the types of capacities that public purchasers need to retain in-house if they are to govern all public services effectively. It may be that the government that gives up 'rowing' in order to improve its 'steering' may end up simply shouting instructions from the towpath.

Responsible private and voluntary providers

Much of the discussion of PPPs rightly focuses on what government needs to do be an effective partner, but this only represents part of the story of successful partnership. Private and voluntary organisations also need to learn new skills, embrace new ways of working and generate trust. Improving quality needs to become the defining mission of all public service organisations. Therefore, operating within the public service sector means accepting a demanding set of obligations. Strong accountability mechanisms should be in place for providers offering services directly to citizens. Often this will involve compliance with legislation which may not apply to firms not operating within the public service sector. As Chapter 10 points out this is already happening, for instance through the provisions of the Human Rights Act. However, other steps need to be taken by public authorities to encourage private providers to put their reputation at stake over the quality of the services they provide. If private or voluntary sector providers have seriously under-performed on a public contract then this information should be made easily accessible to the rest of the public sector. And, perhaps most important of all, is the need for a recognition from the private and voluntary sector of the importance of preserving and cultivating a public service ethos.

There are, however, limits to this approach. There is no point in the public sector entering into a PPP with a private company and then seeking to regulate it into behaving precisely as a public agency would. Self-evidently, for-profit companies will seek to make a profit. They will tend to respond sharply to financial incentives – which is after all, one of the reasons for using PPPs in the first place. This raises some difficult issues about whether or not there are areas of service provision which should be sheltered from the for-profit sector. This issue is taken up in Chapter 6.

Legitimacy among the public and workforce

Polling evidence suggests that the *principle* of public services being delivered in partnership with private and voluntary organisations may be a popular one – though, as with all polling evidence, it is possible to elicit very different responses depending on how the questions are phrased – and even without variation in the questions there seems to be a high degree of variability in views (Chapter 6).

But it is also the case that considerable public scepticism exists in relation to several high profile PPPs. There is a clear problem in the way in which many PPPs are perceived. Someone starting off with a limited knowledge of partnership might easily conclude that PPPs are nothing more than an accounting fiddle, a way of cutting costs rather than improving quality, or a stick used to beat public sector professionals (or a combination of all three). A key argument in this Report is that getting a different message across will require politicians to give a clear and consistent account of the pros and cons of PPPs, accepting when they under-perform, ensuring greater transparency, and critically, coming up with more imaginative ways of engaging local citizens within the partnership process. At the moment partnerships tend to be 'done to', rather than 'done by', local communities.

Ultimately the future of public services will depend on the recruitment, retention and motivation of skilled employees – together with the public's continued willingness to pay taxes to fund them. For both of these reasons it is critical that partnerships are, and are perceived to be, a legitimate way of delivering services. At the moment this is too often not the case. Many public sector workers who feel under-valued, under-paid and under-motivated remain instinctively opposed to the prospect of transferring to a private sector service provider. There are, of course, many counter examples where employees feel that they have benefited from transferring to the private sector; but the term 'partnership' has been applied in too many instances where the only discernible impact of public-private working has been a reduction in the terms and conditions of employees. Even though this is sometimes the result of what is termed 'bargain basement' shopping by the public sector it serves to breed suspicion and hostility about the concept of partnership. Chapter 8 looks at the evidence on the impact of PPPs on the labour force and considers the case for an improvement in the current system of protection for public service employees.

An evidence-based approach

Our lack of knowledge about partnerships applies not just to how well they perform but even to the extent to which they exist. As Chapter 3 makes clear there is currently a woeful lack of publicly available data about the scale of PPPs and more widely the non-public provision of publicly funded services. Until this is rectified, efforts to assess the relative performance of different types of service provider across the public services will be severely impaired. Moreover, much of the relevant evidence that we do have is highly preliminary and patchy. Categorical statements by protagonists on either side of the debate should therefore be treated with great caution.

For these reasons policy-makers should embrace the principle of organised agnosticism. This means that for the foreseeable future there should be a concerted effort to pilot, monitor, and systematically evaluate a spectrum of partnership arrangements. It also means that politicians need to acknowledge that, depending on the evidence which emerges, the use of PPPs could be rolled back as well as rolled out.

Conclusion

This Chapter has argued that PPPs, defined in the way we have suggested, offer an important way of delivering public services. They offer a number of potential benefits, chief among which are outcome-oriented government; improvements in quality and choice through greater diversity and contestability; and enhanced citizen participation in decision-making. However, if these benefits are to be realised there must be a clear understanding of the need for adequate public funding of services, a consistent rationale for when to use PPPs, competent public authorities able to manage partnerships, responsible private and voluntary sector providers committed to quality, reassurance of citizens and employees on the principle and practice of partnership, and a robust evidence base on how partnerships perform. This is quite a list.

At the beginning of the Chapter a number of well-established models of public management were set out. The partnership arrangements that have developed to date in the UK are closest to the 'purchase and provide' approach of the 'new public management' with its emphasis on performance-based incentives and a purchaser-provider split. But the new public management has many shortcomings which need to be, but have not yet been, taken into account by many protagonists of partnership.

- It is too managerialist and technocratic, placing little or no emphasis on the importance of involving the community, both as users and as citizens.

- The desire to reduce costs through the rigid imposition of competitive tendering does not necessarily generate service-improvements (and sometimes achieves the opposite).

- The multitude of centrally set targets can greatly constrain the scope for innovation by managers and front-line workers.

- The exponential growth of inspection, benchmarking, auditing and monitoring brings its own costs and is highly bureaucratic.

In this Report we hope to show how the partnership model of public management could fit into a broader vision of the future of public services than that articulated by the new public management. Our approach is based on the following key points:

Social equity and legitimacy

- *Public funding and control of commissioning.* The core public services should remain publicly funded and should be commissioned and monitored by appropriate public authorities. This is the most important reason why the forms of partnership described in this Report do not amount to privatisation.

Quality and innovation

- *Diversity.* A wide pool of potential providers with different expertise and skills should be encouraged. Where appropriate, this means moving away from an automatic commitment to in-house provision and being open minded in identifying the best providers of a service, regardless of whether they are in the public, private or voluntary sectors.

- *Focus on outcomes.* Wherever feasible contracts for service providers should be set around outcomes rather than inputs. In capital projects the goal should be 'whole life' value-for-money.

- *Decentralisation.* There should be an assumption in favour of thorough decentralisation of operational decisions towards those front-line managers responsible for delivering outcomes.

- *Trust.* Long-term relationships built around shared aspirations for the service for which they are responsible should be encouraged, though these relationships will be balanced by a recognition that a degree of contestability will exist between providers.

Accountability and participation

- *Responsibility.* The roles of commissioners and providers of services, and what each is responsible for, should be clear.

- *Transparency.* Decisions by and the performance of commissioners and providers of public services should be open to full public scrutiny.

- *Responsiveness.* There should be a strong assumption in favour of consultation with service users over desired outcomes, user involvement in selecting service providers and (wherever possible) the linking of payments to providers to measures of user satisfaction.

At the heart of our conception of the public service sector and the role of partnership within it is the conviction that there is a wide range of public services which must remain universal and publicly funded. The greatest challenge of any form of public management is how to deliver these services to ensure the highest possible quality in a cost-effective and accountable manner. We think that PPPs should be an option open to public managers when making these decisions. Before taking our analysis forward we need to attempt to clarify the current order of magnitude of PPPs within our public services. This is the theme of Chapter 3.

Endnotes

1   There is an enormous literature on these topics. The *locus classicus* is probably Williamson (1975, 1985). See also Ouchi (1980); Le Grand and Bartlett (1993); Bartlett *et al* (1994); Bartlett *et al* (1998); Le Grand (1998).

2   Regulators often find it difficult to obtain the necessary data on costs and production processes and they often develop too sympathetic an understanding of the firm's point of view. Although in the British context this tendency may be offset by competition between regulators; see Corry *et al* (1997).

3   Many of the organisations that fall into this grey area are formally categorised as Local Public Spending Bodies and hence are considered here as public.

4   It is worth making the self-evident point that a PPP requires there to be some private component – the existence of joint working between different components of the public sector (for example, health and social services) does not constitute the type of partnership considered here. The only way in which this type of cross-departmental public-public activity falls within the terms of reference of our inquiry is if they themselves give rise to public private partnerships (for example, different departments jointly commission a service).

5   On the other hand, contracting-out some services, such as catering, is viewed as a form of PPP by some government departments. See Corry *et al* (1997) for a discussion of PPPs which does incorporate regulatory relationships.

6   For an overview of the experience in Australia see Commonwealth Department of Finance (1995).

7   As Ham (1996) has put it, 'it is the possibility that contracts may move that creates an incentive within the system, rather than the actual movement of contracts. Of course for the incentive to be real then contracts must shift from time to time, but this is only one element in the process and not necessarily the most important'.

8   See Mulgan (1994) for an exception to this.

9   'The most egregious tales of waste, fraud and abuse in government programmes have often involved greedy, corrupt and often criminal activity by the government's partners – and weak government management to detect and correct these problems' (Kettl, 1993).

II: Economics

3. How significant are PPPs?

Given the degree of political controversy provoked by discussion of PPPs and especially the Private Finance Initiative (PFI), one could easily assume that they already play a large role in the provision of public services and public investment. One could also easily assume that contracting by the state of publicly funded services from the private and voluntary sectors is a relatively recent innovation. Both of these assumptions would be wrong: PPPs are not new, nor do they represent more than a relatively modest fraction of overall public spending.

The main exception is social services where around half of publicly funded care was provided by the private or voluntary sectors by the end of the 1990s. This expansion in the contracting of care with private/voluntary providers predates the use of the term PPP and indeed ministers do not refer to this form of non-public provision as a partnership.

Getting some idea of the relative importance of non-public provision of public services and PPPs is of course very important in setting the background for thinking about the potential for partnership. Given the importance of establishing such a benchmark it is surprising that the evidence on the current scale of PPPs is both fragmentary and incomplete. Nowhere in Whitehall is it possible to obtain a clear picture of the overall scale and impact of PPPs and indeed the first recommendation of this Commission is that the gathering together of such data in Whitehall should be undertaken as a priority.

This Chapter sets out what is currently known about the scale of private and voluntary sector involvement in public services in a number of areas. Data on this is patchy; and the evidence that does exist generally does not allow us to distinguish between a true PPP and short-term contracting (though data on PFI is available). Hence most of the tables in this Chapter refer to total expenditure on private and voluntary sector delivery of services rather than PPPs *per se*. In cases where it is possible to break down the data to identify services provided specifically by either the private or voluntary sectors this is clearly stated. In instances where we simply refer to the 'private sector' this is because there is no (or negligible) voluntary sector involvement in that area of service delivery.

A typology of private/voluntary sector roles

Before assessing the relative importance of PPPs, this Chapter sets out a simple typology of the role of the private and voluntary sector as providers across different public service areas. There are five broad roles that public and private/voluntary providers may perform in key public services. They are:

- *Public Sector Default.* The public sector provides all services.

- *Private/Voluntary Sector Rescue.* The public sector provides all services, except if public providers are seen as failing when the private/voluntary sector acts as provider of last resort.

- *Level Playing Field.* There is no ideological objection to either public, private or voluntary sector provision and the decision as to who provides the service depends solely on a judgement of which provider will provide the 'best' service.

- *Public Sector Rescue.* The private/voluntary sector provides all services, except if they are seen as failing, in which case the public sector acts as provider of last resort.

- *Private/Voluntary Sector Default.* The private/voluntary sector provides all services on contract to public purchasers/commissioners.

Like all typologies, this has elements of over-simplification. But it helps clarify thinking about the role played by the private and voluntary sectors in service provision. Table 3.1 illustrates the five categories as a form of continuum with 'deeper' involvement and integration of the private/voluntary sectors as one moves from top to bottom. It presents examples of the services that can be classified as falling into each category.

The examples given below in Table 3.1 are meant to be illustrative rather than exhaustive. The different roles set out for the private/voluntary sectors are not necessarily clear-cut. For example, in some areas a 'level playing field' may be the ultimate goal, but, where a new market is being established, there may be initial incentives to encourage private or voluntary sector involvement. In other areas of service provision there seem to be unnecessary restrictions on public providers. A further oddity of the table is that there are few areas in which the role of the *public sector* is to provide a 'rescue' service. This does not mean, however, that the public sector could not replace a 'failing' private/voluntary provider – but that this has not, so far, represented the public sector's sole involvement in a service area.

Table 3.1 does clearly illustrate the qualitatively different ways in which private/voluntary providers can be used. It indicates that the majority of non-public sector provision in education and health currently falls into the 'ancillary' category. Private/voluntary sector involvement in core areas remains minimal. In schools and hospitals built under the PFI, private providers are responsible for a restricted range of ancillary services whilst core services are provided publicly. Yet there are exceptions where private and voluntary providers deliver 'core' frontline services, for example Special Educational Needs (SEN) provision and provision of nursing home places to the NHS. What is interesting about these exceptions is that often they apply to some of the most needy and vulnerable service users.

Table 3.1 A typology of private/voluntary sector roles across dfferent service areas

	Education	Health	Personal social services	Prisons
Public sector default	Management of most state schools	Most clinical services	Purchasing and care management	High risk prisoner escort services
Private/voluntary sector rescue	Contracting out of core Local Education Authority (LEA) services (to date)			Management of 'failing' public prisons
Level playing field Ancillary	PFI for schools Contracting for support services by schools and LEAs	PFI for hospitals	Contracting out of support services in local authority nursing and residential care homes	
Core	Contracting out of core Local Education Authority (LEA) services (in the future)		Provision of residential and domiciliary care	Management of new build prisons
Public sector rescue				Management of 'failing' private prisons
Private/voluntary sector default	Supply teachers Special Educational Needs Schools	Community pharmacies Agency nursing Nursing homes		Most escort services All new prisons to be built under the PFI

Over recent years, there has been a shift towards exploring deeper forms of private/voluntary sector involvement in health and education. Although, as yet, insignificant in terms of the scale of impact, this is highly important politically and in its implications for future service delivery. One likely possibility is that under the Best Value regime more Local Education Authorities (LEAs) will explore the scope for partnering with private and voluntary providers for a range of services. The Concordat between the NHS and independent sector, signed in November 2000, could also be of significance in signalling that private/voluntary sector providers should be considered alongside the NHS as potential providers of clinical services. Yet it is questionable whether, in practice, the Concordat will do much to alter the private/voluntary sector's status as the provider of last resort (see Chapter 7). Arguably in personal social services there is already a 'level playing field' for the provision of core services in residential and domiciliary care, though this is disputed.[1]

The Home Office has gone further than either health or education departments is establishing an environment whereby both public and private sectors can compete for the management of some new conventionally procured prisons. At the same time the government is now considering the use of the private sector as a rescue option to manage older 'failing' prisons (Thompson, 2000). However, it is notable that no new conventionally procured public prisons have been ordered since 1992 and the Government has now implied that all new prisons will be built under the PFI (Straw, 1998). This suggests that there is not a level playing field between the PFI and conventional procurement in the prison sector.

There is wide variation in the use of partnerships across different service areas. What remains unclear is whether these differences are the result of a process of consistent evaluation of the possibilities offered by PPPs. Where core services remain largely excluded from the remit of PPPs is this because of inherent difficulties in contracting for these services or because of political sensitivities? If private and voluntary sector providers have long been established in social care and are playing a greater role in the provision of prisons, should they be restricted from playing a greater role in health or education? These are some of the difficult questions that are tackled in Chapters 6 and 7.

Current public expenditure on private and voluntary provision

There is a dearth of centrally held data showing the extent of private/voluntary provision in key public services. This is particularly the case where expenditure is largely devolved, for example in education. In this section the extent of private/voluntary provision in four key public services – health, education, personal social services, and criminal justice – is assessed.

There are two definitional problems in evaluating the extent of public expenditure on private and voluntary provision. Firstly, what constitutes a private or voluntary provider? As Chapter 2 pointed out, the divide between public and private/voluntary providers is sometimes blurred. An example of this is the case of General Practitioners (GPs) and dentists. Whilst often viewed as quintessential public providers they are in fact self-employed 'individual contractors' who sell a service to the NHS. In Table 3.2 (below) we give two sets of figures, indicating levels of expenditure on private provision both when GPs and dentists are classified as private providers and when they are taken to be public sector employees.

The second problem is to decide what represents 'provision' of a service? The government has always purchased from the private sector, for example when private construction firms build conventionally financed schools and hospitals. However, this is a one-off purchase and does not involve services being managed over the life span of the asset. It cannot be considered as private/voluntary provision of key services. In the absence of any clarity on when a purchase becomes a partnership, we put forward our own working definition: to be considered a partnership the private/voluntary sector must involve the delivery of a service over a period of time.

Health warning on the data: The tables below use data from government, private/voluntary sectors and academic sources and some figures are derived or estimated from related data and anecdotal evidence. Figures in bold represent estimates and those in bold and italics indicate a private/voluntary sector source while normal text indicates a government or official figure. This should inform how the figures are interpreted. Unless otherwise stated, the data refers to England and Wales.

Health

It could be argued that the NHS from birth was based on a partnership between the state and non-public providers. As already discussed, dentists and GPs have always been self-employed contractors selling a service to the NHS. They can thus be categorised as constituting either private or public provision and both interpretations are shown in Table 3.2. With GPs and dentists categorised as public, only about 5 per cent of public health expenditure was on private voluntary provision at the end of the 1990s. If we define them as private, then this figure rises to 16 per cent.

Table 3.2 Percentage of expenditure on private/voluntary provision in publicly funded healthcare, 1998-99[2]

	GPs and dentists as public providers	GPs and dentists as private providers
Percentage private/voluntary provision	5	16
Percentage public provision	95	84

Main sources: Laing and Buisson (1999/2000) *Laing's Review of Private Healthcare*; Office of Health Economics (1999) *Compendium of Health Statistics*; NHS Executive Common Information Core (1999/2000) *Department of Health Departmental Report*; Office of National Statistics (1999) *Annual Abstract of Statistics.*

Aside from this historical 'anomaly', another form of publicly funded but privately provided health care accessed by the majority of the population comes in the form of community pharmacies. General ophthalmic services might be said to fall into a similar category where the general population has long used the services of private providers that receive a proportion of their funding from the public purse. The flow of public funds to community pharmacies and general ophthalmic services makes up around two-fifths of all publicly funded private/voluntary provided health care (Table 3.3). Along with the provision of agency nursing, the community pharmacies constitute examples of what we have described as a 'private sector default' position, where there are few equivalent public providers.

Table 3.3 Areas of private/voluntary provision in publicly funded healthcare, 1998-99

Area of provision	Value (millions)
Community pharmacies	440
Ancillary services	**300**
General ophthalmic	239
Agency nursing	216
Acute clinical care	120
Psychiatric	85
Other	279.5

Main sources: Laing and Buisson (1999/2000) *Laing's Review of Private Healthcare*; Office of Health Economics (1999) *Compendium of Health Statistics*; NHS Executive Common Information Core (2000) *Department of Health Departmental Report*; Office of National statistics (1999) *Annual Abstract of Statistics*.

It was the arrival of the internal market in the NHS in the 1990s that opened up the possibility of more services being contracted from the private/voluntary sectors. At the heart of the internal market was the division between the purchasers and providers of publicly funded health care. Despite the ending the internal market, this distinction remains within the NHS in England and Wales, though the Scottish Executive is moving to end it. Compulsory Competitive Tendering (CCT) was the other main driving force for contracting with private/voluntary providers in the 1990s, though for many NHS Trusts contracting-out has long been driven by the necessity to meet annual efficiency gains required by central government.

Table 3.3 shows that at the end of the 1990s minimal amounts of clinical care was being purchased from private/voluntary providers. NHS contracting with private and voluntary sector hospitals for the provision of acute care is perhaps the most politically sensitive category. Unfortunately, no authoritative figure is available. One survey found that in 1997-98 the public sector paid for 84,561 acute patients to be treated independently at a cost of approximately £70 million (Williams *et al*, 2000). However, the Government estimates that NHS expenditure on acute care from private/voluntary providers amounts to £120 million (NHS Executive, 2000). The largest part of this is accounted for by abortions: in 1998-99, 89,000 publicly funded Finished Consultancy Episodes (FCEs) occurred in private/voluntary hospitals, of which 44,000 were abortions (Laing and Buisson, 2000a). For the vast majority of NHS funded acute care, the public sector retains a virtual monopoly. Expenditure on private/voluntary providers of clinical care amounts to less than one per cent of total NHS expenditure on clinical care. Some small areas of expenditure do involve more significant use of private providers. MRI scanner provision is increasingly contracted from private providers. Of 207 MRI Scanners in the NHS, 28 are privately operated which equates to approximately £14-15 million a year spent on private providers.[3]

In contrast with the small-scale use of private/voluntary providers for core services is the more significant expenditure on private ancillary service providers. The figure in Table 3.3 is probably conservative – it is based on a survey of the main private service providers only. Laundry, domestic and waste services are most likely to be outsourced with between 40 per cent and 50 per cent privately provided. A recent informal survey of 376 NHS Trusts indicates that approximately a third of security, catering and non-emergency patient transport are provided privately whilst other support services, such as equipment maintenance and portering, are only provided by the private sector in under 20 per cent of cases.[4] Private provision of ancillary services will be boosted further as more PFI hospitals come on-stream.

Table 3.4 (where dentists and GPs have been categorised as private providers) shows that there is no significant trend away from established patterns of public/private provision.[5] The main differences across time are probably accounted for by trends in expenditure on General Practice and dentistry and not by any significantly expanded use of private/voluntary providers in other areas. The impact of CCT on contracting out of ancillary services and the broader potential impact of the internal market has not fundamentally altered the overall balance of spending in the NHS, even if the impact in certain areas is more significant. The overall pattern is one of continued public sector dominance in provision of publicly funded healthcare.

Table 3.4 Trends in private/voluntary provision of publicly funded healthcare, 1979-1999

Year	1979-80	1995-96	1998-99
Private/voluntary provision	16	12	16
Public provision	84	88	84

Historical trends use previous work by Burchardt (1997) *Boundaries between Public and Private Welfare: A Typology and Map of Services* CASE: LSE

Education

As with health, in education there is not always a clear boundary between public and private/voluntary providers. For example in Voluntary Aided (VA) and Foundation schools the governing body is the legal employer and has primary responsibility for admissions policy. Also the school land and buildings are owned either by the governing body or a charitable foundation. Despite these characteristics, VA and Foundation schools are officially classified as public providers. The 15 City Technology Colleges (CTCs), established from the late 1980s, remain formally independent (voluntary) bodies but are almost wholly publicly funded. Any new City Academies will be formally independent like the CTCs, but their precise governance structure will be negotiated individually with the Secretary of State. Their funding will come direct from the Department for Education and Employment (DfEE), as was the case with Grant Maintained schools, abolished by the Government in 1998, with most becoming Foundation schools.

These ambiguities over the structures of schooling are discussed further in Chapter 7. However, other forces have impacted on the degree of public funding of privately/voluntary provided education services. The now abolished Assisted Places Scheme provided direct public subsidises for a limited number of places in wholly private/voluntary schools. Regardless of their legal status, all locally funded state schools have been subject to the regime of Local Management of Schools (LMS), now superseded by the Fair Funding regime. With increasing proportions of school budgets delegated, schools themselves are been able, in principle, to contract with private/voluntary providers for a range of ancillary services previously provided by the LEAs.

Some 'failing' LEAs have themselves come under pressure to enter into 'partnerships' for the private/voluntary sector provision of some services. The Best Value regime will encourage all LEAs to review the provision of their education services, and with some LEAs wishing to offer their assistance to other authorities, a 'level playing field' could be in sight.

Table 3.5 Percentage of private/voluntary provision in publicly funded education, 1998-99

	Voluntary Aided & Foundation schools as public sector
% Publicly provided	90
% Private/voluntary provided	10

Main sources: DfEE (2000) *Departmental Report 1999-2000; Local Government Financial Statistics* (1999). *CIPFA – Education Statistics 1999 Estimates*; Cambridge Education Associates (1999) *Support Services for Schools.*

If all of the types of state schools detailed above (except CTCs) are seen as public providers, then Table 3.5 shows that 10 per cent of education expenditure was on private/voluntary provision in 1998-99. Table 3.6 shows the significance of public expenditure on different forms of private/voluntary provision. The figures cover school-based education for children aged 5-18 in England and exclude higher education and education for the under-fives.

The clarity of the picture relating to education expenditure suffers from the lack of centrally available data – many of the figures above are estimates. This dearth of information is primarily due to complex funding structures and cash flows, itself a function of the decentralised nature of education provision. Private/voluntary providers can be contracted at the departmental, LEA or school level. The figures in Table 3.6 will be a conservative estimate as information on contracting of the

Table 3.6 Expenditure on private/voluntary provision in publicly funded education, 1998-99

Area	Value (£ millions)
DfEE	
Assisted Places	126
City Technology Colleges (CTCs)	55
National Grid for Learning (NGfL)	50
Literacy and Numeracy	10
LEA	
Transport	**400**
Non-Maintained Special Educational Needs (SEN)	**256**
In Service Training & Curriculum Support	**150**
Schools Meals	*137*
Grounds Maintenance	**111**
Administration –	
Payroll, Finance, Personnel	**350**
School	
Supply Teachers	210
Work Experience	10

Main sources: DfEE (2000) *Departmental Report 1999-2000; Local Government Financial Statistics – 1999.* CIPFA (1999d) *Education Statistics 1999 Estimates*; Cambridge Education Associates (1999) *Support Services for Schools.*

private/voluntary sectors by individual schools is not available. Although many support services are still bought from LEAs, a proportion of schools' expenditure will go directly to external providers.

LEAs have long contracted for a range of administrative services and support services such as school meals, grounds maintenance and transport. The largest single budget identified is for school transport services. About 37 per cent of LEA school meals services were themselves privately provided by sub-contractors in 1998-99, indicating an area of ancillary provision where private providers have a significant market share.

About one quarter of all public expenditure on private/voluntary provision was either for supply teachers or Special Educational Needs (SEN) provision. In both these categories the private/voluntary sectors could be considered the majority or 'default' provider: 70 per cent of supply teacher provision in 1998-99 was private.

At the other extreme expenditure on City Technology Colleges was under one per cent of the overall expenditure delegated to schools in 1998-99. The advent of City Academies, at least in the short to medium-term, does not seem set to increase this figure significantly. Table 3.6 does not cover the contracting out of core LEA services or the private/voluntary management of schools, because none had occurred by 1998-99. However, the figures for this type of activity announced after 1998-99 were, at the time of writing, still very small relative to overall expenditure.

Table 3.7 appears to show an increase in private/voluntary provision in education. This needs to be carefully interpreted as the figures for 1998-99 include a more thorough investigation of the provision of support services. Previous years' figures do not account for supply teachers, maintenance of premises and other support services. Nevertheless, there appears to be a definite upward trend. The increase in private/voluntary provision from 3 per cent in 1979-80 to 7.5 per cent in 1995-96 and then 10 per cent in 1998-99 represents a considerable increase in the absolute value of non-public provision. This can largely be accounted for by increasing outsourcing of support services. Relative to overall expenditure, however, public spending on private/voluntary provision remains low.

Table 3.7 Trends in private/voluntary provision of publicly funded education, 1979-1999

	1979-80	1995-96	1998-99
Private/voluntary provision	3	7.5	10
Public provision	97	92.5	90

Historical trends use previous work by Burchardt (1997) *Boundaries between Public and Private Welfare: A Typology and Map of Services* CASE: LSE

Personal Social Services

Public expenditure on private/voluntary sector provision in social services is far more significant than in health or education. Reforms to social care in 1990 and the payment of benefits for residents of private/voluntary care homes incentivised a growth in non-public providers. The policies of the 1997-2001 Labour Government did not fundamentally alter the incentives that have led to the current balance between public and private/voluntary provision. Table 3.8 shows that private/voluntary providers accounted for just under half of all government expenditure on the personal social services in 1998-99. This does not include income support payments since

---

Table 3.8 Significance of private/voluntary provision in publicly funded personal social services, 1998-99

	Value (millions)	Percentage
Private/voluntary provision	4,929	40
Public provision	7,475	60

Note: Data for UK

Main sources: CIPFA (2000) *Personal Social Services Statistics 1998-99 Actuals*; DoH (2000a) *Health and Personal Social Services Statistics for England and Wales 1999*; Laing and Buisson (2000a) *Laings Review of Private Healthcare*; Laing and Buisson (1999a) *Care of Elderly People Market Survey – 1999*; Laing and Buisson (1999b) *Domiciliary Care Markets 1999*; Department of Health (2000b) *Personal Social Services Current Expenditure: 1998-99*; Department of Health (2000c) *Community Care Statistics 1999*.

these are a transfer payment to individuals rather than a contractual payment between the state and a private/voluntary provider. It is also important to point out that the purchasing and management of care in central and regional social services offices has been assumed to be entirely publicly provided.

Table 3.9 breaks private/voluntary provision down into different client groups. It includes both local authority and NHS expenditure and shows the percentages of overall publicly funded provision for each client group that came from private/voluntary providers in 1998-99. All areas had significant private/voluntary provision. The percentage for 'children and families' was relatively small but remained significant in absolute terms. Two-thirds of provision for elderly people came from outside the public sector, as did three-fifths of provision for people with learning disabilities. There appear to be no major 'no-go areas' deemed inappropriate for private/voluntary providers in the personal social services though these services, by definition, cater for the most vulnerable people in the population.

Table 3.9 Private/voluntary provision of personal social services by client groups, 1998-99

	Value of private/voluntary provision (£ millions)	% overall public expenditure on this client group
Generic services	547	34
Children and families	509	26
Elderly people	2,398	68
Physically disabled	472	63
Learning disabilities	1,686	61
Mental health	609	65
Other adult clients	78	52

Note: Data for UK

Main sources: CIPFA (2000) *Personal Social Services Statistics 1998-99 Actuals*; DoH (2000a) *Health and Personal Social Services Statistics for England and Wales 1999*; Laing and Buisson (2000a) *Laings Review of Private Healthcare*; Laing and Buisson (1999a) *Care of Elderly People Market Survey – 1999*; Laing and Buisson (1999b) *Domiciliary Care Markets 1999*; Department of Health (2000b) *Personal Social Services Current Expenditure: 1998-99*; Department of Health (2000c) *Community Care Statistics 1999*.

The use of private and voluntary providers has been most dominant in the delivery of residential care: accounting for over half of public expenditure on residential and nursing care in 1998-99. In terms of the number of clients who are supported by local authorities, in 1999 188,000 out of a total of 403,000 (46.7 per cent) were in local authority staffed homes and the remainder (53.3 per cent) were in private/voluntary run homes. Residential care has the most established pool of private/voluntary providers for any area of publicly funded service delivery.

The last eight years have seen a dramatic increase in private/voluntary provision of publicly funded domiciliary care. In 1992 non-public providers accounted for only two per cent of contract hours but, by 1997, this his had grown to 44 per cent and then modestly to 46 per cent in 1998 with the figure topping 50 per cent in 1999 (Laing and Buisson, 2000b).

In this area a distinction between private and voluntary providers can be drawn. The increase in non-public provision has predominantly come from the private sector: in both domiciliary and residential/nursing care, private for-profit providers have grown fastest. In domiciliary home-care, for example, the voluntary sector's share of provision increased from under one per cent of overall Local Authority funded provision in 1992 to only five per cent in 1997; while the private sector share increased from two per cent to 38 per cent over the same time period (Laing and Buisson, 1999b). However, for many local authority purchasers, the voluntary sector remains the 'provider of preference' – with a particular foothold in the provision of day care (Knapp *et al*, 2001).

Table 3.10 shows the sharp increase in private/voluntary provision between 1979-80 and 1995-96 and the continued but more gradual increase after 1995, as local authorities continue to contract for provision, particularly of domiciliary care.

Table 3.10 Trends in private/voluntary provision of personal social services

	1979-80 %	1995-96 %	1998-90 %
Private/voluntary provision	14	34	40
Public provision	86	66	60

Historical trends use previous work by Burchardt (1997) *Boundaries between Public and Private Welfare: A Typology and Map of Services* CASE: LSE

The social services look closest, when compared with health and education services, to constituting a level playing field.

Criminal Justice

There is considerable variation in levels of non-public provision in different parts of the publicly funded criminal justice system. Private/voluntary provision within the Prison Service showed a marked increase in the 1990s, while for other areas the impact was negligible. Table 3.11 shows the overall picture in criminal justice.

The criminal justice services covered by Table 3.11 spend relatively little on private/voluntary provision. Data on the police's use of private sector support services is thin; although £112 million may be a slight underestimate, expenditure is predominantly on public provision. The voluntary sector has a long tradition of involvement in probation – the probation service dedicates at least seven per cent of service expenditure to voluntary providers. In 2000-01 approximately £14 million will be spent on drug testing, much of which is expected to go to non-public providers. The Courts have contracted out a range of ICT support services. For example the

Table 3.11 Private/voluntary provision of criminal justice services, 1998-99

		Total expenditure (£ million)	Spend on non-public provision (£ million)	% Expenditure on non-public provision
Total		9,757	459	5
of which	prisons	1,894	270	14
	police	7,070	112	2
	probation	425	32	8

Notes: Expenditure on the Courts and Legal Aid not included. Data for England and Wales.

Main sources: CIPFA (1999a) *Probation Service Statistics 97-98 Actuals*; CIPFA (1999b) *Police Statistics 1998-99 Actuals*: Prison Service (2000) *Annual Report and Accounts 1999-2000*; Home Office (2000) *Departmental Report 1999-2000*.

Resource Accounting and Management Information Service (RAMIS) for the Lord Chancellor's Department and the Court Service has been contracted from a private consortia. However, in all the services in Table 3.11, public provision dominates.

Table 3.12 shows a breakdown of expenditure on private providers by the Prisons Service. The management of prisons is no longer a 'public sector monopoly'. It is notable that although by 1998-99 less than 10 per cent of provision was purchased from privately managed institutions, this seems to have been sufficient to create true contestability (discussed further in Chapter 4). In escort services there has been a more marked switch with the private sector now representing the 'default provider' for all except Category A prisoners.

Table 3.12 Private provision in prisons, 1998-99

	Value of private provision (£ million)	% of overall provision in area
Contracted out prisons	136	7.5
Escort services	119	6
Catering	<2	0.5
Cleaning	3	0.2
Facilities management	10	0.1
Total prisons	*270 (from 1,894)*	*14.3*

Main sources: Prison Service (2000) *Annual Report and Accounts 1999-2000*; Home Office (2000) *Departmental Report 1999-2000*; internal Prison Service data (unpublished).

The nature and scale of the Private Finance Initiative

The Private Finance Initiative (PFI) was launched in 1992 and its evolution is discussed further in Chapter 4. Here we briefly outline the main characteristics of the initiative in order to assess its actual importance in terms of its contribution to the delivery of public investment and public services.

The PFI usually involves a consortium of private sector partners coming together to provide an asset-based public service under contract to a public purchasing body.[6] This might involve the *design* and *build* of a new asset such as a hospital or the significant refurbishment of older assets as in several 'bundled' schools projects. The *finance* for the project will come from a private partner. The project partners will also *operate* elements of the service to be delivered in the new hospital, school or prison. This will usually involve some of the support or 'ancillary' services such as maintenance, cleaning, security and perhaps IT, but sometimes a wider set of 'core' services is included and, in the case of prisons, the whole service.

This then is the classic DBFO (Design/Build/Finance/Operate) model of the PFI, though this is only one of a range of variations of a PPP model that could be used to deliver public services. If the PPP model involves simply procuring an asset and there are no services being operated you can have a DBF model. If the public sector provides the finance but the private sector operates services then the DBO model exists. More conventional procurement focuses on the design and build phase with the operation of services kept separate, a DB model.

The private partners (they are almost exclusively private rather than voluntary) involved in the most common DBFO model will include at the minimum a building contractor (design and build), a facilities manager (operations) and a financial institution (finance and project scrutiny). Other partners might provide equipment or IT services. These partners may or may not come together to form a legal body called a Special Purpose Vehicle (SPV) in order to manage the project and share the risks and rewards.

How important is the Private Finance Initiative?

Our concern here is to assess the scale and importance of the PFI. As a source of publicly sponsored capital investment, and as a charge to public revenue budgets, the importance of PFI grew over the 1990s. However, almost a decade after its inception, the PFI remains a relatively modest part of total publicly sponsored capital investment and total public spending on servicing PFI contracts was forecast to remain small. Moreover, there is no clear evidence that the build up of the PFI, much anticipated by government and dreaded by its critics, is accelerating.

Table 3.13 shows the evolution of the PFI since its launch in 1992. During the first two years of the Labour Government (1997-99) capital spending under the PFI rose modestly. At the time of the 1999 Budget the PFI had been expected to deliver £3.8 billion in capital spending in 1999-00. In fact, PFI capital spending undershot significantly, coming in at just £1.6 billion. Conventionally financed public gross investment had been expected to total £20.3 billion in 1999-00. The actual out-turn was only £18.2 billion. Overall then publicly sponsored gross capital investment undershot by over £4 billion in 1999-00, with over half of that undershoot coming from the PFI.

Over the whole period 1997-2000, PFI capital spending accounted for just nine per cent of total publicly sponsored gross capital spending. The Government forecasts that over the period from 2000-2004, PFI capital spending will average about 12 per cent of total publicly sponsored gross capital spending, though the PFI proportion will actually shrink over time especially as conventional capital spending builds up.

As explained further in Chapter 4, the Private *Finance* Initiative still requires the public sector to *fund* the assets and services being provided. The final two rows of Table 3.13 show the stream of current payments dedicated to funding PFI contracts over the period from 1999-00 to 2003-04. These payments can be expressed as a proportion of Total Managed Expenditure (total public spending). The exact derivation of these figures is hard to trace as the Treasury does not break down the totals by department. On current projections, funding for the PFI will amount to about one per cent of total public spending by 2003-04, with little indication that this proportion will rise significantly in future.

The Labour Government from the start placed great emphasis on increasing public investment and highlighted the expected contribution of the PFI to that objective. Table 3.13 shows that total publicly sponsored gross investment as a proportion of GDP fell sharply after 1992-93 and any modest contribution from the PFI did not significantly arrest that decline in the 1990s. In the first three years of the Labour Government (1997-2000) total publicly sponsored gross capital investment continued to decline as a proportion of GDP. In 1999-2000, total public gross investment including the PFI totalled only 2.2 per cent of GDP, compared with 2.6 per cent in 1996-97 and around 4 per cent of GDP in 1992-93. It is therefore premature to claim that PFI has been part of a resurgence in investment in public infrastructure. Table 3.13 also shows that even with the PFI, total gross public investment as a proportion of GDP will by 2003-04 still be only around 3.5 per cent of GDP.

Planned capital spending under the PFI across different government departments over the period 2000-02 is set out in Table 3.13. It compares the numbers set out in the 1999 Budget with those in the 2000 and 2001 Budgets. The totals build up modestly over time, but more interesting are the significant variations between different departments. Forecast PFI spending in transport and health has decreased significantly, whereas local authorities and the devolved administrations (especially Scotland) are now expected to deliver over half of all PFI capital spending between 2000-02.

Table 3.13 PFI and total public capital expenditure

	Outturn							Estimated outturn	Forecast		
	92-93	93-94	94-95	95-96	96-97	97-98	98-99	99-00	00-01	01-02	02-03	03-04
Total public sector capital expenditure (£bn)	21.6	19.9	20.6	20.0	17.3	17.0	18.5	18.2	22.3	26.7	31.3	35.3
Estimated capital expenditure under PFI (£bn)	–	0.1	0.2	0.4	1.1	1.5	2.2	1.6	4.3	4.4	3.6	2.8
Total publicly-sponsored capital expenditure (£bn)	21.6	20.0	20.8	20.4	18.4	18.5	20.7	19.8	26.6	31.1	34.9	38.1
PFI as a percentage of total	–	0.5	1	2	6	8	11	8	16	14	10	7
Estimated payments under PFI contracts									2906	3595	4084	4478
% of Total Managed Expenditure									0.8	0.9	1.0	1.0

Note: net of sales of fixed assets

Source: HM Treasury Budget Documents

Table 3.14 PFI capital expenditure, 2000-02 (£m)

	Budget 1999	Budget 2000	Budget 2001
Defence	555	865	496
Environment, Transport and the Regions	1621	1544	1268
Home Office	597	175	417
Health	1430	788	1090
Scotland	431	1114	929
Wales and Northern Ireland	152	332	397
Local Authorities	2000	2400	3225
Other	365	602	851
Total	7151	7830	8673

Source: HM Treasury Budget Documents

A summary of current public expenditure on private/voluntary provision

Discussion about the future use of PPPs requires a better base of information on the current scale and impact of private and voluntary sector providers across public service areas.

Recommendations

All public purchasers should publish information on expenditure on private/voluntary sector provision of services. This would facilitate a proper evaluation of the performance (and extent) of alternative forms of service provision.

A 'contestability audit' should be produced as part of the Comprehensive Spending Review. This would map the service areas in which there is currently scope for public authorities to select between different providers and the extent to which this is actually happening.

There are many examples of long standing partnerships between non-public providers and the state. It is even possible to define GPs and dentists as private providers. However, in education, health and criminal justice overall use of the private/voluntary sector remains modest, at only ten per cent of total public spending in education and under five per cent in health and criminal justice. The overall picture is one of the continuing dominance of services that are publicly funded *and* publicly delivered. The analysis of historical trends in health shows the relative scale of private and voluntary delivery not to have increased significantly. Private provision has become more important in certain areas such as prison management and support services in education. However, only in the personal social services, where the market of private/voluntary providers is most mature, has non-public sector provision become a very significant proportion of the whole.

It is important to stress that the Government itself does not refer to private/voluntary sector provision of care services as a form of PPP. Indeed much of the 'partnership' activity suggested by the data reviewed in this Chapter could easily be described as straightforward contracting. The Private Finance Initiative, at the start of the new decade, still makes only a modest contribution towards overall levels of publicly sponsored investment yet most forms of PPP and most especially the PFI remain highly controversial. To understand why this is the case we need to unpack the rationale for going down the PPP/PFI route, starting firstly with the economic arguments.

Endnotes

1   A range of factors may be cited as inhibiting the development of a 'level playing field'. Private and voluntary sector providers, for example, express concern that local authorities favour their own in-house provision (Audit Commission, 1997; Forder *et al*, 1996). Others point out that the stating point for a 'level playing field' – the existence of a mixed economy of providers – varies considerably between localities (Charlesworth *et al*, 1996).

2   Public expenditure on residential care including NHS-funded care, has been categorised under personal social service expenditure in order to be consistent with Burchardt (1997).

3   IPPR survey of private providers carried out for the Commission.

4   A Health Estates Facilities Management Associates (2000) survey was sent to 376 English NHS Trusts with a 52 per cent response rate. The sample respondents were representative of the mix of Trusts, including Acute, Community/Mental Health, Teaching and Ambulance Trusts.

5   Dentists and GPs have been categorised as private providers to ensure compatibility with work on which the table is based (Burchardt, 1997).

6   The organisations involved in PFI deals are predominantly private sector companies so the remaining section refers to the private rather than private/voluntary sectors.

4. The lessons of the Private Finance Initiative

The economic arguments for PPPs and in particular for the Private Finance Initiative have been confused from the start. The price of this lack of clarity has been twofold. Firstly, it has undermined political support for PPPs as people on the ground have been able to see the weaknesses of some of the arguments put forward in their favour. Secondly, it has led to a process of project development that has in many cases limited the scope for value-for-money and innovation. Greater clarity in explaining and justifying the economic rationale for PPPs is a vital pre-requisite for their further successful development.

The debate over PPPs has been dominated by the complex and controversial issues surrounding what has been the most important form of PPP to date – the Private Finance Initiative. Many observers see the term PPP as a synonym or even a euphemism for the PFI. The Treasury, rightly, regards the PFI as one, albeit highly significant, form of PPP (HM Treasury, 2000). The next Chapter looks at other ways in which the Treasury has applied the term PPP. However, the arguments around the PFI serve to highlight the economic rationale for PPPs generally and it is important to explore in detail the evolution and practice of the PFI in order to understand the justification put forward for the partnership approach.

The Private Finance Initiative

There have been few public policy initiatives in recent years that have excited such controversy. When the PFI was launched in 1992, the rationale offered by the then Chancellor, Norman Lamont, seemed fairly clear cut. The PFI appeared to allow *extra* public sector investment by bringing in private finance for public capital projects. This rationale was subsequently taken on board by Labour in opposition and *appeared* to offer the incoming Government in 1997 one way of fulfilling its pledge of delivering significantly higher levels of public investment while maintaining a sustainable fiscal stance.

Parallel to this public finance justification for the PFI was a critique of the perceived costly failures of much conventional public procurement as a result of poor specification of design, poor project management and construction over-runs. The PFI was seen as a means of improving the public procurement process so as deliver better value-for-money and greater innovation in the delivery of asset-based public services, by contracting for the skills of the private sector in designing and managing complex investment projects and their attendant services. This understanding of the rationale for the PFI illustrates why the label Private Finance Initiative could be said to have been a misnomer from the start; the PFI was really a private *management* initiative.

It is important to stress that the term 'value-for-money' when applied to the PFI/PPPs has a meaning that is wider than a simple focus on efficiency. It should be defined as 'the optimum combination of whole life costs and quality to meet the user's requirements' (OGC, 2000), so putting the emphasis on quality as well as efficiency in the delivery of public services.

From the start officials and politicians emphasised one or other or both of the 'public finance' and 'value-for-money' rationales for the PFI and in so doing sowed the seeds of confusion in the minds of those managing, working in and receiving public services.

It is useful to think of PFI as going through several distinct periods of evolution (Broadbent *et al*, 2000). The roots of the PFI lay in the so-called Ryrie rules (after a former Second Permanent Secretary at the Treasury) that had been designed to minimise the impact of Treasury funding restrictions on the investment of public enterprises. The Ryrie rules had an impact on the wider public sector and were seen as a barrier to public bodies seeking solutions involving private finance. Retiring these rules after 1992 the Conservative Government tried repeatedly to get the PFI off the ground, at a time when a key priority was to reduce the budget deficit that had increased sharply in the early 1990s recession.

In 1994 the new Chancellor, Kenneth Clarke, made it clear that the Treasury would not approve *any* public sector capital project unless the PFI option had been explored. This 'universal testing' regime was matched by scepticism about the value of constructing a Public Sector Comparator for PFI schemes (whereby a PFI project is explicitly compared with the best publicly financed and provided alternative to see which offers better value-for-money). Instead the emphasis was on competition as the way of securing value-for-money. There was also institutional innovation in the form of the Public Private Partnerships Programme (4Ps), a body set up in 1996 to encourage the growth of the PFI/PPPs in local government.

Despite these efforts, as Chapter 3 showed, the PFI remained a bit of a damp squib delivering only a marginal addition to public capital spending in the context of a very sharp decline in overall public investment. Surprisingly or not, the incoming Labour Government in 1997 was wholly enthusiastic about the PFI, but even under Labour up to 2000 the initiative had failed really to take off.

The new Government rightly ended 'universal testing' but to make sure that the impetus for using private finance was not lost, also instigated a review of the PFI under Malcolm Bates. The 1997 Bates Review included recommendations over the accounting treatment of PFI projects, the significance of which will become apparent below. The review also led to the establishment of the Private Finance Taskforce within the Treasury designed to encourage the use of the initiative while standardising procurement and contracting arrangements and ensuring considerable central Treasury control over the process. The second Bates review (1999), along with a review by Peter Gershon of civil procurement in central government led to the establishment of Partnerships UK (PUK) and the Office of Government Commerce (OGC), with the former replacing the 'projects' wing of the Private Finance Taskforce and the latter incorporating the 'policy' wing of the Taskforce. Amongst other things, the Taskforce had played an important role in advising ministers on the contentious issues to do with protection of employee rights in PPPs (addressed in Chapter 8). It also presided over a renewed emphasis on achieving value-for-money through the construction of a proper Public Sector Comparator.

It is important then to see the PFI as a constantly evolving process taking up considerable time and attention at the highest levels of Whitehall. However, this official activity did not diminish the voices of the critics. To help see why it is worth outlining briefly the process of the PFI in theory as it would be presented today by, for example, the Office of Government Commerce.

The critical starting point of the PFI process is for the public purchaser, for example a local authority, to specify the outputs (and occasionally the outcomes) it would like to achieve through the development of a particular public service that usually involves a significant capital element. The purchaser should then look at a range of options for delivering those outputs/outcomes, which might include a PPP option with private finance playing a role. The option that delivers the best value-for-money should be chosen. If this is the PFI route, which it need not be, the public purchaser should then manage the project working closely with its private sector partners.

This rational model for public procurement and service delivery largely embodies plain common sense. It is, however, far removed from the way that the PFI has sometimes worked out in practice. The key reason for this is that value-for-money, which is the key focus inherent in this rational model, has not in practice been the driving force behind many PFI projects.

The PFI and the public finances – the only game in town?

In securing new finance for public investment the PFI appears to allow governments to reconcile the desire for higher capital spending with the commitment to maintaining a sustainable fiscal stance. Numerous PFI projects have gone ahead with the public managers involved convinced that they had no alternative and that the initiative was indeed 'the only game in town' (a term used by Price *et al*, 1999).

To understand why the PFI in no way relaxes the resource constraints faced by government it is necessary first and foremost to grasp the difference between the *finance* and the *funding* for a project. The easiest way to illustrate this difference is to use a private sector example. In purchasing a car many people will use private finance, that is, they will borrow from a financing company the sum necessary to drive the car away. However, they will have to find the funding for this purchase from their own income, probably paying monthly instalments back to the financing company. That institution does not in the end provide a single penny of actual resource.

It is the same with the PFI. Although the finance in a DBFO project comes from the private sector all the funding still comes from the public purse, if there are no user charges associated with the project as in some transport schemes for example. A stream of revenue payments has to be set aside to meet the commitments entered into under PFI contracts. Unless the PFI project delivers net savings through greater efficiency, the eventual cost to the taxpayer will be at least the same as under conventional finance where the Treasury borrows in the capital markets.

A more fundamental point is that regardless of how public investment is financed or funded it always carries a real opportunity cost, in that resources are committed which cannot be used for other purposes. This is the fundamental constraint on all public spending. If we want more of the nation's resources to go to health or public transport, then less of the nation's resources are available for other uses – no reforms to the framework of public finances can ever get round this constraint. Too many people, especially on the centre-left, have focussed too much time and attention on trying to find an accounting solution to the problem of ensuring that public services and investment get enough real resources.

In the past the Treasury has contributed to the confusion by not making it clear that the crude public finance arguments usually presented for the PFI are in fact bogus; though it is important to stress that the Treasury now clearly argues that PFI is not about getting capital spending 'off the public sector's balance sheet'. Whether or not this message has filtered out to public managers on the ground is a theme we shall return to.

It is also important to stress that the argument that the PFI in no way relaxes the constraints facing governments holds regardless of the state of the public finances at any point in time. Even if the government faced a budget deficit of eight per cent of GDP, as it did in 1993-94, and the net debt-GDP ratio was rising sharply this would still not make a strong fiscal case for the PFI. In the end concern about the sustainability of the public finances arises because the build up of debt imposes a burden on future generations in the form of the stream of interest payments required to service that debt. But the PFI also sets up a future set of obligations to service the payments that are due to honour PFI contracts. The burden is the same in principle.

Unless the financial markets behave in some way irrationally they will see that capital spending financed through the PFI imposes similar obligations as conventional capital spending. If they think the totality of government spending plans are unsustainable they will react accordingly. It is true, of course, that irrational behaviour by the financial markets is not unknown. But, over time and as the PFI market matures, the markets will become less likely to view PFI liabilities any differently to those incurred through conventional means. Nonetheless, at this point in time it may still be the case that the markets are more relaxed about government financing investment through PFI rather than other means. It is perhaps not surprising therefore that politicians sometimes seek to make the case for PPP/PFI in these terms. It is also true that the political pressure to push investment projects off-balance-sheet will get stronger if and when the fiscal position deteriorates. From our perspective these considerations only serve to increase the need to have clear and credible fiscal rules to ensure that the PPP/PFI route is only selected for the right reasons.

In June 1998, the Treasury published a new set of rules for public spending and borrowing in a revised fiscal framework (HM Treasury, 1998). The main features included two key rules of thumb to guide fiscal policy, the *golden rule* and the *sustainable investment rule*.

- The *golden rule* states that on average over the economic cycle, the Government will borrow only to invest and not to fund current spending.

- The *sustainable investment rule* states that public sector net debt as a proportion of GDP will be held over the economic cycle at a stable and prudent level.

This new fiscal framework, and the way public finances have evolved, have been seen to remove the perceived fiscal justification for going down the PFI route. The golden rule means that borrowing is permitted to finance public investment, in other words it automatically allows, for example, a hospital to be built using finance raised through conventional public borrowing rather than through the PFI.

The sustainable investment rule is more problematic because it depends on the definition of a 'prudent' level of debt. Clearly a debt-GDP ratio which is *rising* remorselessly will sound alarm bells, but there is no strict economic 'rule' as to what level of debt-to-GDP could be regarded as sustainable. In practice authorities tend to set rules of thumb for acceptable debt-GDP ratios. Though acknowledging that levels of net public debt in the UK were not in the late 1990s high by historical or international standards, the Treasury argued that a further modest reduction was desirable. Other things being equal, it suggested as a rule of thumb that the net debt-GDP ratio should be below 40 per cent of GDP over the economic cycle. The main pragmatic argument for this is that it would provide the Government with a buffer to react to major economic shocks. All of this is very sensible and pragmatic. So what are the implications of this rule of thumb for the PFI?

One way to approach this is to undertake a thought exercise: what would have been the implications for the sustainable investment rule of abolishing PFI as part of the Comprehensive Spending Review from 1999 (bearing in mind that the Government had committed itself to the previous administration's spending plans for its first two years in office)? In other words what would have been the implications for the public finances if the (approximately) £11bn of PFI capital spending planned over the period

1999-2002 had been replaced by normal public sector capital spending financed through the traditional method of selling government bonds or gilts?

Table 4.1 The sustainable investment rule with and without PFI

	99-00	00-01	01-02
Public sector net debt (end year, £bn)	355	363	367
Debt as a percentage of GDP	**39.4**	**38.2**	**36.8**
PFI capital spending (financial year, £bn)	3.8	4.1	3.0
Debt assuming all capital spending by public sector (£bn)	358.8	370.9	377.9
Debt as a percentage of GDP with no PFI	**39.8**	**39.0**	**37.9**

Note: PFI capital spending has to be added cumulatively. Ignores any savings from reductions in payments of interest and capital to private sector, and additional interest payments resulting from higher levels of government debt.

Source: 1999 Budget projections and CPPP calculations.

The upper part of Table 4.1 sets out the Government's fiscal plans at the time of the March 1999 Budget and shows the net debt ratio declining to around 37 per cent of GDP by 2001-02. The lower half of the table sets out the amount of capital spending which was planned to be undertaken under the PFI and shows what would have happened to the net debt-GDP ratio if this spending had instead simply been added to the public accounts. The net debt ratio would have declined to around 38 per cent of GDP by 2001-02.

So if PFI had been abolished at the time of the Comprehensive Spending Review and the same capital spending had been undertaken through normal public spending channels, the sustainable investment rule would easily have been satisfied, and by definition so would the golden rule. In this way, the Treasury's new fiscal framework was entirely compatible with not continuing with the PFI in the late 1990s – the initiative was not necessary to secure prudent public finances. In practice the net debt-GDP ratio fell much faster than planned and PFI capital spending undershot in 1999-2000.[1]

Another concern is that government financed capital spending might be inflationary by pushing the economy beyond its capacity limits. But of course a given set of capital projects involving essentially the same set of demands for labour and other inputs would have the same implications for the economy regardless of whether the financing came from the private sector or from the public sector.

It is important then to emphasise a critical point about the PFI – accessing private capital does not in itself make it easier to deliver one extra school or hospital because it in no way alters the real resource constraints faced by the public sector. No change in the financial or fiscal framework can.

The PFI and value-for-money

Putting the unconvincing public finance argument for the PFI aside allows one to concentrate on the real potential benefits of the initiative. The sole convincing argument for the PFI is that it offers the potential to secure better value-for-money and greater innovation in the delivery of public services, with a focus on both efficiency and quality.

Unfortunately, there is widespread concern, in the private and public sector, that the process by which the value-for-money assessment for a particular project is determined has in many cases been highly problematic and lacking in transparency. Past ambiguities about how risk allocation is to be treated and whether the conventionally financed route is really open to the public purchaser have arguably led to calculations being arrived at in order to demonstrate value-for-money and allow the PFI project to go ahead. The construction of Public Sector Comparators has sometimes been half-hearted and too much weight has been placed on simplistic comparisons between the numbers generated in the PSC and the costs of the PFI project. A clear challenge for the proponents of PFI is to create greater confidence across the board about the process whereby value-for-money is determined.

The PFI and risk

At the heart of determining whether a PFI project will offer better value-for-money than its Public Sector Comparator is the allocation of various kinds of risk between the public purchaser and private contractors.[2] These include:

- *Design and construction risks* associated with a project taking longer and costing more than originally envisaged. These are often the risks most easily allocated to the contractors under the PFI and indeed any well-designed contract.

- Risks that *operating costs* may rise faster than expected which should generally be borne by the private partners.

- Risks associated with the *demand for the service* turning out to be lower than anticipated, which can be hard to allocate.

- Risks associated with the *obsolescence of the technology* embodied in the project and the risks associated with the residual value of the asset at the end of the contract.

- Risks involved in *changes to public policy* and regulation that the public sector should generally bear.

The lack of clarity in the past over the rationale for the PFI has had deleterious consequences for the way actual projects have worked out. The *accounting treatment* of a PFI project depends on the extent of the risk transfer achieved. If sufficient risk transfer has been achieved the project will no longer appear on the public sector's balance sheet or as an item of public capital spending. Despite official guidance, it is clear that many practitioners have believed and some still believe a key policy objective is to get enough transfer of risk to get individual projects off the public sector's balance sheet. At least one Department of State believes this – the Department for Education and Employment reviews all PFI schools projects before they are signed and only allows them to go ahead if they deliver value-for-money *and* if the accounting treatment results in them being off balance sheet.

In order to achieve value-for-money it is not necessary for sufficient risk to be transferred so that the project is off the public sector's balance sheet. An appropriate element of risk may be allocated to the private sector while the project remains on the public sector's books. The Treasury now rightly emphasises the importance of securing *optimal* risk allocation; whether this results in the project being off or on the public sector's balance sheet should be *irrelevant* to whether the project goes ahead. The goal should now be to ensure that the practice of all departments conforms to the spirit of Treasury guidance.

The main risks being transferred in a number of PFI deals seem to be the most traditional forms of risk, such as those associated with construction over-runs and their associated costs. Indeed, in the most comprehensive study so far of a range of PFI projects the transfer of construction risks appeared to be the main driver behind the projected value-for-money savings (Arthur Andersen, 2000).[3] The emphasis on the construction risks is noteworthy because these are the kinds of risks most easily dealt with under a range of contracting arrangements other than the PFI, including modified conventional procurement. A Design/Build/Operate (DBO) model, for example, is one that can be structured to deal with construction risk (Palmer, 2000).

There is also some concern about the apparent asymmetry in risk allocation between the public and private sectors. When things go right the private sector appears able to make significant financial gains – this is discussed further below. When things go wrong it sometimes appears to be difficult for the public purchaser to impose very significant financial penalties on the private contractors. This was seen for example in the cancellation of the Benefits Payment Card project where the purchasers (the Benefits Agency and Post Office Counters Ltd) did not in the end demand damages when the project began to slip (NAO, 2000a). This project only seems to have gone ahead because the public agencies involved did not expect to have the capital resources to develop the project themselves and so involved private finance for the wrong reasons.

The PFI and financing

The PFI/DBFO approach is best suited to those circumstances that require private sector expertise in the management of complex public investment projects. In these circumstances a DBFO or PPP approach that puts the equity of the private sector partners at risk, is one way of focusing the skills and energies of those partners.

This then is the justification for using private finance – for putting the 'F' in a DBFO project. The financial institution responsible for raising the finance will exercise 'due diligence' and bring extra scrutiny to the project, both during the procurement phase but more especially through the project's whole life, making sure that the project really will offer significant efficiency gains. This supervision and scrutiny could be separately contracted for, but there are advantages when the financial institutions have had to put their own money on the line. Several PFI projects focused on IT provision have been seen to run into difficulties in part because of the absence of a private financial institution undertaking a rigorous risk assessment.

When partners put their equity into the 'special purpose vehicle' (SPV) that manages a project this may help create the incentive structure necessary to secure efficient management oversight. There are several different models of SPV. In some instances the companies that are the contractors for service delivery also hold an equity stake and this may lead to a truer form of partnership. Sometimes, however, there may be advantages in not having contractors in the SPV, as this is likely to make it easier for the equity holders to themselves change the service providers; meaning that service contracts do not have to be the same length as the whole PFI contract (discussed further below).

The project management expertise and risk assessment that is being 'purchased' through the SPV for potentially high risk projects could be purchased in more conventional ways. However, the DBFO model has the advantage of creating a single point of accountability, with the risk transferred to the private sector of managing and resolving disputes between the different contractors.

Nonetheless, the possible gains from including the 'F' in a DBFO project will have to be sufficient to cover the extra costs associated with securing a return on private equity and using private finance. The fact that private finance will always cost more than finance raised by the Treasury has been a significant line of attack against the PFI. It is true that as the PFI market has matured the difference in borrowing costs between conventionally financed projects and carefully designed PFI projects has fallen. However, the typical cost of finance for a well-designed PFI project may still be 1-2 per cent higher than the rate at which the government borrows and the difference will be higher for riskier projects.

The above discussion suggests that the reason why private finance costs more is because the risks in the project are explicitly priced. The costs to the UK government of borrowing in the financial markets are relatively low because the markets know that the UK government is not going to default – it is almost a risk-free investment. When government finance is used for a risky investment project, the costs associated with the risks of that investment turning out to be imprudent are still there but are passed on to current and future taxpayers rather than being separately identified and paid for.[4]

If the typical cost of private finance for a well-designed PFI project is about one to two per cent higher than the interest on government bonds or gilts, this will lead to an apparent increase in capital costs of up to 10 per cent over a 25-year contract. The capital element of a project may in turn be 20-25 per cent of the total cost, the rest being the service or operating element. In these circumstances, the extra cost of private as opposed to public finance may amount to about two per cent of the total cost of the project. Clearly if the PFI project can deliver significant efficiency savings it should not be hard to cover these extra financing costs.

The discount rate

In comparing the costs of the PFI project with its Public Sector Comparator, allowance has to be made for the fact that payments from the public purse for the capital element of a PFI scheme will be made at a later date than is the case under conventional procurement. A payment made later effectively costs less so these future payments have to be discounted, using the Treasury's long established six per cent real pre-tax discount rate. A considerable debate has raged over whether this rate is appropriate for appraising PFI schemes. The lower the discount rate, the more attractive would be the conventional financing route (other things equal); a higher discount rate would favour the PFI. Some economists argue for a higher rate and some for a lower rate and some for using different discount rates for different projects (Grout, 1997). It should be noted that the private sector tends to use similar 'rough and ready' rules of thumb as the Treasury's six per cent rate.

On balance, there appears to be merit in the argument for slightly lowering the benchmark discount rate now that the real costs of public borrowing have come down. For a typical PFI project, lowering the discount rate by one per cent would make the whole project about five per cent more expensive over its lifetime relative to the PSC. This would not stop PFI deals that offer significant value-for-money gains from proceeding though it would be sufficient to tilt the outcome for projects where the value-for-money case was very marginal. It is interesting to note that the NAO reported that London Underground examined the impact on its analysis of the Government's proposed PPP for the Tube of using a real discount rate of 3.5 per cent (NAO, 2000b).

Re-financing

The considerable gains that have resulted from the re-financing of some PFI projects over recent years has generated considerable controversy. Early PFI projects have had more expensive financing costs in their initial stages as the capital markets have priced in the somewhat uncertain costs of the private partners bearing risks. When the construction stage of these projects has been completed some contractors have been able to go back to the markets and re-finance the deal at significantly lower cost, resulting in additional financial gains for these organisations. These amounted to £10.7m in the case of the re-financing of the Fazakerley Prison PFI project (NAO, 2000c) of which the Prison Service received only £1m.

These financial gains have been seen to be at the expense of the public purchaser. They are often, however, defended as the return to the private contractors for having taken on the financial and political risks in the first place – though the apparent lack of willingness to share these gains with the public purchaser has soured the atmosphere around the PFI. In theory the scope for such gains should diminish as the market matures and the prospective gains from re-financing will be priced into the original contracts.

The Treasury has issued explicit guidance to public purchasers to ensure that all relevant contracts incorporate more explicit gain-sharing arrangements and the OGC and PUK have also been keen to reinforce this message. However, there appears to be a lag between the issuing of such guidance and public purchasers implementing it. In the earlier deals in which explicit provisions of re-financing are missing, private partners will need to show more political sensitivity in sharing out any excess financial gains – indeed this may be taken as one criterion for identifying a true 'partnership' arrangement.

The PFI and service operation

Under traditional procurement for asset-based services the public sector finances the project itself, contracts separately for the build and design of the asset, and then runs services in-house. Under the PFI these different components are bundled together into a single package. Combining these elements of service provision may help overcome difficult incentive problems that may have led to the poor performance of some conventional procurement projects in the past.

One such incentive problem relates to ensuring that new assets are maintained to a high quality over their life-cycle. Under conventional models of procurement and service provision politicians and public managers often face pressures to restrict maintenance budgets in order to increase current spending or to build new high-profile capital projects. The argument that long-term PFI contracts can be an effective way of ensuring that asset-quality is not allowed to deteriorate over time is valid, though the application of Resource Accounting and Budgeting (RAB) should (at least in principle) help ensure that this is now the case for conventionally financed projects as well.

Another incentive argument for agreeing long-term contracts for the operation of services – the 'O' within a DBFO project – is the strong synergy that often exists between the design and operation of capital projects. Linking the operator of a service with those responsible for designing and building the underlying asset through a 'special purpose vehicle' should lead to more innovative and cost-effective designs. This is because integrating the D, B and O elements of a PFI project may encourage the different parties to make risky 'asset-specific investments' (Williamson, 1985) in the project that they would not be willing to make if they were contracting in isolation from each other. The benefits of this approach were reflected in some of the evidence that the Commission received which stressed that a smooth interface between the design and operation of an asset-based service, rather than anything inherent about financing, is the key to successful PFI projects.

The importance of this synergy between design, build and operate will vary across sectors. The prison sector is often cited as an example where the integration of service operation and the design and build of the underlying asset could have significant benefits. In other sectors, such as schools, the relationship between the design of the school infrastructure and desired outcomes such as educational attainment may be more difficult to establish.

In practice there is a shortage of hard evidence on the role that service operators play in influencing design within PPP projects. As Chapter 7 discusses the available evidence from the hospital sector suggests that the PFI has not had a strong positive impact on hospital design. One reason for this may well be the limited nature of the service provision allowed within hospital PFIs. However, the evidence from the prison sector is also mixed on this point. There are examples of prison operators working side-by-side with builders and architects on all questions of design (for example Altcourse prison). But there is also anecdotal evidence that service-operators have had little impact on the design of the buildings; others have told us that the Prison Service has been more involved than private providers in discussions about prison design.

In any case the benefits of integrating the operation of services within long-term PFI/PPP projects needs to be compared against the costs. There is a danger that the public procurer will be 'locked-in' to a single service provider over a long period of time. This may lead to a lack of pressure for improvement in quality and the possibility that a service provider can get away with 'coasting' rather than striving for continual improvement. The removal of the possibility of changing providers within the lifespan of a PPP contract cuts against the grain of the argument made in Chapter 2: namely that one of the potential gains from the use of PPPs in public services is that they allow for a degree of contestability in service provision. One-off contestability at the beginning of a contract is unlikely to make up for the 25-30 year period in which a single provider has an effective monopoly.

Of course, within conventional PFI contracts there should be mechanisms in place to encourage the service provider to perform to a high standard over the life of a contract. Benchmarking and payment deductions help prevent under-performance. The fact that a contract termination due to persistent under-performance could have a seriously deleterious effect on the reputation of the service provider is another form of safeguard. It is also the case that public authorities reserve the ultimate sanction of terminating the contract at their own discretion – though this tends to incur a great expense.

These safeguards clearly have a role to play in ensuring reasonable performance but they can be rather blunt instruments. A service provider may be able to perform fairly poorly over a long period of time before they would be replaced. The economic costs of this – in terms of the loss of pressure for improvement that contestability might spur – may well outweigh the benefits that might flow from integrating the operation (O) with the build (B), design (D) and finance (F), in a DBFO PFI contract.

To date little evidence has been collected on this issue. Given that the prison sector has experience of both 'full' PFI (where the private consortium runs the whole prison) as well as contracting for the management of conventionally built and financed prisons, it provides an ideal test-bed for examining whether the full PFI model outperforms the option of using contestability for the operation of a service over a shorter time-frame.

Evidence of this type is much needed. It would provide an insight into the inevitable trade-off between contestability and commitment within PPPs. In some instances, long-term term agreements for service operation may be beneficial so long as the contract allows for adequate safeguards to prevent under-performance. The advantage of this approach is that it offers the service provider the timeframe necessary to make investments in the partnership relationship. The type of safeguards necessary to reduce the risks inherent in long-term contracting are discussed below and further in Chapter 8.

However, in other areas the potential pitfalls of the public sector being tied to a single service operator may be too great. This is more likely to be the case if core services are included within a PPP. In relation to a school, for instance, parents and governors might only be willing to enter into a PPP which includes some core services such as teaching if they know they have reserved the right to switch to a different educational provider in the event of under-performance. This could be done by building a school conventionally and then contracting separately for the management, or alternatively by undertaking a 'full' PFI/DBFO contract where the 'O' refers to a rolling 5-7 year contract for key services including school management (discussed in Chapter 7).

Clearly all PPP contracts should provide the public sector with clear safeguards against under-performance. The public procurer should *always* retain the option of introducing new service providers if performance is persistently inadequate. Consideration should always be given to whether value-for-money and quality improvement are more likely to be achieved if there are contractual break-points where the public procurer has the option of introducing contestability for service provision. The grounds on which termination can occur, and the level of any compensation payments incurred, should always be clearly agreed at the outset and factored into value-for-money calculations. The performance of DBFO prisons should be compared to those in which only private management has been contracted for. This should inform the future use of long-term contracts for the operation of PFI prisons.

Value-for-money – a consensus?

The different 'key drivers' of value-for-money in PFI contracts were explored in a report commissioned from Arthur Andersen by the Treasury Taskforce (Arthur Andersen, 2000). A sample of NAO reports and the anonymous case studies put together by Arthur Andersen suggest projected value-for-money savings in PFI projects in the order of 10-20 per cent. These projected savings are arrived at by comparing the cost of the PFI project with its Public Sector Comparator; they of course refer to long-term projects that by definition are not yet complete. We will not know the actual outcomes for many years – hence the headline number quoted by Arthur Anderson of a 17 per cent average efficiency gain is in danger of gaining a reputation for 'settling the issue once and for all' which it does not deserve.

A significant problem with the Arthur Anderson study is that the researchers were unable to break down projected value-for-money savings by sector. The NAO reports

Table 4.2 Estimated savings from PFI projects				
	PFI Cost (£m)	Public sector Comparator (PSC) Cost (£m)	Saving (£m)	Saving on PSC (%)
First Four Roads*	698	797	99	12
A74/M74	193	210	17	8
Bridgend and Fazakerley Prisons**	513	567	54	10
Dartford and Gravesham Hospital	177	182	5	3

* One project was showing a higher PFI cost than the PSC
** Savings all came from Bridgend prison

Sources: NAO Reports.

suggest that the PFI appears to be achieving significant efficiency gains in some prison and road projects. However, in two critical areas – schools and hospitals – the gains appear marginal.

The projected efficiency savings in the prison PFI projects of around 10 per cent appear to result from two significant features. Firstly, the prison PFI projects are 'full' DBFO models where all of the operation and management of the public service is part of the contract. There is no separation out of ancillary and core services. This should enable the contractor to integrate thoroughly the design and build of the prison with its operation and make productivity gains through the way it manages the single most important input in any public service – the workforce. It should be pointed out that prisons may be a special case, to some extent, in that there are long-standing staffing problems in some conventionally procured and managed prisons. A second key feature might be the clarity of the contractual model in prison PFI projects. The Prison Service is the sole purchaser and has over time built up expertise in contracting; arguably, the Highways Agency has developed similar expertise in relation to contracting for PFI road projects.

Both of these key features are absent in education and in health. In these cases a very restricted model of DBFO is being used with the operating element encompassing only a narrow range of ancillary services such as maintenance, cleaning and occasionally IT. The main labour intensive forms of service provision are excluded and the possible gains from greater efficiency are thereby limited. In school PFI projects in England the relationship between the Local Education Authority and the school governing bodies as joint purchasers is unclear (see Chapters 6 and 7). In health the main public purchaser – the health authority – has had limited input into the PFI process, which largely involves the Department of Health acting directly with NHS Trusts. The consequences of this are explored in a CPPP commissioned comprehensive review of the operation of the PFI in the NHS (Boyle and Harrison, 2000). Recall that the critical starting point of the PFI process is for the public purchaser, which in this case should be the health authority and/or the NHS Executive, to specify the outcomes it would like to achieve through the development, for example, of a new hospital. In practice their appears to be little connection between PFI hospitals and the wider strategy for improving health outcomes within a health authority – though this is an indictment of NHS planning processes rather than the PFI *per se*.

The NAO report on Dartford and Gravesham (NAO, 1999a) suggested that it would deliver only marginal value-for-money (see Table 4.2). This scheme is in fact representative of PFI hospital projects on which data exists, none of which show significant value-for-money savings when set against the Public Sector Comparator. In the case of most NHS hospital PFI schemes the small projected savings could easily disappear if some assumptions relating to risk, or the discount rate, were altered (as

Table 4.3 Comparison of costs under PFI and PSC options (£m)

NHS Trust	Capital value of scheme	Net present cost		PSC minus PFI	Net risk added to PSC
		PSC	PFI		
South Manchester[a]	65.6	2,126	2,124	2	20
Norfolk & Norwich[b]	143.5	1,682	1,642	40	76
Greenwich Healthcare[a]	93	1,427	1,410	17	46
Calderdale Healthcare[a]	64.6	1,362	1,342	20	37
Bromley Hospitals[a]	117.9	1,179	1,166	13	30
Worcester Royal[a]	86.6	1,098	1,095	3	10
Dartford & Gravesham[b]	94	944	928	16	42
Barnet & Chase Farm[a]	54	198.2	193.2	5	15.5
Carlisle Hospitals[b]	64.7	174.3	173.1	5.9	21.8
South Buckinghamshire[b]	45.1	169.2	162.1	7.1	9.3
North Durham[b]	61	180.9	177.0	3.9	20.4

a Data source: House of Commons Health Committee HC629, 1999. The figure for Dartford & Gravesham does not reflect the subsequent correction to the PSC which resulted from the NAO's review (NAO, 1999b). A substantial inconsistency was uncovered relating to the estimation of building cost inflation. This reduced the estimated savings under the PFI from £17.2 million to £5.1 million;

b Data source: House of Commons Health Committee HC959, 1998 (a, b). For consistency the values for Norfolk and Norwich which were reported then are used.

Source: Boyle and Harrison, 2000

argued by Boyle and Harrison, 2000; Sussex, 2001; and Price *et al*, 1999). This is illustrated in Table 4.3 which shows how the estimate of the net risk retained under the PSC was the crucial factor in determining PFI as the preferred option.

Boyle and Harrison (2000) also point to the high transactions costs that have been a feature of PFI deals in health and across most sectors. Indeed they calculate that payments by Trusts to external advisors have averaged over three per cent of the value of the schemes, not significantly different from the projected value-for-money savings. However, improvements to the PFI process, such as contract standardisation, may lead to reduced transactions costs in the future.

Some of the deficiencies highlighted around PFI hospital projects are misplaced in that they also apply to conventionally financed hospital projects. Certainly the poor NHS planning framework would throw up problems for conventional hospital projects. Likewise, some of the problems that have been laid at the door of the PFI, such as reduced bed numbers, are really the result of wider NHS policies, though the lack of effective linkage between the planning of large hospital projects and wider NHS strategy for bed numbers can be criticised (Boyle and Harrison, 2000).

The lack of convincing value-for-money gains from PFI hospitals would lead one to wonder why 19 out of 23 major hospital projects that had reached financial closure by summer 2000 were commissioned using the PFI route? The most likely answer is that the NHS bodies involved believed that the PFI was 'the only game in town' and the hospitals would not have been built any other way. For example, the NHS Plan for future hospitals published in February 2001 suggested that almost all new hospitals would be built using the PFI without providing an analysis of value-for-money in existing schemes (DoH, 2001a).

School PFI schemes also appear to have been driven first and foremost by the lack of any conventional alternative.[5] The Treasury's own report on Colfox school in Dorset revealed that financial pressures on the local authority were the driving force and that the PFI project was only three per cent lower in cost than the Public Sector Comparator (HM Treasury, 1999a). The large 'bundled' PFI scheme for 29 secondary schools in Glasgow was also driven first and foremost by financial constraints in that the Council was clear that there was no alternative option involving conventional finance. However, in this case when the PSC was originally constructed the PFI project was expected to deliver five per cent efficiency gains, and subsequent developments in the project may further have increased the scope for value-for-money.

The DfEE has published no evidence on value-for-money in PFI schools projects, though two projects involving Voluntary Aided schools are expected to cost four per cent and two per cent less than their Comparators. The evidence to date suggests that expected value-for-money gains in school PFI projects will be of a similar order to those in hospital PFI projects.

Again it should be stressed that part of the reason for marginal gains in health and education may be the restricted nature of the DBFO model being used, where the bulk of the costs of the service, the staffing costs, are outside of the control of the contractors. Whether or not more services might be incorporated within future PPP deals is explored in Chapters 6 and 7.

Affordability

There are two different meanings attached to the use of the word 'affordability' in the debate over the PFI/PPPs. The first refers to the problem faced by most public purchasing bodies where the publicly financed and provided option is ruled out because it is not 'affordable' under traditional budgetary controls as a result of the need for a high up-front commitment of finance. This is the problem of the PFI being perceived as the 'only game in town' because conventional finance is seen not to be available.

The second meaning of the term follows from the observation that any PFI project sets up demands for future funding streams from the public purchaser. This raises the issue of how far those funding needs will prove 'affordable' and the possible constraints that servicing PFI contracts may place on other areas of service provision. It is critically important to note, however, that any long-term investment entered into by any public body will require a stream of revenue payments to be set aside to meet the capital, depreciation and maintenance costs and associated service requirements. The problem of 'affordability' in this sense applies to any form of public investment in public service projects and is the mirror at the micro level of the need to secure 'sustainability' in the overall public finances.

Some observers have criticised the fact that NHS Trusts have to put aside a significant proportion of their budgets to service PFI contracts as being a possible constraint on service provision in the future (Gaffney *et al*, 1999). Many of these criticisms conflate the impact of the PFI with the wholly separate introduction of capital charges into the NHS in 1991. These were designed to encourage NHS Trusts to use assets more efficiently by requiring them to pay for their capital (at the Treasury's six per cent real rate). So a conventionally financed new build hospital would require the NHS Trust to set aside a stream of revenues to pay for these capital charges – in effect paying the Treasury for borrowing public money – along with associated depreciation and maintenance costs. A PFI built hospital would require the NHS Trust to set aside a similar stream of revenues to pay for the private capital being used. This stream will be somewhat higher, reflecting the higher cost of private capital. In addition, the stream of payments under the PFI contract will include the costs of maintenance and depreciation and service provision included in the contract. Thus the stream of capital payments under a conventional build and the stream of capital and service payments under a PFI scheme are not directly comparable.

To understand whether the PFI hospital project is more or less 'affordable' than the equivalent conventional hospital relies once again on a comparison of the Public Sector Comparator with the PFI project. We have seen that PFI hospital projects offer marginal value-for-money savings. In this sense they are only marginally more affordable but they are no more 'revenue hungry' than any conventional hospital scheme. The problems raised by having to set aside significant revenue streams to service lengthy contracts may be more acute for schools, but for reasons more to do with the structures of locally delivered education and the inappropriateness of the PFI for routine refurbishment and maintenance.

For instance, in the London Borough of Brent a 'bundled' PFI scheme for the refurbishment of schools required the governing bodies of those schools to set aside 10-12 per cent a year of their delegated budgets to be paid back to the Local Education Authority (Thompson, 2000). This was to pay for that element of the PFI contract involving the school services that would normally be paid for out of the schools' budgets delegated under the Local Management of Schools and Fair Funding regimes. In this case problems arose because of the lack of clarity over the contractual position of the schools vis-à-vis the LEA. In addition it was not clear that a 25-year contract made sense for a project geared towards routine refurbishment and maintenance. Many eligible schools chose not to take part.

Similar problems arose at Pimlico school, originally set to be a simple refurbishment project. However, because such simple projects are not readily 'PFI-able', the LEA and

DfEE made strenuous and ultimately unsuccessful attempts to persuade the governing body of the school to opt for complete demolition and rebuilding. This is the most worrying case of an attempt to alter a project simply to go down the PFI route against the wishes of the service user, so that the project would be 'off balance sheet'. This clearly breaches the 'social equity' criteria set out in Chapter 1.

A significant problem raised by the need to set aside revenue streams for conventional or PFI contracts is that central government has deliberately created pots of revenue that can only be accessed by local authorities for PFI schemes and not for other forms of capital investment. This was the case with Pimlico school, effectively denying the governing body any real choice over which route to take. This is part of the general problem of a lack of 'level playing field' between different forms of investment.

The future for the PFI

Time and again the Commission on Public Private Partnerships has been provided with accounts of PFI projects that have gone ahead first and foremost because there was in fact no conventional alternative. Not only has this contributed to a process of developing PFI projects that may have led to a sub-optimal approach to the allocation of risk and the achievement of value-for-money; it has also undermined political support for the initiative and other forms of PPP – it is hard to win people around to a particular policy if they feel they are being forced to do it. This lack of a 'level playing field' has contributed to some of the scepticism that the PFI sometimes attracts.

The pre-requisite for taking the PFI model and other forms of PPP forward is to make value-for-money – defined in efficiency and quality terms – the sole driving force and to remove the incentive for going down this route solely to avoid constraints on public finance. Creating a 'level playing field' means having a transparent set of public finance rules that do not set up artificial barriers or incentives to benefit one type of provision over another.

The framework for public finances

The first important reform would be for the overall framework for the public finances to reflect the fact that privately financed public investment has the same implications for the sustainability of the government's finances as conventionally financed investment (Hawksworth, 2000a; Robinson, 2000). The sustainable investment rule should be modified to ensure that it would still be satisfied even if all PFI projects had instead been financed in the traditional way. This would simply be a matter of the Treasury regularly presenting a calculation (for example in the

Budget Red Book) that showed whether or not this modified sustainable investment rule would be met over the period normally used for public finance projections. It would produce a more robust test of fiscal sustainability while removing the temptation for politicians to use the PFI to 'hide' investment that makes claims on public revenue resources.

A second recommendation logically consistent with the first is that, in addition to resource budgets, government departments should be set an overall capital spending budget that encompasses both traditionally financed public spending and the capital value of PFI spending. There might also be an indicative split between the PFI and traditionally financed capital spending (in part as a form of target to encourage departments to make adequate use of the PFI) but there would have to be considerable flexibility to move capital spending between the two sub-categories. The objective would be to remove the incentive that currently still exists to use the PFI to evade departmental capital budget constraints.

Our proposed changes would in no way affect the actual accounting treatment of individual PFI projects. After a project had been shown to offer significant value-for-money and the contract had been signed, an accounting judgement would still be needed on whether the project was on or off the public sector's balance sheet. Deciding this *after* the event would be consistent with the accounting treatment of any private sector transaction and would be in line with Treasury and National Audit Office guidance that the accounting treatment of a PPP project should play no role in deciding whether it goes ahead or not.

This new financial framework would apply equally to local government. The Local Government Finance Green Paper (DETR, 2000a) appeared to offer local authorities a 'level playing field' by freeing them of direct controls over capital spending. Instead authorities would be able to borrow subject only to 'prudent' limits; that is, the ability to service from revenue streams any capital investment undertaken. This would mirror at the local level the logic behind the sustainable investment rule at national level. The Green Paper also explicitly accepted that central government should not restrict the funding available to authorities to force them to go down a partnership route. Rather it should encourage authorities to plan positively for diversity and explore a range of different options.

However, the Green Paper also signalled the continued ring-fencing of financial support for PFI projects, thus continuing to tilt the playing field in favour of the PFI. This was justified as being necessary at least 'until private finance achieves more general acceptance' (DETR, 2000a). There are, however, more subtle ways of helping and encouraging public bodies to explore different PPP options (see Chapter 8). Even more worryingly the Green Paper almost invited authorities to develop PFI projects that would be off-balance-sheet by saying that in this case they would not count against an assessment of whether the authorities' borrowing was prudent. This is inconsistent with the framework outlined here, as well as with the principles of Best Value, and NAO, OGC and Treasury guidance. Local authorities should go ahead only with those projects that promote Best Value, not those that result in them getting capital spending off balance sheet so they can avoid the DETR's controls.

All of the changes proposed here are consistent with the evolution of Resource Accounting and Budgeting (RAB) in the public sector. RAB should help create a more rational planning of public capital investment, and encourage the proper management and maintenance of public sector assets over the life-cycle, possibly involving private sector partners. In itself RAB should have neutral implications for the PFI, because it does not influence the value-for-money judgement. It will, however, reinforce the pressure on departments to use their existing assets more efficiently, using where appropriate the commercial skills of the private sector through the wider markets initiative (see Chapter 5).

Recommendations

The framework for public finances should be revised so that privately financed public investment is taken into account in deciding the 'sustainability' of the public finances.

Government departments should be set an overall capital spending budget that encompasses both traditionally financed public spending and the capital value of PFI spending. Public authorities need to have a clear policy planning framework which integrates all forms of investment and service provision.

The process of public contracting

Operating a transparent set of rules in public finance offers the chance of generating a model for public contracting that would offer the best opportunity for achieving value-for-money and innovation in the delivery of public services. The Office for Government Commerce has developed a Gateway Review Process to promote the successful management of large, complex or novel projects so as to deliver value-for-money (See Appendix 8.1). This sensible process is consistent with the simple rules and procedures set out below that are designed to make value-for-money the 'only game in town'.

If a project is going ahead under the PFI solely because the relevant public authority believes there is no conventional alternative and wants to get the project off-balance-sheet, the process should be brought to a halt right there and then. This should be the first 'golden rule' of the PFI to ensure that there are no more examples like Pimlico school. It would help ensure that projects are not distorted in order to make them 'PPP-able'. Only when this golden rule is firmly in place, can a rational process for determining the possible suitability of the PFI/PPP route for a particular project, be put in place.

The starting point for such a process is for the public purchasing authorities to clarify their strategy and the public policy planning framework within which all investment and service provision has to take place. Once the public policy framework is right and the outcomes for the service have been specified, a Public Sector Comparator can be constructed that provides the benchmark against which to assess possible partnership solutions. The PSC needs to be regularly discussed throughout any negotiation process and needs to be fully disclosed at the appropriate time.

The point of disclosure will depend in part on the extent of competition in the bidding process. Ideally, there should be a competitive procurement process – involving a number of serious bids going through to the final stages. Competition in bidding for PFI contracts has been variable in the past, though as markets have matured and the public purchasers have improved their own skills, the extent of competition has grown. The public sector needs to concentrate on specifying outcomes sensibly, but could show greater flexibility in terms of different models of provision. The greatest problems arise when the public purchasers cannot accurately specify the outcomes they want to secure and then show a lack of imagination in obtaining the best form of provision.

It is important to recognise that the comparison of a PPP with the PSC is not a 'pass-fail' test. Rather any PPP proposal needs to be subjected to a sensitivity analysis to see whether different assumptions, for example about different forms of risk allocation, would significantly alter the value-for-money assessment. This process should be as open to public scrutiny as possible. For large projects a final verification of the contract by an independent outside body might be factored in from the start, with that body reporting directly to council members in the case of a local authority contract, for example. It can be prudent to have a second opinion in appropriate circumstances and this may in itself improve public confidence in the process.

Finally, after a decision to go ahead has been made the accounting treatment of the PPP/PFI can be decided upon. Deciding on the accounting treatment after the contract has been signed is the second golden rule consistent with making value-for-money the 'only game in town'.

Some other specific changes would alter the value-for-money comparisons. Lowering the benchmark discount rate by one per cent will tilt decisions marginally in favour of conventionally financed projects but should not prevent PPPs offering really significant value-for-money gains from going ahead. Building into contracts options for sharing the excess gains from re-financing deals might make PPPs marginally less attractive for some private contractors but would be seen by most as a price worth paying for reducing the popular perception of PPP projects leading to excessive gains in some cases.

It is important to stress that many of the lessons of the PFI could be applied with benefit to conventional procurement and indeed this will be one of the main goals of the Office of Government Commerce. This includes positive lessons such as arriving at a better understanding of the identification and pricing of different forms of risk and the approach to whole life costing developed in the PFI. It also includes negative lessons to do with clarifying who exactly the public purchaser is and how the project does or does not fit in with wider public policy objectives. It is important to recognise that in this sense the benefits of the PFI may extend further than those arrived at by a simple comparison of the cost of individual PFI projects with their Public Sector Comparators.

In areas such as health the 'mono-culture' of the PFI/DBFO model has had more of an impact on asset procurement practices than actual service delivery, though, arguably, it is in service delivery – the 'O' in DBFO – where the real scope for greater value-for-money and innovation lies. Clearing the ground in terms of the public finance framework and the public procurement process is the necessary pre-requisite for encouraging a wider range of models of PPP which should act as a further spur to innovation.

It seems likely that some of the problems with the financial framework and approval process for the PFI have contributed to the significant undershooting in capital spending identified in Chapter 3. The absence of a 'level playing field' between the PFI and conventional capital spending has encouraged public bodies to go down the PFI route as a way of avoiding government spending and borrowing controls. However, the development of PFI projects has proved long and drawn out, with many projects being very slow to come on line. In the meantime conventional spending on public assets is delayed in anticipation of the successful completion of PFI contracts. This has led to the odd situation in which public managers can simultaneously complain about the PFI being the 'only game in town' while it also remains a relatively small proportion of total capital spending. In addition the PFI is more often – and more appropriately – used for the building of new assets rather than refurbishment. Much conventional capital spending is used for maintenance and refurbishment of housing, schools or hospitals and indeed this makes up a large proportion of total publicly sponsored capital spending. Hence the PFI can simultaneously be a small proportion of total capital spending while being the dominant model of procurement for *new* hospitals or prisons.

Recommendations

PFI projects should not go ahead just because a public authority believes there is no alternative and it is therefore determined to get the project off-balance sheet.

The accounting treatment of a PPP/PFI project should be settled after a decision to go ahead on value-for-money grounds has been made.

All PPP/PFI proposals need to be subjected to a sensitivity analysis to see whether different assumptions, for example about different forms of risk allocation or a different discount rate, would significantly alter the value-for-money assessment.

All contracts should have explicit provisions for sharing super-profits arising from re-financing deals.

Consideration should be given to reducing the discount rate used by the Treasury from six to five per cent.

Generating diversity

A key aim of a new approach to PFI/PPPs should be to encourage public purchasers to choose the appropriate form of PPP or indeed conventional procurement for a particular service, as part of a more explicit aim of encouraging a much greater diversity of forms of provision. The Treasury has itself set out criteria for when the PFI, and by extension other forms of PPP, might be most suitable.

The high transactions costs often involved in PPPs might make them more suitable for large-scale projects though this may not be the case in relation to particularly innovative small deals. The PFI/DBFO route involving a SPV may be most appropriate for the most complex projects, involving significant risks in the design and construction phase that carry over into the operational phase. Here the project management disciplines derived from involving a financial partner and having some or all of the partners putting their equity at risk are most relevant and there is the strongest case for the integration of the contractors. This model is also appropriate for projects where there is considerable scope for greater innovation in design and above all in operation. In these circumstances including more of the 'O' within the DBFO model should be explored (see Chapter 7).

Where there is considerable scope for commercial use of assets the DBFO/PFI approach may also be appropriate, which explains its extensive use by the Ministry of Defence for services such as the sea transportation of military equipment. The DBFO route is also clearly most suitable where there are third party payments and where the private partners can bear a significant part of the demand risk, as in the case of DBFO road projects.

The corollary is that more routine projects, where the emphasis is on the delivery of an asset and routine maintenance but with a modest operational element, may be best dealt with using a Design/Build/Operate (DBO) model with the finance coming from the public sector. This is a good description of many recent hospital projects delivered under the PFI, where the allocation of design and construction risks may not require a full-blown DBFO project. Routine refurbishment and maintenance – for example of schools – may not involve significant risk and may not require long contractual arrangements at all and so may be best suited to more conventional forms of contracting.

Other PPP models have yet to be tried extensively. A Design/Build/*Guarantee*/ Operate (DBGO) model would involve a financial institution ensuring that project scrutiny skills are being exercised and guaranteeing the completion of the project on time and to budget. The private partners here are taking on board the construction risks identified as one of the main sources of value-for-money savings in conventional PFI models. There is no reason why there could not be a pick-and-mix approach to the involvement of different proportions of private and public capital and debt and equity – a 'mixed finance model'.

In practice the decision between a DBO, DBGO and a DBFO project may sometimes be a marginal one, which raises the obvious question as to why we do not see more DBO projects and so many PFI/DBFO projects? The answer of course is that the 'F' in DBFO in the past has been driven largely by spurious public finance arguments.

There is no need to set out some kind of fixed framework for when a particular model should apply. Rather the policy framework outlined here should encourage private providers to vary the models they offer for different projects and for public purchasers to consider a range of different models and be guided by value-for-money considerations, and not financing or accounting issues, in choosing the appropriate option.

How would we know that this new framework was being applied successfully? One key test would be when a major spending department such as the Department of Health or the Home Office announces a tranche of big capital projects they make clear that several might be PFI/DBFO projects, several would be DBO and several would be conventional projects. The fact that the latest plans for hospitals and prisons appear to entrench the PFI as the 'only game in town' shows how far we still have to travel in this regard. A second test would be when departments stopped looking at the accounting treatment of PFI projects *before* contracts were signed.

Right up until the final singing of the contract the option of going ahead with a more conventional public procurement as outlined in the Public Sector Comparator should always remain open. This will only be the case if the public purchaser could be assured of public finance if that could be shown to be the best value option and the same revenue streams would be available regardless of the option chosen. Indeed there is a very strong case for re-naming the PSC the *Public Sector Alternative* (PSA) to emphasise that it is precisely that: an option that should always be open if it is the one that would deliver value-for-money.

Operationalising this framework would give public purchasing bodies real choice, would make the procurement process more competitive, and would deliver a greater diversity of outcomes. We would still see DBFO/PFI models but probably fewer of them as a more diverse set of other forms of PPP emerged.

Recommendation

A 'mono-culture'of procurement models should be avoided. Government should promote diversity in procurement by encouraging a range of different PPP models without undue emphasis on the conventional DBFO/PFI model.

Conclusion

There is some concern in Whitehall that this framework, combined with large planned increases in conventional capital budgets promised in the spending reviews, will diminish the flow of PPP projects. But the flow of PPP/PFI deals is in itself not a good performance indicator: £1 billion worth of innovative PPP/PFI projects offering significant value-for-money would be better than £2 billion worth of PFI projects offering marginal value-for-money. However, the current incentives for ministers and officials are to deliver deal flow not significant value-for-money. On the other hand, the public purchasers who have complained that the PFI model is the only game in town might be seen to have failed in their duty to deliver value-for-money if, following the implementation of the above framework, a wider range of PPP models did not emerge.

The key political argument behind these recommendations is that one cannot successfully develop policy innovations by putting forward arguments for them that do not stand up to scrutiny. A policy based on denying a full range of choice to public managers will not succeed in generating either the intellectual or political support that will make PPPs a long-term success. In the long run getting the economics of PPPs right will be a key factor in convincing people that partnership has a role to play.

Endnotes

1   If capital spending under the PFI had been replaced by conventional forms of public finance, the selling of an extra £11 billion of government bonds over this period would have posed few problems. Indeed financial institutions and particularly the pension funds were complaining about the relative dearth of long-dated government bonds.

2   This is discussed further in NAO (1999c).

3   The estimated projected savings were sensitive to the risk transfer valuations that accounted for 60 per cent of forecast cost savings, but in only 17 projects out of 29 was there sufficient data available to identify a risk transfer valuation.

4   Quasi-government institutions such as the European Investment Bank are also able to borrow at low rates, but only because the financial markets believe that the institution is guaranteed by EU governments. Using the EIB to finance the debt in PFI deals, which is common practice, is almost exactly equivalent to the government borrowing the money in the first place (and should be treated as such).

5   This was explicitly acknowledged to be the case by the Deputy Prime Minister in relation to the Victoria Dock School in Hull, though this may have been a particularly interesting example of an innovative small-scale project involving a local company (Prescott, 2000).

5. PPPs and public enterprise

In 1997 the Labour Government inherited a drastically reduced public enterprise sector following over a decade of privatisation by the previous Government. Labour faced the question of what to do with the remaining revenue generating public enterprises. Almost by definition these were the enterprises which, for various technical and political reasons, were less obvious candidates for straightforward privatisation.

For several of them the Government's response was to promote solutions described as 'Public Private Partnerships'. Others saw the models proposed for London Underground and for the National Air Traffic System (NATS) as part-privatisations. By using the language of PPPs in this way the Government associated the term PPP with 'privatisation', a move that many thought unhelpful. The Government also inherited and took forward moves towards encouraging the public sector to extract more value from its existing assets base. A key element in this was the wider markets initiative involving public agencies working in partnership with the private sector to exploit the latent commercial potential of public assets – another application of the label 'Public Private Partnership'.

Hence a three-fold approach to PPPs emerged: the Private Finance Initiative, which focused primarily, though not exclusively, on the construction of *new* assets; the wider markets initiative focused on the more efficient use of *existing* assets; and new models of partnership for key public enterprises (HM Treasury, 2000). These were all major initiatives but they by no means exhausted the range of partnership options available to (and being used by) the Government.

The wider markets initiative

In November 1997 the government published a National Assets Register and announced its intention of disposing of assets it no longer needed. For those assets that remained the question was how better to exploit their value. Departments and agencies were to be encouraged to work in partnership with the private sector, where appropriate, to exploit the commercial potential of physical assets such as land, premises and equipment as well as the skills and intellectual property of the public sector.

The justification for the wider markets initiative was two-fold:

- To bring commercial disciplines to bear in exploiting public assets through contracting and partnering.

- To raise additional revenue, albeit often on a small scale, to fund public services such as basic research.

With a large inheritance of land and premises, the Ministry of Defence has faced a particular challenge in managing its asset base effectively and has used private management where appropriate. The Defence Evaluation and Research Agency (DERA) had developed partnership approaches to exploit commercially its intellectual property. It was proposed that DERA itself should become a PPP, but in the end it was decided that the larger part of the Agency would become a Public Limited Company instead.

Other examples of the initiative included the potentially very ambitious partnership involving the British Waterways Board and Partnerships UK to establish a canal-based national water grid for the transfer and sale of water. PUK would also be involved in other initiatives including the commercial exploitation of the skills and intellectual property of the Forensic Science Service. The famous creation of Dolly the cloned sheep by a Scottish public research institute was followed by the spinning off of a company, to which the patents were transferred for further commercial exploitation.

One of the main areas thought to be particularly relevant to the wider markets initiative was the output of government funded Public Sector Research Establishments (PSREs) – such as the one responsible for Dolly the sheep. There has been a long history of attempts to exploit the commercial potential of government funded research, to give research establishments greater freedom to make use of their intellectual property and the incentive to do so by allowing establishments and their staff to share in the proceeds. A practical issue here is how to allocate the appropriate commercial risk to the private partner.

There is also a more profound challenge. If government funded research has more or less obvious commercial applications, it may be asked why it should be publicly funded in the first place. In many instances, of course, the future commercial possibilities of research will be so uncertain that private funding may be difficult. But it is critical that the wider markets initiative avoids the potential problem of diverting PSREs away from their duty to pursue research aimed at those public goals that the private sector by definition does not have an incentive to pursue.

Although it is at an early stage of development, there is clear potential for the wider markets initiative to develop and extend the more creative use of public sector assets. Aside from the problem of maintaining the necessary but difficult separation of the pursuit of pure public goods from the commercial exploitation of public research it is perhaps one of the least disputed forms of PPP.

PPPs for the public enterprises

The 1997 Labour Government's proposals for the public enterprises have been a matter of considerable dispute, giving rise to more difficult political and policy debates than just about any other domestic issue during the 1997-2001 period. Labour's position in 1997 was clear in one important respect: it had no intention of reversing any of the privatisations that had occurred under the previous Government. The reform of 'Clause IV' had moved Labour decisively away from any lingering focus on public ownership as a solution to market failures in industry. There was also a general acceptance that some of the privatisations undertaken by the previous Government had eventually proved successful – with the exception perhaps of water and especially the railways. As always with Labour governments, pragmatism played an important role: any re-nationalisation, even of the railways, would take up precious legislative time and was perceived to involve the use of financial resources better used for higher priorities.

The Government's approach to the public enterprises certainly followed the principle of encouraging diversity. Whether this diversity was the result of choosing rationally the right model for each public enterprise is a matter of some debate. The PPP label has been attached to two particularly high-profile initiatives:

- The proposed PPP for the London Underground would involve private consortia taking over responsibility for investment in and maintenance of the infrastructure assets of the Tube under 25-30 year contracts, while the public sector remained in control of the operation of services. This would draw private finance and management skills into part of the functioning of the Tube.

- Just under half of the equity (46 per cent) in National Air Traffic System (NATS) is set to be sold to the private sector strategic partner chosen in March 2001, with the public sector retaining a 49 per cent share and 5 per cent being offered to the workforce through an employee trust. Safety and economic regulation would be the separate responsibility of the Civil Aviation Authority.

The PPP model was also applied to the Commonwealth Development Corporation with the sale of a majority stake. It has been proposed to sell a minority stake in British Nuclear Fuels Limited (BNFL), but with the public sector continuing to bear the main risk that can not be transferred: that of the costs associated with decommissioning obsolete sites. The new body to promote innovative PPPs, Partnerships UK, is itself a PPP (see Chapter 8).

By contrast a different model was chosen for another important public enterprise:

- The Post Office was turned into a Public Limited Company (PLC) in spring 2001 under the new name of Consignia, with the government as sole shareholder, and with a separate regulator, the Postal Services Commission. This in many ways mirrored the logic of the 'privatise and regulate' model implemented by the previous government for most of the utilities, but with continued public ownership (Robinson and Rubin, 1999). In practice the fact that the sub-post offices have always been run privately means that the Post Office has long been a form of PPP.

In the case of each of the PPPs the same set of arguments associated with the PFI arise. Is the PPP approach necessary because the public finances require it or is it a route to bring in the skills of the private sector (where appropriate) to manage complex investment projects and to deliver value-for-money?

The fiscal rules and public enterprises

There is, however, one critical difference with publicly funded services such as health and education where the PFI has played a role. In the case of the public enterprises all or a significant part of the revenue funding comes from charges to customers. Although in recent years fare revenue has been sufficient to cover London Underground's operating costs it has never been enough to fund all of its investment needs and significant additional public funding has been required. NATS, however, is wholly self-funded from charges. The Post Office in the 1990s was generating net revenues to be paid back to the Treasury.

To understand the Labour Government's approach it is necessary to go back to the public finance rationale for the PFI, and indeed to go back further to one of the rationales offered for privatisation, to the Ryrie rules, and the Government's new fiscal framework (see Chapter 4). The investment of public enterprises has generally counted as part of total public investment. Governments have traditionally used their control of the borrowing of the public enterprises as a lever of macroeconomic management. From the late 1970s the borrowing and investment of the public enterprises was constrained to help reduce the government's deficit, contributing to the under-investment that characterises much of the public infrastructure.

The microeconomic case for imposing arbitrary public borrowing constraints on public enterprise investment is weak (Hawksworth, 2000b). There is no reason why the level of public investment considered prudent by the government in terms of the overall management of the economy should be consistent with the amount of investment considered necessary and efficient by the public enterprises. Investment by public enterprises should instead be judged on whether it can deliver value-for-money in comparison with the option of not investing and with alternative methods of provision, including the PFI and other forms of PPP.

The Ryrie rules were an attempt to relax the constraints on public enterprises. However, for many public enterprises, privatisation proved a more successful way of escaping Treasury controls, even when necessarily accompanied by more or less tough regulatory regimes designed to tackle those market failures that had been a significant rationale for public ownership in the first place.

One of the rationales for privatisation never really stood up to serious analysis. Asset sales were seen as a less painful revenue raiser by politicians and were bizarrely treated as negative public expenditure in the public accounts from the 1980s. In fact the selling of assets has the same macroeconomic implications as the selling of government bonds or gilts and is another way of financing a budget deficit not of reducing it. This was rightly recognised by the Government in the fiscal framework established in 1998, with the new key measure of fiscal policy, Public Sector Net Borrowing (PSNB), treating the sale of shares in public enterprises as a way of financing a deficit in the same way as bond issues.

It is clear, however, that public finance arguments have been one of the main driving forces behind the Government's PPP plans for the London Underground and NATS just as they have been key in the PFI. The Department of the Environment, Transport and the Regions (DETR) appears in each case to have accepted the argument that the PPP model was the only way to finance the necessary investment and that the sale of assets generates finance more painlessly than the selling of government debt.

The argument that there is a need to get the financing of public enterprise investment 'off balance sheet' was particularly unconvincing in the case of NATS. Here the amounts involved, just over £1 billion spread over about seven years, could easily have been financed conventionally (Hawksworth, 2000b). In the case of London Underground, estimated capital and maintenance work of £12-13 billion spread over 15 years would be more significant but still manageable. In each case, borrowing to finance investment would satisfy the Government's golden rule and would alter only modestly the declining trajectory for net public debt and so would not affect the sustainability of the public finances.

Although the DETR had originally hoped that the Tube as a PPP could become self-funded from fare revenue it came to recognise that some continued public funding would more than likely be necessary. A great deal of the debate around the Government's PPP centred on whether London Underground's investment should be financed by government bonds (or gilts), government-guaranteed bonds, revenue bonds or via private finance. This diverted attention away from the far more important issue of how that investment would be *funded* from a mix of fare revenue and continued public revenue funding either from general Treasury sources or dedicated funding streams such as congestion charges, for example. Regardless of the model of *financing* chosen, the need for some public *funding* would remain.

The Government's slowness in coming to accept the need for continued public funding of London Underground was matched by an inconsistent approach to bond financing. In the case of the Channel Tunnel Rail Link (CTRL), Government stepped in to rescue a troubled major transport infrastructure project that was *privately managed under the PFI* with government-guaranteed bonds that might raise £1.1 billion on top of £2 billion of direct grants. The decision to use government-guaranteed bonds rather than simply issuing gilts was justified on the basis that the CTRL would remain a 'flagship PPP' and to avoid signalling to other PPP bidders that the government would be willing to take on financial risk. It was also taken to keep the project off the public sector balance sheet, though going down this route would cost the project an additional £80 million (NAO, 2001a).

The Treasury decided that these government-guaranteed bonds would not count as public borrowing on the grounds that there was a small chance of the project failing and the guarantee being called on. Though the restructured PPP for the CTRL was in many ways more robust than the original PFI deal, the complex mixture of public and private finance and guarantees now underpinning the CTRL leaves the taxpayer exposed to considerable financial risk (NAO, 2001a). With investment in the London Underground almost certainly less risky than the CTRL some commentators asked why the Treasury's logic could not be applied to government-guaranteed bonds for the Tube (Glaister et al, 2000). A more substantive point is that whether borrowing for investment in the transport infrastructure is on or off the public sector's balance sheet is of course irrelevant for securing value-for-money, which ought to be the key driver.

Private finance for London Underground and for NATS will cost more than the equivalent public finance, a point emphasised by critics of these PPPs.[1] This matters especially for London Underground because capital costs are such a large proportion of total costs. At first sight it would appear that efficiency savings of around 20 per cent may be required to make the PPP option value-for-money (Industrial Society 2000), which is at the high end of likely savings from other PPPs. However, as emphasised in Chapter 4, the apparently lower cost of capital to the public sector is in part a function of some of the risks being passed on in a hidden form to current and future taxpayers rather than being separately identified and paid for. This is effectively what happened with the costs of the overrun on the Jubilee Line Extension on the Underground.[2]

The real case for PPPs for public enterprises

The basic arguments for using private finance for these PPPs are much the same as those for using the DBFO/PFI approach in the public services. The extra costs of private finance have to be outweighed by the benefits resulting from the skills, risk assessment and expertise that the private sector may have in running complex investment projects involving significant risk, particularly where there is the greatest need for the integration of contractors. The experience of the CTRL and Eurotunnel would lead one to question whether private management of large transport infrastructure projects is necessarily more efficient than public. However, the advantages of having a PPP as one option are clear, not least because the contestability this brings places pressure on public sector management to raise its game.

This then is the primary argument for bringing private equity and management into NATS. It is not the private finance *per se* that was being sought, but the due diligence and project management disciplines derived from having the private partners putting their equity at stake. Similarly it is believed that the financial risks borne by the private partners in the case of London Underground will lead to more efficient oversight of maintenance and investment in the Tube, which in the past has been a widely acknowledged failure of London Underground's management. Design and construction would be integrated with maintenance, but not operations. A significant degree of construction risk would be transferred. In both cases the necessary project management skills could be separately contracted for, and in the case of the building of the Jubilee Line Extension, this was indeed the model chosen, though only after the project had run into significant problems.

However, the other key argument for the PFI/DBFO approach is that significant value-for-money gains can flow from the integration of the design and build of the assets with the operation of services using those assets. This may be the case with the PPP for NATS, but the proposed PPP for London Underground would involve the separation of investment from operations. This resembles the model of the PFI that in health appears to date to have delivered unimpressive projected outcomes in terms of value-for-money, compared with prisons or indeed the PFI/DBFO model for roads.

There are, of course, very significant differences between health and transport, most notably the relatively greater importance of capital investment in transport versus the relative importance of labour input in health services. Nevertheless, the separation of investment and operations in the proposed PPP for the London Underground seemed strange in the light of the emphasis on integration inherent in the PFI. It is also problematic when set against the problems created by the fragmentation of the rail industry. The issues raised by having a fragmented management structure were not surprisingly those that the body that would take over responsibility for the Tube in the summer of 2001, Transport for London (TfL), emphasised in relation to the proposed PPP.

There were other plans for different forms of PPP that would have maintained this desirable integration of investment and operations while also fostering contestability between privately and publicly managed parts of the network (Osmon, 2000). A significant criticism then of the Government's proposed PPP model for the London Underground was the failure to consider publicly a diversity of different PPP models, as well as comparing the preferred PPP model with the best publicly financed alternative and indeed full privatisation.

Transparency and the public sector comparator

Another obvious parallel with the debate over the PFI was the perceived lack of transparency in the process of developing the PPP for the Underground. In this case there was an added complication. The body originally responsible for evaluating the PPP bids and making a recommendation to the Secretary of State – London Transport – would have transferred its responsibilities for the Tube in the summer of 2001 to Transport for London, answerable to the new Greater London Authority and its Mayor. These new bodies would have had to manage and be responsible for complex PPP contracts that they themselves had not drawn up.

The ideal model of the PFI involves the construction of a Public Sector Comparator in the early stages of policy planning, setting out the best publicly financed and provided alternative alongside the proposed PPP, so that they can be explicitly compared to see which offers best value-for-money. Following a recommendation from the Environment, Transport and Regions Select Committee, the National Audit Office looked at London Underground's financial analysis and found that it had gone through a thorough process in estimating the costs of the public sector and PPP options (NAO, 2000b). However, the NAO also recognised that the likelihood of developing real 'partnership' had been compromised by the exclusion of the staff of Transport for London from the procurement process though they would assume overall responsibility for the Tube.

Although a PSC for London Underground was constructed and eventually subjected to independent scrutiny, a PSC for NATS was never constructed. Without a PSC in each case it is impossible for outsiders to judge the relative merits of the different models. Given the scale, complexity and above all the contentious nature of the PPPs for London Underground and NATS, they best illustrate the case that full and honest scrutiny of all the options for a particular enterprise or service needs to be undertaken to secure public confidence in the process.

The absence for a long period of time of a full and open consideration of the public sector alternative to the London Underground PPP was a consequence of the decision that the preferred PPP plan was indeed 'the only game in town'. The PPP for NATS appears to have been driven largely by public finance arguments; the potentially more convincing arguments for the management of complex investment projects have often not been articulated. Both examples provide case studies of how the public finance framework gives individual government departments incentives to use PPP options as a way of evading their capital budget constraints, rather than exploring a range of options solely with the aim of securing value-for-money.

The right model for public enterprises?

All of this directs attention to the question of whether it is possible to apply a consistent set of principles to help formulate the right model for each public enterprise in the same way as it is possible to identify the circumstances in which different PPP models might apply in the public services? In this case the 'right' model could be continued public ownership, finance and operation, or various different models of PPP, or indeed outright privatisation which, for revenue generating enterprises, should remain an option – even for a Labour government – if the analysis is strong enough.

The following criteria provide a basis for assessing the suitability of partnership models to different public enterprises (Hawksworth, 2000b).

- The degree of direct competition possible in the market, with more competition tending to favour private ownership, as was clearly the case with the first tranche of privatisations in the 1980s.

- The significance of non-commercial objectives such as social, cultural or environmental considerations, that may support some degree of public ownership where the market would not deliver these outcomes and regulation is problematic.

- The scale and complexity of the required future investment programme, which may benefit from private sector management skills although not necessarily private sector ownership.

- The extent of uncertainty as to required future service provision, which will require flexible contracts if a PPP option is to be effective.

- The extent to which the business can be broken up without losing significant economies of scale and scope, which may limit the menu of viable options in some cases.

These criteria are applied to London Underground, NATS and the Post Office in Table 5.1.

Ironically, perhaps, the Post Office is the one example where the degree of direct market competition creates the strongest case for privatisation, made stronger by the fact that in Germany and the Netherlands, privatisation has been the chosen route. The speed of movement in postal and related markets would seem to require precisely those commercial and management skills thought to be prevalent in the private sector. Rather than bringing those into the Post Office through a PPP, the Post Office has entered into joint ventures with private partners and effectively acted like a private sector company, while remaining publicly owned.

In postal services the key issue is getting right the degree of liberalisation that fosters competition without undermining the significant economies of scale and scope that characterise mail delivery (Robinson and Rubin, 1999). Liberalisation will be taken forward by both the domestic regulator (the Postal Services Commission) and the European Union.

NATS has many of the features of a natural monopoly; it is also the case that public confidence in safety is central to the credibility of any proposals for its future. As has already been explored above, the case for involving private sector skills in the

Table 5.1 Key characteristics of London Underground, NATS and the Post Office

	London Underground	NATS	Post Office
Degree of direct market competition	Low (for peak time commuters)	Very low (80% natural monopoly)	Increasing (from various directions)
Non-commercial objectives	Safety; reducing road traffic congestion	Safety is critical; national security issues also arise	Universal service; support rural areas
Scale and complexity of future investment programme	Large and complex, with a history of delays and over-runs	Large and complex, with two major new centres using state-of-the-art technology	Less capital intensive than LU or NATS, but looking to invest in new markets
Uncertainty about future pattern of service provision	Traffic numbers uncertain but basic pattern is set for existing network	Traffic set to rise steadily over time – new routes likely	Significant due to new communication modes
Economies of scale and scope	Significant network effects	Significant – mostly a natural monopoly	Significant for mail collection/delivery
PPP adopted?	Yes	Yes	No
Overall approach	3 long-term franchises to be let for infrastructure; operations still in public ownership	Sell 46% to strategic private partner; 5% to employees; 49% golden share for government	PLC model with increased commercial and financial freedoms
Other notable features	Need for complex contracts between parts of business; potential conflict with London Mayor	Looking to exploit future opening of EU air traffic control to competition for national franchises	Increasing use of acquisitions and joint ventures with private partners in UK and overseas

management of large and complex investment projects was the clear argument in favour of the PPP approach in the case of NATS. However, one alternative was to contract separately for those skills.

A place for trusts?

Another option for NATS would have been to transfer ownership to a not-for-profit trust, as in Canada (Institute of Professionals, Managers and Specialists, 2000). This would have included the airlines as one group of stakeholders. Interestingly, the final choice of a consortium of airlines as the private partner in the PPP in March 2001 appeared to deliver a solution not far removed from the trust model, as the consortium's bid was based on a 'not for commercial return' approach.

The trust model for NATS had considerable attractions. In an industry such as air traffic services that is primarily a natural monopoly and where safety is such an important feature, a not-for-profit model would have definite advantages in avoiding the perception of any conflict between profit and safety while allowing for the involvement of all the stakeholders. There would still be scope for separate contracting for management skills. With regard to the PPP model, concerns relating to potential conflicts of interest have been raised in regard to all the private sector bids. In the case of the airlines, as customers of air traffic services they would be interested in low charges, when lower charges might not be in the interests of safety. The trust model as it operates in Canada with the airlines nominating 5 out of 14 directors on the trust board, also appears to result in the airlines exerting similar downward pressure on costs. In the case of the PPP for NATS the airlines will be putting their equity at stake and therefore bearing significant financial risk in managing contracting arrangements with, for example, equipment suppliers. A not-for-profit solution for NATS has the merit of reducing the potential for these conflicts of interest, though the solution relies on there being an effective regulatory regime.

A not-for-profit trust model was also proposed for London Underground (Industrial Society, 2000). London Underground also has strong features of a natural monopoly and a similar record to NATS of complex investment projects indifferently managed. Central to its operation is the complex relationship between London Underground and the contractors that have to carry out the necessary maintenance and investment under any model. Under the Government's proposed PPP model these contractual relationships would necessarily be long-term, though with periodic reviews every seven and a half years, emphasising the difficulties of contract negotiation, monitoring and enforcement. This puts a premium on the management skills of London Underground, though it is the alleged deficiencies in those skills that were a major argument for the PPP in the first place.

More generally there has been a lack of imagination in thinking about when and where alternative models, such as trusts, have a role to play in the remaining public enterprises and beyond (Grayling, 2001). In instances where safety and the perception of safety is key, a natural monopoly (or something approaching it) is inevitable, and access to the capital markets outside of Treasury controls is viable, then trust models should always be considered alongside the other alternatives.

The right models for NATS and London Underground?

The problem with the PPP models for London Underground and NATS was not that they clearly failed to stand up to scrutiny on the basis of the criteria outlined above. In each case the PPP model had merits, though not the one most highlighted by some ministers (that is the raising of private finance). Rather, in each case there was a failure to explore publicly the full range of options including other forms of PPP or trust models as well as the best public sector alternative. The price of this omission, added to the emphasis on a public finance argument that does not hold up, has been the relative failure to convince public and professional opinion of the merits of the proposed models.

Critics of the PPPs for NATS and London Underground suggested that they amounted to part-privatisations and of course they were right relation to NATS where more than half of the equity was sold. The political problem raised for the PPPs in the public services is that having allowed the term privatisation to be associated with one form of PPP it becomes easier to associate that term with all other forms of partnership. However, in the case of the public enterprises the issue of both ownership and whether investment is on or off the public sector's balance sheet should be irrelevant – only value-for-money should count in deciding on the right model.

We have not been convinced that the proposed models for NATS and the London Underground were the best available options – though at the time of writing there is still uncertainty as to the nature of the final model that may emerge for London Underground. It is true that some of the risks of going ahead with the PPP for NATS would seem to have been assuaged somewhat by the choice of a partner working on a 'not for commercial return' basis. However, a not-for-profit trust combined with the appropriate contracting for private management skills could have delivered the objective of efficient and safe air traffic control services and should have been explicitly considered alongside the PPP model chosen. The Government's proposed PPP for London Underground was not the best model, primarily because of the separation of investment and maintenance from operations. This is not to deny that some form of PPP might have been a viable option but the initial model offered by the Treasury and the DETR was not it. One should only proceed with a particular PPP structure once it has been openly tested against all the alternatives, both other PPPs and the best public sector alternative. Not doing so explains some of the difficulties that the proposals for NATS and London Underground have encountered.

A better framework for the public enterprises

Serious consideration of the publicly financed and provided alternative would necessitate looking again at the Treasury rules that have led departments to go down the PPP route in the first place as a way of avoiding constraints on capital budgets. One solution would be the changes in the fiscal framework for departments discussed in the last Chapter.

Since 1998, there has been some relaxation of the rules for certain self-financing public corporations including the Post Office and selected local authority owned airports. Where these airports can demonstrate that their revenue streams are sufficient to fund any investment undertaken, traditional Treasury controls over borrowing have been relaxed. There seems to be no obvious reason why NATS in a publicly owned or trust model, for example, could not have been given the same flexibility. We have also seen the Treasury being flexible in the case of the CTRL and bond financing. There seems to be no obvious reason why similar logic could not to be applied to London Underground.

Any changes to the framework for public enterprises would probably be subject to the Treasury being satisfied that these enterprises could meet a number of prudential tests and demonstrate a track record of financial responsibility over a significant period of time (Hawksworth, 2000a). The Local Government Finance Green Paper (DETR, 2000a) appeared to offer local authorities just such a prudential framework in place of direct controls over their capital spending. It would seem logical to extend the same framework to public enterprises, allowing them direct access to capital markets outside normal Treasury controls, possibly up to some pre-set maximum limit or subject to prudential controls including demonstrating how investment will be funded through adequate revenue streams.

This framework would eliminate or at least significantly reduce the incentive to pursue PPP options purely as a way of evading controls on capital budgets as opposed to securing value-for-money and quality. They might also allow more innovative forms of PPP to be pursued such as those involving giving minority equity stakes to private partners.

The more radical step of allowing revenue generating public enterprises to 'opt out' of Treasury control would require an effective form of 'public sector bankruptcy' to be introduced that allowed failing management teams to be replaced without threatening continuity of provision. This would be the necessary safeguard to accompany the adoption of General Government Net Borrowing (GGNB) as the key measure of fiscal policy in place of the current measure, Public Sector Net Borrowing (PSNB), a change long advocated by a range of observers and organisations. The difference in principle between the two is that the former excludes the borrowing of revenue generating public enterprises. In practice the difference has in recent years been negligible: GGNB and the PSNB were identical in 1999-2000.

This change would mean that from the point of view of managing the public finances to ensure macroeconomic stability and fiscal sustainability, the key measure targeted by the Treasury, would not include the borrowing of public enterprises. Given that these two measures are now almost identical in practice this should not impinge on the credibility of fiscal policy. However, such a change would inevitably increase the cost of finance to these enterprises through the addition of a risk premium as government would no longer be guaranteeing their borrowing. Indeed this is the best test of whether public enterprises really are at arms length from the government: their cost of capital should be little different from a private company facing a similar set of risks and opportunities. In this sense freedom from the Treasury comes with a price.

Similar frameworks have been suggested in the past (Hawksworth and Holtham, 1998; Radcliffe, 1998). Some observers see this option as unlikely at present given the lack of trust that central government has in the ability of many bodies to run their finances without some central oversight (Hawksworth, 2000a).

Recommendations

Public enterprises that demonstrate they could fund investment through revenue streams should have direct access to capital markets outside normal Treasury financial controls.

The option of public enterprises 'opting out' of Treasury financial controls also needs to be considered. This would require an effective form of 'public sector bankruptcy' to be introduced so long as failing management teams could be replaced without threatening continuity of provision.

Conclusion

The future of revenue generating public enterprises, whether as PPPs or other models, is a separable debate from the role of PPPs in the delivery of publicly funded services such as health and education. NATS is self-funded. One almost certainly unrealisable goal for the London Underground PPP was to eliminate the need for public revenue subsidies. By contrast PPPs in health and education are in no way meant to qualify the nature of these services as publicly funded and free at the point of use. Intellectually it is perfectly consistent to argue the case for part or even full privatisation of some revenue generating public enterprises, especially those that are self-funded, while remaining committed to tax funded core public services free at point-of-use. Whether or not this is appropriate will depend upon the particular circumstances in each instance. Whatever happens with the remaining public enterprises – and we would strongly suggest that a range of structures including trust models are considered – the government will rightly keep up the pressure on all public bodies to utilise all their assets more effectively. The scope for PPPs here is clear.

Endnotes

1   The key criticisms of the PPP for the London Underground can be found in Glaister *et al* (2000); Gaffney *et al* (2000) and The Industrial Society (2000).

2   However, this particular example involving new tunnelling may be of limited relevance to the plans for the PPP for London Underground where no new tunnelling is envisaged (NAO, 2000b).

III: Practice

III. Practice

6. Where is partnership appropriate?

The debate on whether partnerships should be used for the provision of core public services (front-line services) rather than simply the building and maintenance of physical assets and related ancillary services typically generates great passion but little understanding. Whether or not PPPs improve the quality of services for citizens often gets lost in discussions of the danger of profiteering, the threat of privatisation, and prejudices about the public, private or voluntary sectors. Rarely is there even agreement on the criteria that should be considered in evaluating whether or not it is appropriate for PPPs to play a role in key services.

Our objective in this Chapter is to clarify the real issues that should determine the use of PPPs for the delivery of public services. This means building on the general argument made so far. Part I of the Report examined why, in principle, partnerships may have a role to play in public services. It clarified some of the broader conditions for effective partnership. Part II examined the extent to which the private and voluntary sector are already involved in the delivery of services. It separated out the serious from the spurious *economic* arguments surrounding the use of partnership. It is the role of Part III to consider the types of partnership arrangement that may be desirable in key areas of the public services as well as identifying some of the practical barriers that need to be overcome if these models of partnership are to work.

A key issue is to establish the *types of services* that it is appropriate to consider delivering through partnership arrangements. The first section of the Chapter sets out existing rationales for determining the types of services that can and cannot be delivered through partnerships. It argues that these rationales are unsatisfactory. Chapter 3 demonstrated that the circumstances in which partnerships can be used to deliver services vary considerably across sectors. These variations often seem to be the result of seemingly arbitrary rules which demarcate the boundaries of non-public sector involvement in key areas of service provision – rules which often reflect a political compromise struck in a bygone era more than the best interests of today's service-users.

A more suitable approach to identifying public-private boundaries would include a case-by-case assessment of the method of service provision most likely to secure a high quality and value-for-money service for all citizens. Such an approach would involve assessing whether partnership arrangements are well placed to overcome some of the difficult issues that arise in the provision of complex services. These include:

- How possible it is to specify and monitor service outcomes?

- Are potential service providers suitable?

- Is there a clear purchaser-provider relationship?

- Will greater diversity in delivery lead to the fragmentation of services?

- Will greater diversity of providers weaken commitment to publicly funded services?

These are the issues considered in the second section of the Chapter.

What is wrong with current public-private boundaries?

The facts and figures set out in Chapter 3 indicate that, despite wide disparities across service-areas, the reach of private and voluntary providers within the public services has long extended to some sensitive elements of service delivery, though in many areas the public sector retains a near monopoly position. It remains unclear why policies have promoted partnerships in some areas of direct service provision but not in others.

A rescue service

Across the public services government is increasingly embracing the view that when existing public sector institutions are deemed to be 'failing' private sector companies should be used as a service provider of last resort. In effect the private sector offers a 'rescue service'. In some, though by no means all areas, it seems that the role of the private or voluntary sector could be limited to this rescue function. Indeed, in a number of areas the private sector is now on the verge of occupying a 'monopoly' position in relation to this rescue function. This can be seen most explicitly in relation to 'failing' prisons, where the Prison Service has been threatened with being formally excluded from entering their own bids when prisons are market tested (Prison Service News, 2001). A pre-disposition towards the use of the private sector in instances of public sector under-performance has also been seen in relation to local authority services including Local Education Authority (LEA) services and schools, and has been discussed in relation to under-performing hospital trusts and benefits offices.

We have argued that, where possible, there should be a level playing field between alternative forms of service provision. The 'rescue only' approach sits uneasily with this stance for a number of reasons.

- First, it is highly restrictive and limiting. If it is thought possible to devise PPPs for the highly complex task of addressing service failure it is not clear why they should not also be considered in other more normal circumstances. Moreover, imposing a 'rescue only' approach towards the use of private providers also risks obscuring the potentially more important role that partnerships with private or voluntary sector providers may play in *preventing* under-performance and helping good performers to further improve standards of service.

- Second, it is based on a very restrictive approach to the public sector. Experience shows that public sector institutions can be effective at remedying failure given appropriate incentives. LEAs in Tower Hamlets, Manchester and Barnsley have all improved significantly without contracting out services to the private sector (Audit Commission and OFSTED, 2001). The ability of public authorities to provide supporting services has been at least partially acknowledged with the inclusion of Camden LEA on the DfEE's list of 'preferred bidders' for service provision. Likewise, the capacity of the Prison Service's in-house teams to match private sector competitors (for non-failing prisons) has been established by its ability to win back the management of both Manchester and Blakenhurst prisons (in 2000), which were previously contracted out. Indeed, this makes the Home Office's threat to exclude the Prison Service from bidding for 'failing' prisons, as well as to build and manage all new prisons through the PFI, seem all the more unbalanced.

- Third, private sector experience, even success, in running some public services does not demonstrate that it will be able to remedy deeply ingrained problems in a failing institution. One of the most important factors in securing efficiency gains and some improvements in quality within the prison service, for example, has been an ability to create a different culture within new prisons, aided by a new population of inmates and staff. It is by no means clear that similar improvements would follow if private companies had to address the problems of an established institution. Where problems with a service are deeply embedded, the private sector may at best be no better placed to remedy these difficulties than the public sector.

- Fourth, presenting the private sector as a form of punishment used for 'failing' public institutions is likely to entrench an adversarial approach to public-private relations. The use of 'private sector hit-squads' seems likely to fuel suspicion among public sector workers and managers about the very notion of partnership. In many cases this approach leads to a private sector organisation seeking to hire public sector managers who are then contracted, often at considerable expense, to an under-performing public agency. We do not see why more sharing of expertise could not take place *within* the public sector.

- Fifth, it seems highly likely that some of the potentially more dynamic private sector providers will be unwilling to enter a market which is restricted to dealing with public sector 'problems'.

> Recommendation
>
> The private sector should not be restricted to providing services after a public sector agency has been deemed to have 'failed'. Equally, successful public authorities should not be excluded from helping improve services delivered by other public providers.

The core/ancillary distinction

Another apparent inconsistency in the way in which partnership arrangements are used in core public services is that, in the health and education service, there is a barrier between those services that can be procured through the Private Finance Initiative (PFI) – those classified as 'ancillary' – and those 'core' services which are ring-fenced for delivery by the public sector. In other areas, such as the prison service, a full range of services can be procured through the PFI, including the management of prisons and their staff. This apparent anomaly is even more striking when we consider that outside a PFI contract the private sector can provide management, employ staff and deliver publicly funded education and health services. Thus NHS Trusts can already contract with independent providers to run their pathology and radiology services, private hospitals perform elective surgery services for publicly funded patients and voluntary organisations run independent schools for publicly funded students (see Chapter 3).

The distinction drawn between core and ancillary services raises the question of whether certain services have characteristics that make them inherently unsuitable for delivery through the private or voluntary sectors. It is often argued that services such as cleaning, catering, and security can be relatively easily specified in a contract and therefore can form part of the package of ancillary services included within a PFI deal. The Government's position on this question appears ambiguous. On the one hand, policy continues to use a model of PFI which stipulates that clinical and curriculum related activities should be excluded from projects. On the other hand, the recent compact with independent health providers, together with the proposals to contract for school management, suggests a desire to use partnerships to push diversity into the core areas of service provision (DfEE, 2001, DoH, 2000d).

The key issue for a reassessment of the boundary between functions that can and cannot be included within health and education PFI deals (and other partnerships) should be the impact that this will have on the *quality* of services experienced by service-users. A broad cross-section of groups providing evidence to the Commission took the view that the current core/ancillary distinction is sometimes an obstacle to innovation (though opinions differed sharply on how this issue should be addressed). A range of organisations noted the strong inter-connection between the 'ancillary' and 'core' services produced by a hospital or school (for example, catering in a hospital or ICT in a school) which made it hard to arrive at a sensible risk allocation between the public and private sectors. They argued that the existing public-private interface in PPP projects risks stifling innovation by creating artificial barriers within public service institutions that will inhibit new thinking about how to configure and deliver services (CPPP, 2000). Others stressed that ending the core-ancillary distinction within PPP projects would create a 'partnership benchmark' for service quality which could be compared to standards of provision for similar services that are delivered by the public sector. It was also pointed out that there is a serious danger of sending the message to employees classed as 'ancillary' that they are of secondary importance to the success of a service.

The implication of this is not that all services should be provided by the private or voluntary sectors, nor that the delivery of core services should be necessarily included within PFI projects. This prospect raises complex issues which are discussed in Chapter 7. Rather, it is that public sector purchasers should keep an open mind about the bundle of services that are incorporated within PPPs. They should seek to identify patterns of delivery that offer citizens a unified and high quality service that represents value-for-money.

Recommendation

Broad categorisations of core and ancillary services should not be used to determine the right boundary between those services that can and cannot be provided through partnerships.

A different approach

A number of arguments have been used to suggest that insurmountable problems confront those seeking to deliver core services through partnership arrangements based on contract. These problems take a number of different forms. Some concern the difficulty of writing a contract that covers every possible aspect of service delivery. Attempting to specify contracts in exhaustive detail can generate perverse effects as well as escalating transaction costs. Another problem is that an opportunistic organisation may exploit gaps in a contract at the expense of service users or taxpayers. Others emphasise that introducing a diversity of service providers will lead to fragmentation and impede accountability.

In this section we examine these potential pitfalls and assess whether or not they can be overcome. Two key points need to be kept in mind. First, we need to be careful to avoid the assumption that all of these challenges only apply when services are provided through partnerships with the private or voluntary sector: many of them also apply to public agencies. Secondly, it is important to consider whether a move from a narrow contracting-out model of service provision towards a longer-term partnership may help in addressing some of these concerns.

Specifying, measuring and monitoring service outcomes

In relation to health, education and other core services, the greatest barrier to contracting with any provider is the difficulty in specifying and monitoring outputs and outcomes. The outcomes of time spent at a school, hospital or in a prison are acutely difficult to codify let alone measure and monitor. It can also be difficult to establish the 'value-added' by the provider in achieving these outcomes. Many of the outcomes are affected by numerous variables outside of the provider's control. Sometimes it will only be possible to evaluate the impact of the provider's behaviour fully at some stage in the future (for example, the impact of prisons on rates of recidivism).

It is often felt that contracting for emergency health services represents the greatest challenge in relation to contract specification (Nicholson, 2000). In treating emergencies a provider must undertake constant prioritisation and re-prioritisation of treatment. Demand and case complexity are unpredictable – so it is difficult to draw up conditions or guidelines to cover every eventuality. This leaves many decisions firmly in the hands of the provider and increases the danger of behaviour that is not in the best interests of the users of the service or of citizens.[1] One example of this would be hospital consultants selecting to undertake a more expensive course of patient treatment than is actually necessary in order to increase payments. Another would be a private firm cutting back on safety measures in a way which is hard for an external body to detect through inspection.

Despite these problems, there are numerous examples of the use of partnerships for the provision of highly complex services. In the US, emergency services have been one of the services most frequently outsourced (Moore, 1996). In Denmark, emergency services such as fire protection are provided through a partnership with a private firm. In Sweden, a private company currently runs an emergency hospital that provides publicly funded care for a population of 300,000 people in Central and West Stockholm. And in Australia there are five privately financed and privately operated hospitals currently caring for publicly funded patients, with another two being constructed and six projects being tendered (Foley, 2001). Many of these hospitals provide the full range of services found within a district general hospital including intensive care and emergency services. Operators provide a range of financial, data and quality reports, with an independent audit assessing the accuracy and validity of the hospital's reports, against which claims for payment are made.[2]

One of the most interesting developments in the new generation of partnership arrangements that have emerged over recent years is the concerted push by some public authorities to give incentives to service providers to focus on outcomes rather than measures of input or throughput. This means developing measures of health gain, educational attainment, effective rehabilitation of prisoners (see Case Study 6.1) and user-satisfaction. None of this is easy – it presents challenges in relation to the public sector's capacity to write, manage and monitor contracts and the private sector's willingness to accept outcome-based risk (discussed in Chapter 8).

Case Study 6.1 Innovative contracting: HMP Dovegate

The Prison Service and the private sector have agreed to a highly innovative contract. Two hundred of the places within this eight hundred person PFI prison will form a therapeutic community with its own director. A joint public-private committee of five, chaired by a Prison Service nominee, will support the director. The aim is to share the risks associated with meeting the needs of those prisoners in the therapeutic community – whose care must be innovative and cannot be tightly specified. The contract itself includes a number of unique elements:

- For the first time in a private prison, the contract includes a performance bonus that is linked to the reconviction rates of prisoners from the therapeutic community after release.
- The operator will be penalised if a prisoner does not complete a twelve-month treatment programme or does not have the opportunity to complete a resettlement programme after therapy.
- The contractor must also contract with a suitable organisation for a research programme into the effectiveness of the therapeutic community's programme to be carried out – comparing this with another therapeutic prison run by the public sector.

The extent to which it is possible to specify and measure desirable service outcomes and agree payment mechanisms that encourage providers to deliver them is a key issue in determining whether partnerships are likely to produce real improvements in service quality. Once again, it is important to stress that similar challenges are faced in the development of service agreements between *public* sector providers and purchasing authorities. It is true that using PPPs for core services does raise particular issues and partnering techniques are still in their infancy. In any case, the fact that partnership agreements for complex services are feasible does not mean that they are necessarily desirable. But the claim that it is simply not possible to deliver complex services through partnerships and achieve high quality outcomes does not appear to be borne out by experience.

Guaranteeing social equity

The introduction of service delivery partnerships often gives rise to concerns about social equity. The clearest risk occurs when the provider of public services is able to select service users. This can result in the problem of 'cream-skimming': when providers chose to offer services to the most able pupils, the healthiest patients, the most reliable tenants, the most employable jobseekers – so they can most easily meet the terms of their service agreement. If this happens social inequity will result: those most in need will be unfairly treated.

The extent to which cream-skimming is likely to be a problem will depend in part on the nature of the contract and the payment structure. Flat-rate payments linked to key outputs (for example, number of patients treated) or outcomes (for example, number of job-seekers in employment) may encourage some providers to try and select service users who are unlikely to be costly. One way of avoiding this problem is to make a higher payment to providers if they assist 'expensive' service users. The difficulty with this approach is that it requires the purchaser to be able to make an assessment of the service user's circumstances which may itself prove costly. On the other hand, sometimes it may prove straightforward to link extra payment to easily observable characteristics that will not add significantly to the price of a contract.

Once again it should be stressed that these problems could affect all forms of providers. The use of performance indicators, league tables and quasi-markets *within* the public sector has long given rise to some of these concerns (Le Grand and Bartlett, 1993). Ensuring that state schools do not just admit pupils that are likely to be easy to teach at the expense of more difficult pupils is a perennial problem. Similar difficulties are also well established in contracts with public, private and voluntary providers of employment and training programmes for job-seekers. We draw two lessons from this. First, where appropriate public purchasers should seek to circumvent the problem of cream-skimming by using payment formulas that properly reward service providers (whether they are public, private or voluntary) for working with users whose needs generate higher costs. Second, public purchasers should play close attention to the ethos and culture of all potential service providers as this will have a strong bearing on the extent to which issues such as cream-skimming arise. It is to this issue that we now turn.

The ethos of service providers

As has been pointed out, there are inevitably aspects of service quality that will be hard if not impossible for purchasers to observe and monitor. In the operation of a prison, for example, every detail of the appropriate use of force by prison guards or the duty to appoint high quality personnel cannot be specified and monitored – particularly in a contract based on outcomes (Hart *et al*, 1997). Similarly, even a contract that has been well drafted will leave some scope for cream-skimming. In almost any service area, scope will exist for behaviour that increases rewards for the provider organisation without violating the formal terms of the agreement, often in a way which is unlikely to be detected through monitoring.

So is one type of organisation more likely to exploit these opportunities than another? One well established school of thought assumes public sector employees possess a particular type of ethos – an inclination to act with integrity and in the interests of the user rather than the producer – that make them uniquely placed to deliver public services. Another perspective maintains that it is the voluntary and community sector that is especially well placed to deliver services to many of the most vulnerable groups in society. This is due in part to the assumption that the motivations of those who work in the voluntary sector are benevolent.[3] But it is also due to the governance structure of voluntary organisations which, although sometimes criticised for being unwieldy, helps service providers to develop high trust relationships with vulnerable citizens. Freedom from large-scale bureaucracy, direct political interference, shareholder demands and the threat of take-over help to ensure that managers and front-line staff have the space to forge collaborative relationships with service users (Hansmann, 1996; Billis and Glennester, 1998).

Others take a more critical view of voluntary sector provision of services, arguing that voluntary agencies can be as easily 'captured' by the interests of their producers as any other type of organisation. The goals and values of voluntary organisations may be idiosyncratic, meaning that some citizens may be negatively affected if they do not sign up to the social 'mission' of their service provider. This issue becomes more acute in service areas where providers hold strong discretionary powers over users (such as personal advisers/case workers). Indeed, some commentators – including those who are sceptical about the role of the private sector – argue that in these areas it will be easier for public authorities to regulate for-profit providers as their motives are likely to be more predictable and transparent than their not-for-profit counterparts (Goodin, 2000).

Research into these issues is relatively limited. Some work has shown that the motivations and aspirations of public sector managers differ from those of private sector managers working *outside* of the public services in areas such as engineering or financial services (Steele, 1999). This is hardly surprising: we would anticipate that managers working in core public services (whatever the nature of their employer) would have different motivations to someone in the commercial traded sector.

Of more direct relevance is the research into the motivations and behaviour of public and private sector residential care providers. This has indicated that private sector care providers do not conform well to the textbook stereotype of the profit-maximising provider (Kendall, 2001). It emphasises the importance of a wide range of motivational factors: among them 'meeting the needs of elderly people', 'professional accomplishment' and 'independence and autonomy'. An analysis of 'revealed motivations' based on the actual behaviour of care workers supports these findings.[4]

In order to further explore the ethos and motivations of public service employees, and whether or not they vary between public and private sectors providers of public services, the CPPP undertook qualitative research with nurses (some of whom had worked within both public and private sectors), patients and health managers. We set about examining whether or not these groups perceived a difference in the nature of service provision across different sectors (a summary of the work is set out in Appendix 6.1). The research highlighted that healthcare workers themselves – both nurses and health managers – strongly felt that there was no difference in ethos between providers. Nurses were adamant that there was no divergence in attitude or approach between those working in the public and private sectors. Interestingly, patient responses were more ambiguous. Most were quicker to describe the commitment and dedication of nurses working in the NHS than in the private sector. Patients felt that nurses working in the private sector were understandably motivated by better salaries and working conditions. Ultimately, however, they maintained that the attitude of nurses towards patients did not differ significantly between sectors. Many of the managers interviewed emphasised that there was little significant difference in ethos between the public and private sectors although they highlighted the importance of people's perception of this difference.

It is impossible to reach a definitive judgement on these issues not least because of the paucity of research that has been conducted and the huge diversity of experience that exists within all sectors. We might expect that, as managers and personnel transfer between sectors, it will become increasingly difficult to make assumptions about the ethos of providers based on the sector in which they work. This discussion points towards the following tentative observations. The ethos and culture of providers is a key factor determining the quality of public services, particularly in relation to services for vulnerable groups. It is also notable that diversity in provision tends to be most established in areas where services are being provided to the most vulnerable groups (social services, mental health care, long-term care). Although it is the case that if not properly regulated the profit motive can sometimes conflict with the interests of users, it is wrong to suggest that any one sector – public, private or voluntary – has a monopoly on the public service ethos. Organisational cultures and ethos will vary widely within and across sectors.

Purchasers of public services therefore need to be more adept at assessing the suitability of different organisations to provide key services – the assumption should be that service users must have a substantive role to play in this process wherever possible (see Chapter 8). Factors such as track record, employee motivation and measures of user satisfaction will help provide a guide to this assessment. On this basis, organisations should not be prevented from providing public services because of their legal structure or whether or not they are profit-making.[5]

Clear purchaser-provider relations

Partnerships for service delivery are predicated on the existence of a clear relationship between purchasers and providers. The public purchaser should always and everywhere be the body deciding on the priorities for public services, responsible for the key resource allocation decisions and for specifying the outcomes to be delivered. This is crucial if public accountability is to be maintained (see Chapter 10). In addition, the available evidence suggests that the effectiveness of PPPs depends to a considerable degree on the nature and clarity of the purchaser-provider relationship that exists. A number of benefits seem to be associated with sectors such as prisons and road-building where there is a single public sector purchaser.

- The contracting process is (comparatively) easier as there are fewer public sector stakeholders and, typically, fewer potential bidders.

- It is easier for the public sector to develop and retain expertise in commissioning.

- It is easier to integrate investment decisions about individual PPP projects within wider policy priorities.

In many ways these clear relationships are the exception rather than the norm. In relation to the Employment Service regional offices have acted as the purchasers of services which are delivered at local level, an approach not considered ideal by some observers (Finn, 2001). More acute problems exist in health and education where the purchaser-provider split is far less clear. In these areas there is a complicated set of relationships *within* the public sector as well as less expertise within the commissioning authorities. This seems to be one of the reasons why value-for-money gains have been less clear and the contracting process more protracted.

The education service provides two contrasting examples. A great deal of misleading discussion has taken place about the provision of Local Education Authority (LEA) services by private and voluntary providers. In each case the LEA retains all of its statutory functions intact and is merely contracting with private providers for the delivery of a range of services. These can include helping the LEA with its strategic management functions by contracting for private management skills and/or the provision of discrete services such as administrative functions or support for school improvement. These contracts tend to be for five to seven years after which the LEA can choose whether or not to retain the provider. Not only is this not 'privatisation', it illustrates a fairly clear purchaser-provider relationship and the emergence of a public service characterised by a healthy diversity in provision.

In school PFI deals, the picture is far more complicated and less satisfactory. LEAs are the signatories to most PFI deals, but school governing bodies must agree to pass back a proportion of their delegated budget – around 10-12 per cent – to the LEA for the whole of the contract period. The Pimlico schools project gave a clear example of the scope for conflict between the LEA and the governing body in deciding on the suitability of a PFI proposal (see Chapter 4). In the case of Brent's 'bundled' PFI project a lack of clarity about the degree to which schools could hold the LEA to account for its part in monitoring the contract emerged as a significant issue and barrier to the project (Thompson, 2000). The underlying problem here is that there are two key public purchasers: the LEA and the school governing body, with potentially different interests and different capacities for handling contractual relationships.

A similar difficulty arises in the NHS where there are a range of purchasers – Regional Offices, the Health Authorities and Primary Care Groups or Trusts. For care services the problems created by having local authority social services departments and Health Authorities as separate purchasers has long been documented and lies behind the proposals to develop integrated Care Trusts.[6] However, the issue of having the *provider* organisations, Hospital Trusts, both driving and being signatories to PFI hospital deals has been less extensively discussed. This has resulted in procurement expertise being very thinly spread within the health service (see Chapter 8). Also the focus on provider organisations as the drivers and initiators of PFI deals has meant that these projects have rarely been integrated into the wider plans for service development drawn up by Health Authorities (Boyle and Harrison, 2000). In effect the public purchasers have not been driving the partnerships and their fit with wider health service goals has suffered as a result.[7]

Pointing out that clear purchaser-provider relations can be beneficial certainly does not mean that partnership arrangements should not involve close working between the different parties. This will always be a key ingredient of partnerships. In the case of joint ventures, both the purchaser and provider will be shareholders and board members of the partnership. This approach brings its own challenges but can work if there is clarity in relation to the respective roles of the different parties and a shared commitment to problem solving. Other contractually based service partnerships are increasingly using 'partnership boards' (Chapter 8) as a key forum at which purchasers and providers can agree on strategic issues as they arise over the life of the contract. Again, this approach has much to offer in helping generate high-trust relations so long as it is based on a clear agreement about the respective roles of the different partners.

Avoiding a fragmented service

A move towards greater plurality in service provision could make it harder to ensure that citizens benefit from a unified service. There is a risk that ill-conceived partnership arrangements within a single service area can lead to fragmentation or forms of competitive behaviour between providers that do not benefit citizens. The result could be a drop in the quality of services as users (as well as public service employees) have to navigate a path across different organisational boundaries. Public accountability can also suffer as greater complexity can make it harder to establish who is responsible for what (see Chapter 10).

It is already the case, however, that many parts of the public services rely upon the co-ordination of the activities of a range of different provider organisations. This co-ordinating role is clearly a central function of modern public managers. Partnership arrangements can either act to integrate or fragment services depending on the circumstances. This point was brought out clearly in a visit we made to a public sector prison whose managers reported that one of the most significant challenges they faced was managing a range of contractual relations with public, private and voluntary organisations who provided many of the key services in the prison – often under very rigid short-term contracts. Yet despite this, the senior management of the prison did not wish to bring these services in-house, arguing that this would distract them from their core activities. In contrast at a *privately*-operated prison we visited, the management team indicated that it was very reluctant to enter into further partnerships for any areas of service provision: it wished to keep as much control of the prison and its staff as possible.

Ensuring that diversity in provision does not lead to the fragmentation of services requires that there is a strong public sector purchaser able to shape, regulate and integrate the market for service provision. In the absence of such a purchaser the introduction of a diverse set of providers could undermine service quality and accountability.

What does the public think?

A further factor that needs to be taken into account when thinking about the types of services in which partnership arrangements may be used is public opinion. The National Health Service and state schools are key social assets and we would expect citizens to have strong views on how these services are delivered. Polling work investigating attitudes towards diversity in the providers of public services yields varied results.

A recent MORI poll exploring public attitudes towards the use of public private partnerships within the health service revealed widespread support for the notion of the NHS working in partnership with private and voluntary providers (MORI, 2000)[8]:

- 79 per cent of respondents agreed with the statement that 'the country's healthcare needs would be better served if the NHS and private sector worked hand in hand';

- 69 per cent said that they would be more or equally willing to pay taxes for an NHS provided by a range of providers – a significant indication that involvement of private providers would not undermine public commitment to a universal, tax-funded health system;

- 84 per cent of people are confident about a future health service in which there is some degree of partnership between public and private sectors;

- 59 per cent agreed that private health companies should be brought in to run a local NHS hospital when the NHS management had failed to run it satisfactorily.

These findings echo other pieces of evidence. A poll conducted in 1995 asked the question 'who should provide health services, assuming that the NHS continues to be publicly funded?' The majority of people – including a majority of supporters of all the main parties – were not concerned about whether NHS services were provided publicly or privately (Harris Research Centre, 1995).

The suggestion, then, seems to be that the public are more interested in service quality than in the sector of the provider organisation. From this perspective, we might expect public attitudes to increase the pressure for experimenting with partnerships in new areas of service provision, so long as this is seen to work towards improving service quality.

On the other hand, other polling evidence indicates public opposition to private sector involvement in service delivery – particularly if it is pointed out that a profit will be made. One recent ICM/Guardian poll found that:

- 66 per cent of the public agreed that 'in general' public services should not be run for profit;

- 48 per cent of people thought that public services should always be run by the public sector;

- 25 per cent supported the view that they should be run in partnership with the private sector;

- 6 per cent maintained that public services should usually or always be run by private companies.

If the predominant public attitude was one of wariness; if PPPs were felt to endanger public services or to erode the values on which they were based, this would weaken the case for their use. This is not just because politicians would be reluctant to speak out in their favour (it is to be hoped that sometimes policy-makers would seek to shift or challenge public opinion) but, more importantly, because it would call into question the wider legitimacy of a move towards greater diversity. Given that our starting point for considering PPPs was the desire to deepen commitment to publicly funded universal services, we would want to avoid shifts to patterns of service delivery which threatened this goal.

Public opinion, this data suggests, is volatile. Wide variation between polls is likely to reflect the significance of how questions are ordered and phrased. Ultimately we would presume that public opinion depends on a range of factors: experiences of diversity in provision of public services; perceptions of current standards of service provision and confidence in the ethos of the proposed provider.

Conclusion

The existing rationale for distinguishing between the services that can and cannot be provided within a partnership does not hold up to analysis. Both the 'core-ancillary' distinction and the 'rescue only' approach have severe limitations. In future, a more flexible approach should be taken in which public purchasers are allowed to make a case-by-case assessment of the package of services that they want to incorporate within a PPP.

The issues raised by providing core services through partnerships can be challenging but seem not to be insuperable. There are significant practical issues that need to be carefully thought through, particularly in relation to preserving social equity. Contracts must be clearly specified and devised so that they prevent cream-skimming. Purchaser provider relationships must be clear-cut. Public authorities need to think about the fit between the type of service they want provided and the ethos of different provider organisations. The limited evidence that we have which examines the motivation of providers from different sectors when delivering similar services does not substantiate a simple distinction between the motivations of for-profit, not-for-profit and public providers. It also seems that citizens show pragmatism in their approach to the involvement of private providers in the core public services, so long as they are shown to deliver effectively. However, different polls give very different results on this issue.

Recommendations

Purchasers should take a case-by-case approach towards assessing the package of services that are included within a PPP.

A partnership approach may be appropriate if the following criteria are satisfied:

- service outcomes can be clearly specified and measured

- value-for-money can be demonstrated – indicating that transaction costs and costs of monitoring the contract are offset by efficiency gains

- clear purchaser-provider relations exist

- contract terms do not allow scope for the provider to select only the most 'profitable' clients

- an integrated service can be provided, with close working and clear communication between providers

- providers demonstrate an appropriate public service ethos.

Endnotes

1   See Vining and Globerman (1999) for a study of the issues involved and experiences of contracting for healthcare services.

2   See, for example, report of the Auditor General Western Australia (1997) for details of the contracting process and terms for the Joondalup Health Campus, a private hospital with beds for 265 publicly funded patients or Corben (1997) for a peer review report of Port Macquarie Base Hospital, a 219 bed, privately built, owned and operated hospital treating publicly funded patients in New South Wales.

3   See for instance some of the submissions to the Employment Select Committee inquiry into the New Deal that argued that voluntary organisations are best placed to deliver the New Deal (ESC, 1998).

4   An analysis of care pricing in 1996 revealed that, on average, residential care providers were setting prices below those levels that would maximise profit. Actual mark-up rates were averaging less than two thirds of the profit-maximising level (Forder et al, 1996). A more recent study of the domiciliary care providers examines how far providers' accounts of their motivations translate into practice (Kendall et al, 2001).

5   The one exception to this might be where safety issues are paramount – this is discussed in relation to NATS in Chapter 5.

6   Care Trusts, proposed in the Health and Social Care Bill, will be organisations established to strengthen joint working between NHS and local government agencies (HMSO, 2000a). They are intended to build on provisions for joint working permitted by the 1999 Health Act, which allowed NHS organisations and local authorities to pool funds, jointly commission services and engage in joint service provision. It is likely that, if implemented, Care Trusts will take a variety of forms ranging from being organisations responsible for commissioning services for a particular client group to being bodies responsible for commissioning all health and council functions for across a range of partner agencies. (See www.doh.gov.uk/caretrusts.index.htm for further details.)

7   In Scotland the purchaser-provider spilt in health is to be ended, making the whole concept of PPPs problematic, though the implications of this for PPPs do not appear to have been thought through. In Wales the five Health Authorities are to be abolished, with 22 local health groups, equivalent to Primary Care Groups becoming the sole purchasers, which at least brings greater clarity. In England, the NHS Plan largely fails to address the issues raised by the problematic planning framework surrounding PPPs in health, as discussed further in Chapter 7.

8   A nationally representative quota sample of 1,907 adults aged 15-plus were interviewed throughout Britain between 21 and 25 September 2000. The data has been weighted to reflect the national population profile.

Appendix 6.1 Qualitative research

The Commission's programme of qualitative research, carried out by a Senior Researcher in IPPR's Public Involvement Team, was motivated by two key concerns. Firstly, that the Commission's discussions should be informed by a sense of whether and under what conditions the public and public service professionals support the use of partnerships to deliver core services. Secondly, to explore in greater detail the notion of the 'public service ethos'. In meetings and consultations, the 'erosion of the public service ethos' was often raised as a potential, negative consequence of the use of PPPs. Yet we identified a deficit of research investigating whether the ethos and motivation often attributed to those working in the public sector, such as a concern that their work should benefit the wider community, could also be shared by those delivering similar 'frontline' public services within the private sector. We therefore wanted to examine whether patients, professionals and managers with experience of both private and public hospitals identified a difference in the motivations and attitudes of providers from different sectors.

The goals of the research were:

- to explore the attitudes of health managers, the public and health professionals towards partnership between public and private sectors for the provision of health services;

- to gauge whether nurses from both public and private sectors were seen by the public as sharing a common 'public service ethos';

- to investigate whether nurses themselves perceived a difference between the motivations and 'ethos' of the public and private sectors.

The qualitative research programme involved:

- focus groups with patients and nurses with experience of both the public and private sectors;

- in-depth interviews with senior managers with experience of commissioning health services from a range of sectors.

In the first stage of the research a total of six focus groups were conducted: four with patients and two with nurses. Respondents were recruited by an agency with specialist experience of medical recruitment. Respondents were paid for their time. Each focus group lasted an hour and a half and followed a flexible discussion guide. Focus groups were conducted between 3 and 8 August 2000.

In the second stage of the research eight interviews were conducted with NHS executives – four with Health Authority Chief Executives and four with Primary Care

Group	Details	Specification	Location
Patients	Inpatients	Men, 18 – 40, BC1	London
	Inpatients	Women, 40 +, C2D	Sutton Coldfield (Birmingham)
	Day patients	Men, 40+, C2D	Oldham (Manchester)
	Day patients	Women, 18 – 40, BC1	Sutton Coldfield (Birmingham)
Nurses	Nurses who have experience of both private and public hospitals Mix of ages and experience		London
	Nurses who have experience of both private and public hospitals Mix of ages and experience		Oldham (Manchester)

Trust Chief Officers. Participants were randomly selected from a database and approached to take part. Interviews were conducted in eight different locations, ensuring some geographical spread. Each interview lasted for around an hour and followed a flexible discussion guide.

Further details of the work can be obtained from the IPPR.

7. PPPs and key public services

It has already been suggested that, in principle, contracting for complex services such as the provision of clinical care or the operation of a prison is possible, though there are many challenges involved. This Chapter draws on these arguments to consider the role that partnership could play in core public services such as health, education and local government. It builds on the account of the current public-private split in the provision of services identified in Chapter 3, and makes suggestions as to where, when and how greater diversity in provision could help improve services in the future. Again it must be stressed that these core services should remain publicly funded and free at point of use. What is being discussed is whether there is a case for greater diversity of provision.

Policy makers interested in assessing the potential scope for diversity are faced with a range of possible approaches. Given that almost every type of public service has been contracted at some time or another, it could be argued that we should not be too concerned about the feasibility of contracting with different types of providers. According to this rationale, the focus should be on ensuring that public sector purchasers are encouraged to contract with a plurality of service-providers in all areas of provision. It is sometimes suggested that 'a one-size-fits-all' rule be adopted which forces public authorities to deliver a fixed proportion of their services through partnership arrangements.

This is not the approach adopted here. The degree to which it will be possible for partnership arrangements to meet policy objectives whilst safeguarding social equity, value-for-money and accountability is likely to vary considerably between different service areas. The argument made in this Chapter is that there can be *coherence* in our approach towards the use of PPPs without uniformity. Coherence should flow from using a shared set of criteria across different service areas to determine the use of partnerships.

The conclusion we reach is that policy-makers should be willing to promote a degree of diversity in most areas of provision. In some areas, there will be justification in arguing for a 'sector blind approach' – based on the idea that the role of the purchaser is to select the most appropriate provider regardless of whether they are based on the public, private or voluntary sector. In these cases putting in place measures to ensure that there is a genuine level playing field between providers will be critical. This will bring its own policy challenges: ensuring that the policy or financial framework is not skewed towards one type of provider over another and that public managers are adept at dealing with different types and sizes of organisations. In other areas, such as clinical services in health, the arguments are much more complex and the evidence is patchier and more contested. Consequently our recommendations are far more tentative. Here the policy challenge is of a different type. The aim should be to pilot innovative approaches towards the use of partnerships that will allow lessons to be learnt about the merits of alternative forms of service provision. The extent to which partnerships are used in these areas in the future should depend upon evaluations of these pilots.

Health

Moves towards a greater use of partnerships in the health service must be informed by a view of the direction in which the health service is and should be moving. Thinking about the potential contribution of different types of service provider must be integrated into a wider understanding of changes in the nature of health care: the opportunities provided by new technologies; the moves towards care closer to home; the emphasis on linking professionals and specialists into 'networks' that cut across health institutions and provide a pathway of care for patients; and an awareness of the evolving relationship between district general hospitals, regional centres, community hospitals and primary care providers. The following sections develop some concrete proposals on ways in which an element of diversity may sensibly be introduced given this unfolding context.

The fact that partnership is on the health agenda is itself notable. Much attention has been given to shifts in the Labour party's approach towards the private and voluntary healthcare sectors. In 1983 the Labour Party pledged to 'remove private practice from the NHS and take into the NHS those parts of the profit-making sector which can be put to good use'. Even at the start of New Labour's first term in office, NHS Executive guidance stated that commissioners should use private hospitals only as a last resort (NHS Executive, 1997). Yet in November 2000, with the signing of the Concordat between the Department of Health and the Independent Healthcare Association, we saw a political commitment to ending any ideological obstacles preventing joint working with the private sector where this might be in the interests of NHS patients (Department of Health, 2000e).

At the moment it remains unclear what the practical, as opposed to the symbolic, significance of the Concordat will be. It has been driven by the view that the major problem facing the NHS is a shortage of capacity. The hope was that, due to lower bed occupancy rates in the private sector, there would be opportunity to lease beds and theatre space from independent providers or to negotiate block contracts for services. If the NHS bases its use of independent providers on the premise that they simply represent spare capacity which can be drawn on in hard times, the scope for partnership will only stretch as far as the existing numbers of spare beds. If, on the other hand, the rationale behind the greater use of PPPs in publicly funded health is to allow providers, regardless of sector, to become involved in the task of providing high quality, cost effective health services, a number of wider issues arise.

The starting point for thinking about how partnership could play a more ambitious role in the health system should be the local Health Improvement Plan (HimP) drawn up by the Health Authority in co-operation with the local authority, the Primary Care Group or Primary Care Trust and other local stakeholders. This will set out the outcomes in terms of improvements to the health of local people that all agencies will work towards attaining. It is in this context that plans for the development of health care provision, including the physical infrastructure, should go forward.

Primary care

Many of the most important structural changes affecting the health service over the past decade have occurred in primary care. The role of GPs and other primary care professionals as purchasers has been a focus of health service reform since the early 1990s. In 1997, GP fundholding was discontinued, but the simultaneous establishment of Primary Care Groups attempted to preserve the benefits of practitioner led commissioning, whilst reducing the inequalities in provision for patients and the high transactions costs that were seen to have emerged out of the internal market.

Primary Care Groups/Trusts (PCG/Ts) represent a new level of organisation for the NHS. They are local boards of GPs, community nurses and other stakeholders with responsibility for improving the health of their community, developing health services and commissioning hospital services on behalf of their population.[1] There is considerable scope for them to work in partnership with other groups. Yet, equally, there is a risk that partnerships within the primary care sector are developing before the role and remit of the PCG/Ts has been fully established.

The first role that private and voluntary providers could play is in helping Health Authorities and PCG/Ts with their strategic management functions, offering the kind of services that some providers offer to Local Education Authorities (LEAs). There is also already acknowledged to be a role for private providers with experience of planning the development and management of assets in the health field to work with PCG/Ts to develop the physical infrastructure in primary care (Department of Health, 2001a). As in education, the Health Authority and PCG/Ts could then decide whether they might then *separately* contract with a range of providers for the actual delivery of new and refurbished premises for example. The scale of demand for capital modernisation is considerable. The NHS Plan suggests the need for investment of £1 billion to refurbish or replace 3,000 GP premises and develop 500 one-stop primary care resource centres by 2004 (Department of Health, 2000e).

An important model of partnership that has recently emerged from the Department of Health and Partnerships UK – called NHS Lift – raises some important issues. On the one hand, the initiative appears to be innovative, representing a significant shift away from the conventional PFI model of PPP. It is also based upon the laudable objective of improving the infrastructure of primary care facilities within inner city areas. It may well provide a route for injecting new (and much needed) management resources into the planning and running of vital public assets. On the other hand, the proposed structure seems to be complicated and risks conflating the role of purchaser and provider (see the discussion in Chapter 6). The main proposition is that there should be a national joint venture between the Department of Health and PUK, with further mini joint ventures involving this national body, private providers and the 'local NHS'. The local joint ventures would plan *and* deliver investment in the primary care infrastructure. The ultimate purchaser – the Department of Health – as well as local service commissioners, will enter into joint ventures with service providers. This will succeed in getting all the key parties involved in the process but it may lead to a lack of clarity over who is responsible for what. It is also the case that, with NHS Lift having Departmental backing, local bodies may see it as representing the only viable option for capital investment.

This not to say that the concept of a 'joint venture' at the local level may not offer substantial benefits. But it would be preferable if it were one of a range of options explored alongside the development of longer-term partnering contracts (see Chapter 8), as well as contracts for service management or other forms of PFI. There is also a real need for independent advice for PCG/Ts as well as support in developing the procurement capacity of PCG/Ts.

The role of PPPs is not restricted to physical assets: partnerships may also have a significant role to play in the future delivery of primary care services. PPPs may be used to offer greater co-ordination for services that can be provided across GP practices or PCGs/Ts. There is clearly scope for this in relation to payroll, administration, facilities management and IT. More contentiously, as PCG/Ts and Health Authorities move towards closer joint working with local authorities through Care Trusts, there will be increasing attention given to the possibility that Best Value could be applied to the provision of health and community services – with the obligation this brings for re-assessing existing models of service delivery.

Independent providers may, within this new context, seek to demonstrate their ability to provide health and community services on a contracted basis with the PCT or Care Trust. In this case, the provider would be required to deliver on specific outcomes – either maintaining and improving the health and social care of a local population or co-ordinating services to meet a specific set of health needs, such as diabetes or intermediate care services. Broadening the range of potential providers could assist commissioning bodies in defining and implementing local objectives, improving and monitoring quality and cost-effectiveness and providing a stimulus to innovation. Yet the extent to which this approach offers real potential depends heavily on the future role adopted by PCTs – the extent to which they take on a strategic and commissioning role, as well as on trends in primary care more broadly. No definitive judgment can be reached at this point in time. Only once there is more certainty about the role and remit of the public agencies involved in primary care will it be possible to set out more fully the scope for partnerships.

Recommendations

There must be greater clarity about the future role of PCTs and Care Trusts and their relationship with other purchasers or commissioners of health care. The 'purchasing' side of health care needs time to bed down before the full potential of partnerships for service 'provision' can be assessed.

Independent advice and expertise on procurement strategies and the possible use of PPPs should be provided. This needs to be factored into the emerging NHS Lift model.

As PCTs become more established and Care Trusts emerge consideration needs to be given to the application of Best Value to primary health and community services.

Intermediate Care

Intermediate care services are specifically designed to provide 'a bridge between hospital and home' and to prevent inappropriate admission to acute hospitals or long-stay residential care (King's Fund, 2000). Services must be designed to respond flexibly to patients' needs and be sensitively geared towards rehabilitation and recovery. The intention is that, in the long term, high quality intermediate care will reduce demand for expensive hospital stays and long-term care. At the moment, although rapidly developing, intermediate care policy is in its early stages.

Existing nursing, residential and domicillary care services are largely provided in the private and voluntary sectors. The development of the intermediate care sector will inevitably involve partnership working as much of the existing expertise and capacity lies outside the public sector (Peck and Bowers, 2000). NHS organisations and local authorities now have an imperative to consider the contribution of voluntary and private sectors (Department of Health, 2001b). Intermediate care will also offer a test-bed for the wider aim of bringing the private and voluntary sector into the collaborative process of planning intended to characterise relations in the NHS. Partnerships will require the development of locally agreed protocols for referral, admission and discharge in and out of NHS and private and voluntary sector facilities and greater exchange of information between the sectors about workforce capacity issues and clinical activity.

A number of generic challenges face those seeking to develop intermediate care services. In England and Wales the distinction between 'nursing' care (funded by the

NHS in all settings) and 'personal care' (that will continue to be means tested) increases the imperative for pooled funding between Social Services and local NHS bodies. Not only is achieving this problematic but there is also currently considerable difficulty in specifying the nature of the intermediate care 'product' that should be 'bought'. Meanwhile, all providers require a payment mechanism that takes into account the levels of dependency of service users and the intensity of care provided. Particular challenges in working in partnership include:

- The need for a significant change of attitude towards the private sector from some health purchasers.

- An inclusive and agreement-based approach will require that small and large, (and potentially competing) service providers are willing to work together. Some issues, such as workforce planning are likely to present a particular challenge, given the lack of capacity in some providers.

- Finding ways of agreeing longer-term partnering arrangements (rather than short-term or 'spot' contracts) which facilitate higher levels of investment and greater trust between purchasers and providers.

- Most importantly, ensuring that health authorities or PCT/PCGs find the appropriate balance between forging co-operative relations with providers whilst also ensuring a degree of contestability between them. Relationships will have to be transparent if conflicts of interest are to be avoided.

Recommendations

A number of pilot sites should be developed to establish models for Local Level Concordats to:

- explore new forms of joint strategic working between public, private and voluntary sectors

- establish models of longer-term partnering agreements

- overcome barriers to clear communication between the purchasers and providers of care

---

The opportunities and barriers to partnership working could be identified and learnt from through the creation of a set of pilot sites in which different methods of involving stakeholders can be evaluated and explored.

Secondary care

In recent years the configuration of hospitals in general and acute services has come under review (Ham *et al*, 1998). New technology is enabling more routine hospital treatment to be carried out at home or in community settings. At the same time, there are suggestions that services – such as cardiac surgery, neuro-surgery and radiotherapy will be provided increasingly in specialist centres. A theme of the 1995 Calman-Hine report into cancer services, echoed within National Service Frameworks and the National Beds Inquiry, was that healthcare should increasingly be based around co-ordinated networks that manage clinical conditions across services and hospital sites, rather than fitting into existing structures and buildings (Kelly and Whittlestone, 2000).

To date, thinking about the potential contribution of PPPs has not been closely integrated with wider thinking on the re-configuration of health care services over the next decade (Boyle and Harrison, 2000, 2001). As a result there has not been a concerted effort towards using partnerships to achieve serious changes in the way in which services are provided. The corollary of this is that there is little hard evidence to suggest significant innovation resulting from the use of the PFI which, in its existing form, is not well designed to play a major role in realising the goal of a seamless and patient-focused NHS service. Without change it will continue to produce the same services in new buildings.

Although NHS Trusts have, since 1983, been able to tender for the provision of support clinical services, the use of private/voluntary providers has so far been limited and has followed a short-term 'market testing' approach. The emphasis has been on cost-cutting with outsourcing being led by NHS Trusts outside the context of a regional or local investment and service strategy. The use of longer-term partnership arrangements – as long as they pass the value-for-money test – would increase the choice of providers available to health service commissioners, allowing them to specify more clearly the service outcomes they want. New management techniques, greater economies of scale, more effective use of assets and technology and a stronger synergy between the design and operation of services could follow.

The ease with which greater diversity in provision could be introduced will vary across service areas: those where barriers to entry are low, organisational interfaces are not too complex and where moves towards substantial reconfiguration of services are being considered, are obvious candidates. Diagnostic and Treatment Centres aimed at providing same-day testing and diagnosis or performing dedicated elective surgery in order to reduce waiting times for surgery are a key service area in which it would be viable to introduce a degree of diversity in provision.

One way of doing this would be through a full DBFO/PFI model (see Chapter 4 for a discussion).[2] The challenge here would be to ensure that the partnership was premised on the need for continuous improvement in service quality throughout the life of the contract. It should also provide the scope for the commissioning health authority to switch to a new service provider (at agreed points in the life of the contract) if key performance indicators had not been achieved. Alternatively, the centres could be built conventionally, with the management and operation provided separately through a partnering style contract (see Chapter 8). In both instances private management needs to be compared with the NHS option. A new programme of capital investment in these facilities would benefit from utilising these different approaches and the learning that would result.

The scope for partnership in the provision of support-clinical services should also be developed. Currently, the NHS is undertaking a pathology modernisation programme that is aimed at region-wide service reconfiguration. If implemented, this will involve the establishment of regional service centres providing a range of testing facilities. Different consortia of providers could tender for the establishment of such centres.

These approaches are not entirely new in that NHS Trusts can already subcontract service provision to a private and voluntary health care provider and, as Chapter 3 pointed out, health authorities commission elective services directly from private and voluntary providers. What is different, however, is the recognition that the design of new facilities around clinical needs and the ability to alter the deployment of staff are vital if provider organisations are to be able significantly to improve the nature of service delivery. This means that, in the future, when health authorities have identified a need for Diagnostic and Treatment Centres, or reconfiguration of other support-clinical services, they should encourage bids from a range of providers, including NHS, voluntary, private sector and partnership organisations, including the option of staff transferring.

Recommendations

The operation of Diagnostic and Treatment Centres by public and private providers should be piloted using a range of approaches – including PFI and non-PFI models. Contracts should be designed to encourage continuous improvement and to allow a degree of contestability in the provision of clinical services.

Several development sites should be created to pioneer the introduction of regional pathology services – with the provider selected on the basis of their ability to demonstrate continual improvement in service quality and value for money. The development sites would explore different procurement processes and contribute towards the establishment of cost and quality benchmarks.

Equipping the PFI process to meet health need

We have made a number of arguments in relation to the PFI in health. The debate about the value-for-money offered by health PFI projects was addressed in Chapter 4 where we noted the restricted opportunities for innovation and efficiency offered by the prevailing DBFO model. We have also noted the anomaly whereby hospital trusts cannot incorporate clinical services within PFI projects (due to the core-ancillary split) even though they could contract for these services with the private/voluntary sector outside of a PFI contract. We have suggested that partnership arrangements be piloted in new areas of health care including support clinical services as well as (aspects of) clinical care. These proposals raise the question of whether it would be desirable to consider using a PPP arrangement for the operation of a full District General Hospital, including accident and emergency services and intensive care.

It is in relation to these services that the most difficult issues arise. The experience of other countries with a mixed economy of provision in publicly funded healthcare – from France to Canada and Australia – suggests that the challenges that arise in specifying outcomes, devising payment mechanisms and monitoring quality and cost are surmountable. We have also suggested that the introduction of partnership arrangements have the potential to generate pressure for genuine innovation and continual improvement, to challenge established patterns of staff demarcation and working practices, and achieve a better fit between asset design and service configuration.

Against this, there remain serious question marks over whether it would be desirable to implement a full-hospital PFI scheme in the UK at the present time. These doubts take a number of forms. The evidence from Australia is important in this regard both because full hospital PFI schemes are in existence and because a model of the PFI similar to that in the UK has evolved (with the exception of the inclusion of full clinical services in some instances). To date there is no clear evidence that full PFI hospitals are producing significant value-for-money defined in terms of both quality and cost, though the evaluations themselves are limited (Victorian Auditor General, 1996-97).

In any case very careful thought needs to be given to whether current models of PFI offer an appropriate vehicle for the inclusion of core services. One concern is that this approach would bind a health authority to a single health provider for a long period of time. The argument made in Chapter 4 was that if a PFI contract is for the provision of key services this increases the need to ensure the possibility of contestability in service provision over the life of a contract. It is also unclear that the private/voluntary health sector would currently wish to enter into such a project, not least because of the significant political risk involved and their lack of capacity. Finally, and most significantly of all, there would be a major crisis of legitimacy if such a model was imposed on local communities against their wishes. These reasons, together with the inadequate evidence, mean that it would be inappropriate to *insist* upon any future PFI hospitals including a full range of clinical services.

This view is based on pragmatic rather than ideological grounds. As the evidence base develops and the practice of PFI improves, it is possible that the balance of the argument may shift. At the present time, however, public sector purchasers should not be constrained in the range of services they may seek to procure through PFI projects: blanket restrictions on the inclusion of clinical services should be removed. Health managers should be allowed freedom to determine the most appropriate package of clinical and non-clinical services and the organisations best placed to provide them in a procurement project. Any decision to include clinical services in pilot projects needs to be carefully monitored and evaluated before this approach could be extended.

Finally, there are other ways in which PFI projects need to evolve. The next generation of PPP contracts should include more flexible projects in which the focus is on packaging together investment requirements for a whole health care system – encompassing primary, intermediate and acute care – over a period of 10 to 15 years.[3] These investment needs might span a range of health care sites and include both capital and non-capital elements (see Kelly and Whittleston 2000 for a discussion). Decisions as to where and how the planned investment should be allocated should be taken at agreed points during the life of the relationship.

Recommendation

The operational element of a PFI hospital should not be limited to the provision of ancillary services and the inclusion of a wider range of services should be an option for purchasing bodies. The inclusion of more clinical services in PPPs must not be imposed by central government.

Private sector management in NHS Trusts

A challenge for the health service is how to use its management expertise to best effect. Currently it is proposed that the management skills of all clinical staff are to be developed through the NHS Modernisation Agency. At the same time, increasing scrutiny is being placed on standards of provision and on disparities in standards between NHS organisations. The Secretary of State is likely soon to have the authority to 'intervene' in problem organisations (HMSO, 2000a).

The last Chapter discussed the shortcomings of relying exclusively on the private sector to 'rescue' under-performing public institutions or management teams. Hence the use of private sector 'hit-squads' for under-performing hospital trusts should be avoided. An alternative approach would be for the NHS to draw on both public and private sector skills in order to develop a standing managerial capacity for the provision of consultancy services which will help spread best practice, prevent failure and assist in crisis situations. In order to do this the Modernisation Agency should encourage the formation of a number of pilot 'partnership teams' made up of senior figures from successful NHS Trusts and, where appropriate, private sector managers with expertise in financial management and asset/facilities management, systems administration and contract design. Public and private managers would be seconded to these NHS partnership teams and their employers properly compensated.

Recommendation

The Modernisation Agency should establish a number of 'partnership teams' which involve public and private sector experts. These teams can be drawn upon to improve management and commissioning across the board and, where necessary, to help improve under-performing NHS trusts.

Local government services

In many local government services the use of different types of providers is already firmly established. This trend has been reinforced by legislative changes that make it clear that the primary responsibility of local authorities is the promotion of the social, economic and environmental well-being of the area and its people rather than the provision of services per se (HMSO, 2000b).

The change in the legislative framework is being accompanied by a new attitude in local government. Councillors of the left, right and centre are coming explicitly to reject both the 'size is everything' model that councils must at all time maximise their direct service delivery, and the 'night watchman state' model that councils should meet once a year to hand out contracts. There is a greater willingness not just to accept but to welcome a future in which councils 'lose a service delivery empire but rediscover a community leadership role'. Such a sentiment would lead councils to pride themselves neither on the proportion of services that they retained in-house nor on the scale of the PFI/PPP deals they had secured. Their concern would be whether or not citizens were receiving services tailored for their needs and which represented value-for-money.

Developing new strategies for improving well-being necessitates working with others: councils are expected to plan, set their strategic objectives and design services in consultation with other public, private, voluntary and community groups. However, in relation to service delivery the argument as to whether a partnership route is appropriate or not is essentially the same as in other public service areas. A service delivery partnership should only be adopted if it offers 'best value' for local citizens.

Best Value (discussed below), which replaced the Compulsory Competitive Tendering regime, is not the only policy driver encouraging local authorities to think about partnership. The e-government targets are likely to necessitate more partnerships with the private sector. Local Public Service Agreements (PSAs) are also designed to encourage authorities to question the traditional approaches to service delivery. Local Strategic Partnerships (discussed in Chapter 9) will see public, private and voluntary groups being involved in discussions of how to co-ordinate the delivery of mainstream services. There is no doubt that policy from the centre is pointing towards a greater use of partnerships and that many authorities are acting on this agenda. A recent survey of local authority managers and chief executives revealed that a majority of local authority personnel (59 per cent) agreed or strongly agreed that 'the modernisation of local government will not be possible without significant private sector involvement' (Figure 7.1).

These wider changes fit our argument that diversity between different types of provider can be a key factor in achieving high-quality services. Our approach seeks to identify the barriers that still prevent the creation of a genuine level playing field between these different forms of service provision, including different models of

---

The Best Value Framework

Since April 2000, local authorities, police authorities and fire authorities have had a statutory duty to deliver best value; securing continuous improvement in the exercise of all the functions that they undertake, having regard to the goals of economy, efficiency and effectiveness.[4]

Authorities are obliged to undertake five-yearly Best Value Reviews (BVR) of all their functions. To do this they need to consider what are called the '4 Cs':

- Challenge why, how and by whom a service is being provided;
- Compare services with the performance of others taking into account the views of both service users and potential suppliers;
- Consult local tax payers, service users, partners and the wider business community in the setting of new performance targets;
- Use fair and open competition wherever practicable as a means of securing efficient and effective services.

Authorities must also publish annual Best Value Performance Plans (BVPPs) the principal means by which an authority is held to account by local people for both the efficiency and effectiveness of its services and for its future plans. All functions will be subject to external inspection the frequency of which is at the discretion of the Inspectorates carrying them out, though the expectation is that they will be aligned to the five-yearly Review cycle. The result of this is a report for the Audit Commission, which may be referred to the Secretary of State when auditors are not persuaded that serious efforts are being taken to secure best value (Audit Commission, 1999a).

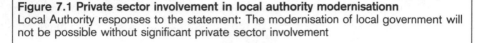

Figure 7.1 Private sector involvement in local authority modernisationn
Local Authority responses to the statement: The modernisation of local government will not be possible without significant private sector involvement

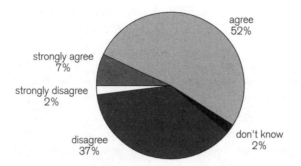

Source: Responses of 167 local authorities to a postal survey of the Society of Local Authority Chief Executive (SOLACE) members, conducted in September 2000 by Zurich Municipal Management Services and SOLACE

partnership. At the moment a range of barriers – legal provisions, the fiscal framework and management cultures – stand in the way of diversity. These barriers work in both directions: sometimes pushing authorities towards a particular partnership option such as PFI, at other times pushing them towards retaining services in-house. We are aware, however, that creating a level playing field is a necessary but not sufficient condition for securing quality services. Chapters 8 and 9 consider further necessary steps – improving commissioning skills among public managers; ensuring that groups of local authorities (and other public bodies) are encouraged to consider commissioning services jointly and offering citizens real influence over the nature of service contracts.

Building diversity into Best Value

The Best Value regime is premised on the notion that diversity in service provision is key to improving the quality of local services. Authorities are supposed to 'plan positively for diversity' and work with the best providers from all sectors. The expectation is that the 'future for public service provision is one where there is real variety in the way services are delivered and genuine plurality among providers' (DETR, 1999a). But there are a number of ways in which the existing regulatory framework for local government needs to be reformed if all forms of service delivery are to be assessed on their merits. It is not clear, for instance, that the existing framework really requires authorities to 'challenge' themselves. A vital first step in the process of building on the Best Value regime is to ensure that information is collected and published – an annual 'diversity statement' – showing the levels of expenditure channelled into different forms of service provision. Currently the lack of any such reliable data makes it impossible to assess the extent to which authorities are utilising different service delivery vehicles. Given the importance that Best Value attaches to working in partnership this is a notable omission.

A diversity statement would provide the basis for a more rigorous assessment of the patterns of service delivery that are being adopted in pursuit of Best Value obligations. It would help elected members and, if need be, other bodies such as the Audit Commission, to make a clearer assessment of whether there is a link between inadequate service quality and patterns of service provision. Drawing attention to the prevalence of different models of service delivery would in some instances reveal the dominance of expenditure on internal forms of provision, in others it would show the extent to which some authorities are reliant upon a single company for the provision of a broad cross-section of services. Both of these 'mono-culture' approaches can be problematic. The aim here is not to establish another area of central regulation and local box ticking but simply to provide signposts to possible action where there is evidence of under-performance.

Diversity should inform councils' strategy on service commissioning. Examples of this do exist. In cities such as Montreal, Phoenix and New Orleans, authorities have made a point of intentionally fostering a degree of contestability between in-house and private or voluntary sector providers across a range of services. The goal has been to avoid either a public or private monopoly in service provision (Savas, 2000). The concept of diversity should inform the commissioning strategies of *all* authorities: it is not just applicable where there is evidence of under-performance. Nonetheless, the question of what, if anything, the existing Best Value regime will do to help persuade a recalcitrant authority to consider different models of service provision is particularly pressing where there is evidence of service failure.

At the moment – short of the extreme measure of central intervention by the Secretary of State (or the threat of it) – it is not clear what bite Best Value will actually have in these instances. The Audit Commission should have the ability to set a 'diversity target' for an under-performing authority where it is felt that poor performance is linked to a mono-culture of service provision. This could mean authorities whose Best Value Reviews reveal under-performance should be encouraged to consider new forms of service delivery. This would apply to both in-house and external providers of services.[5] Diversity targets must be tailored to reflect the needs of local circumstance. A single 'diversity target' – with a fixed target for alternative forms of service provision – would be a highly arbitrary way of seeking to improve services. But if such a target is tailored to the service needs of an under-performing authority and backed up with support on how it could be met, it could be a major addition to the existing toolkit for realising Best Value.

In addition to clear information and a focus on the link between patterns of service delivery and quality in different service areas, authorities must use a fair and transparent process for assessing external bids with those from in-house service organisations. It is vital that tendering is a genuine exercise and not used merely to create a benchmark for in-house cost and performance. If this is not the case, an authority will not be seen as a credible partner. By this we do not mean that there should be a return to the highly prescriptive approach towards the regulation of the tendering process that was adopted by the CCT regime.[6] The paradox of the CCT formula was that despite its intentions it was relatively unsuccessful at encouraging external provision and was easily subverted by authorities that wanted to resist the move to contracting out.[7]

However, there is a need to ensure that authorities treat external bids fairly. At present, the evaluation of bids that fall outside EU Directives are regulated by each individual authority though there is some external guidance as to the approach that should be taken.[8] Intervention only occurs when complaints are made and usually works in favour of the authority. Again, if political leaders within an authority, or external inspectors, felt that the objective of Best Value was being subverted by a lack of partiality in comparing in-house and external bids then explicit guidance would be required.

Avoiding a new mono-culture

Over the last couple of years there have been several high profile and ambitious partnership arrangements struck between authorities and large service companies who provide a wide range of services. There is currently an interest in extending these agreements into key areas of governance and strategic management and encouraging many more authorities to follow this route. It is too early to reach firm conclusions on the performance of these agreements, though it is clear that some have the potential to reap the benefits from economies of scale and to bring about much needed innovation, particularly in back-office functions. It is also true that even in the larger deals that are currently taking place many key services will remain with the authority.

Nonetheless, we think that there are considerable risks inherent in this emerging model of partnership. The prospect of 'one-company towns' sits uneasily with the principle of diversity which is supposed to inform Best Value. If the private partner under-performs, or the relationship between the authority and its partners deteriorate (say, following a takeover), this could have a major impact on the services offered to local citizens. There is also a risk that local political leaders will invest so much in the relationship with their strategic partner that they will find it hard to remain impartial about whether it is really benefiting local citizens. If this happens then democratic accountability would be imperilled.

This is not to oppose the shift towards these large scale partnering arrangements or to say that they should be stopped. But it does suggest the need for caution and careful thought. In five years time we do not want authorities to look back and regret the fact that a new mono-culture of provision has emerged. As a matter of priority authorities, supported by DETR and the IDeA (whose remit is to improve all forms of local service delivery), should establish how large partnering agreements for multiple forms of service delivery can accommodate sub-contracting to in-house teams, smaller local firms and social enterprises.[9] Authorities should think hard about the potential benefits and costs of bundling together different areas of service provision. Central government should be careful not to push authorities too far in this direction before there is better evidence of how existing deals are performing and a clearer understanding of how accountability issues are being resolved.

Recommendation

Local authorities, supported by DETR and the Improvement and Development Agency (IDeA), should establish how large partnering agreements for multiple forms of service delivery can accommodate sub-contracting to smaller local firms and social enterprises.

Encouraging SMEs and social enterprise

There needs to be a recognition of the problems that small firms, social enterprises and voluntary organisations can face in seeking to bid for service contracts. These stem from the way that providers are 'approved' by authorities, the costs to smaller organisations of entering into pre-contract negotiations and the type of contract specifications used for service delivery. Too restrictive an approach to the use of approved suppliers and too great an emphasis on financial strength and history militates against smaller organisations. It is also the case, however, that a shift by authorities towards partnering arrangements could potentially benefit smaller providers. A point made by voluntary organisations is that they have sometimes been expected effectively to subsidise local authority activities, as they have not received grants that cover the full costs of the services they deliver. Bidding for work under partnership arrangements should help to ensure that voluntary bodies receive proper funding. Block contracts, in which there is a fixed payment for a specified quantity of service, will also help provide a guaranteed income stream and therefore be attractive to small providers (in the past these contracts have often been the preserve of public sector providers). In contrast, 'spot contracts' – where price is agreed on a case-by-case basis – provide little security. In this sense, the long-term nature of most partnership arrangements is likely to assist providers with a smaller financial base. But it would be mistake to think that all of the responsibility for supporting smaller firms and voluntary bodies rests with authorities. The representatives of these sectors need to step up their efforts to help ensure that their members (or consortia of them) are in a position to work in partnership with public authorities.

Recommendations

All Best Value authorities should publish an annual 'diversity statement' as part of their Best Value Performance Plan. This would specify by service category the volume of services provided in-house, externally, and through different partnership arrangements.

Diversity statements should be the basis for informed consideration of the impact of an authority's commissioning strategy on small firms and voluntary and community organisations. Authorities need to consider whether these organisations are unfairly affected by the short timescale imposed on bids and the types of contract they are offering.

Authorities, supported by the DETR and the IDeA, should establish how partnering agreements for multiple forms of service delivery can accommodate sub-contracting to smaller local firms and social enterprises.

The Audit Commission, where appropriate, should be able to set a 'diversity target' for authorities who under-perform or fail to improve where this can be attributed to a lack of diversity in service provision. Support on how to respond to this requirement would be provided by the IDeA.

A level playing field for capital investment

Over recent years some models of partnership, most notably PFI projects, have benefited from legislative, institutional and financial support that has made them a highly attractive option to local authorities. Most importantly, central government has 'ring-fenced' financial support for the PFI, so that many authorities have felt that the initiative was the 'only game in town'. As Chapter 3 pointed out, central government has increasingly relied on devolved and local government to deliver an increasing proportion of PFI spending. The Local Government Finance Green Paper (DETR, 2000a), while offering local government a highly welcomed 'prudential' framework for capital investment, also signalled the continued ring-fencing of support for PFI projects (see Chapter 4).

This 'ring fencing' results in a distortion between the PFI and other models of partnership which have not received a similar degree of policy attention. The Commission has received sharply differing views on the strengths and weaknesses of the PFI vis-à-vis other forms of partnership such as non-PFI joint venture companies (JVCs). Both approaches have their advantages and disadvantages and will suit different circumstances. The role of the policy and financial framework should be to avoid distorting the choice between these vehicles and to support public managers in selecting the most appropriate form. At present the legal and institutional forms of support for partnerships in the form of JVCs remain fragmented and unduly restrictive compared to that for the PFI.

Under the new Local Government Act (2000) it is clear that authorities now have the power to participate in JVCs in commercial fields such as leisure facilities and regeneration. What remains unclear is the position in relation to JVCs that are created to deliver other services. The type of legal protection offered to investors in PFI projects through the 1997 Local Government Contracts Act does not apply to the share capital that a private company might invest in a JVC. It is likely therefore that investors in JVCs are less certain about their security than they would be in a comparable PFI deal.

Recommendations

As a matter of priority the prudential framework for local authority capital spending as outlined in the Local Government Finance Green Paper should be instituted. PFI projects and JVCs should be treated in the same way as conventionally financed projects, with them counting against an assessment of whether an authority's borrowing was prudent.

The accounting treatment of a local authority PFI project or JVC should be decided after it has been determined that it offers Best Value and contracts have been signed. This should make the issue of the accounting treatment of JVCs less problematic.

Capital invested in other forms of PPPs such as JVCs should benefit from equivalent legal safeguards to that invested in PFI projects.

Creating companies with the private sector

There is a risk that existing capital finance rules distort the structure of JVCs. Currently the capital transactions of JVCs that are deemed to be under the 'effective control' of a local authority count against the local authority's borrowing approvals.[10] At the moment a stringent definition of 'effective control' is used. Even if the authority has a minority of the equity and a minority of directors, all the company's capital transactions are still regulated. Consideration should be given to a new definition of 'effective control' for joint ventures. In addition a *proportional system* of risk-allocation could be considered whereby there is a direct link between the proportion of a JVC's capital transactions which counts against an authority's borrowing capacity and the proportion of the equity and control that the authority holds in the JVC.

Recommendation

Consideration should be given to a new definition of 'effective control' for joint ventures and the introduction of a proportional system of risk-allocation.

Sharing expertise within the public sector

So far we have spoken of the need for a genuine choice between different models of service provision. One crucial element of this involves ensuring that local authorities are themselves able to develop expertise in particular areas of service provision and share this capacity through the use of trading arrangements with other *public* bodies.

Ensuring that unnecessary constraints are removed from local authority enterprise also fits those arguments in favour of a level playing field. The greater use of contracting for local authority services, combined with restrictions on the ability of public agencies to bid for them, could easily increase the prevalence of a 'private sector default' approach towards the delivery of local services (see Chapter 3). On the one hand, private enterprise is free to acquire expertise, recruit staff, generate economies of scale and trade freely with the public sector. On the other, public enterprise (in the form of local authority organisations) is constrained in its capacity to share its expertise through trading arrangements with other authorities. This imbalance needs to be rectified.

If there were a genuine level playing field it would be possible for the expertise of one authority to be sold on, or franchised, to others. This would mark a decisive shift away from the implausible view (that still receives much support) that each and every authority should seek to develop expertise in all areas of service provision. We do not think that this is tenable. Instead, local authorities could develop an in-house specialist 'brand' in particular areas of service provision. In some cases this could take the form of a partnership between a local authority and a private or voluntary sector organisation which would facilitate risk-sharing as well as skill-pooling. An example of this would be a successful Local Education Authority working together with a specialist educational company bidding for a contract to provide services to another LEA. In other cases the private sector could lead a franchising arrangement with an authority playing an advisory role.

The current law does not prohibit local authorities working together in this way but it by no means facilitates it. The legal framework is restrictive in relation to the nature of the goods and services that can be traded as well as the type of bodies with whom an authority can trade. There is also considerable uncertainty about the type of contractual risks that an authority can assume without falling foul of District Auditors.

Of course, some of the existing restrictions are there for good reason. Local authorities' primary concern must be securing the well-being of local citizens. They should not embark on any activities that imperil this objective, nor should they enter into commercial transactions that result in local citizens bearing undue financial risk. Equally, however, authorities with recognised expertise should be able to benefit from sharing their approach with others. A reform of local authority trading provisions should give clear freedoms to local authorities who have performed well in Best Value inspections to enter into agreements with other public and private bodies in order to provide services. Any risks incurred through these arrangements would need to be transparent and kept within 'prudential' limits.[11]

Recommendations

Authorities who have performed well in their Best Value inspections should be allowed greater freedom to trade, within prudential limits, with other public bodies.

DETR together with the IDeA should produce guidelines about the types of contractual provisions which are acceptable in terms of financial and managerial risks, clarifying those that are (un)likely to be acceptable to auditors.

Creating a level playing field in social housing?

Social housing exemplifies the policy of encouraging public bodies, in this case local authorities, to focus on their strategic role as planners and purchasers of services on behalf of tenants, focusing on outcomes and moving away from the position of direct provision or management of social housing (DETR 2000a, 2000b).

It also exemplifies the important distinction to be made between the funding and financing of public services. Much of the funding for public housing comes from user charges, that is rents (themselves underwritten by housing benefit), but some councils also receive general public revenue subsidies designed to keep rents below market levels. The finance for investment in public housing can come from conventional public borrowing or from private sources. However, in all instances there is an opportunity cost to the nation of investing more in any form of social housing.

The Government has set an ambitious target of raising all council housing to a decent standard by 2010. Within the DETR Housing Green Paper four ways in which investment and efficient management could raise the quality of social housing were outlined (DETR, 2000b). Under the first three the housing stock would remain in local authority ownership.

● The local authority could continue to directly manage the stock and finance repairs.

● It could establish an 'arms length management company' to manage its stock, thus formally separating its functions as a landlord from its strategic commissioning role in housing.

● It could use the PFI to bring in private management and finance.

● It could transfer stock to registered social landlords (RSLs) who would manage the stock and finance any investment.

The first two options could also involve the authority contracting separately with private providers solely to manage housing stock, which has occurred in a small number of authorities. In deciding which option to go for, tenants should be able to exercise a real choice based on their judgement of which option would provide the most efficient and responsive *management*. How any investment is *financed* should be strictly irrelevant for tenants whose only concern will be prospective rent levels.

The DETR has separate ring-fenced pots of money to facilitate all the options. For some local authorities with a small disrepair backlog, the introduction of the Major Repairs Allowance will mean tenants could see a sustainable future for their homes remaining in council ownership. But for other local authorities, current DETR controls over local government capital investment and borrowing can effectively rule out the first two options. Tenants are then faced with a non-choice: either stay with your local authority and have little money spent on your property, or transfer to an RSL, or agree to a PFI proposal, and receive new investment. Not only is this approach analytically unattractive it is also inconsistent with the DETR's Local Government Finance Green Paper which offered local authorities a 'level playing field' by freeing them of direct controls over capital spending (DETR, 2000a).

The proposals in the Local Government Finance Green Paper would enable authorities to borrow subject only to 'prudential' limits, that is the ability to service from revenue streams any capital investment undertaken. Applied to housing this would mean that as long as authorities could show that they had sufficient revenue streams from rents and general subsidy they could undertake borrowing for capital investment without any form of government approval. This is a major step in the right direction: it would make the first two options for the management of social housing more tenable and help establish a 'level playing field'.

The Finance Green Paper also explicitly accepted that central government should *not* restrict the funding available to authorities and hence force them to go down a PFI route. However, it went on to signal continued ring-fencing of revenue support for PFI projects and appeared to invite authorities to develop PFI projects that would be considered as 'off balance sheet'; PFI projects would not count against an assessment of whether an authority's borrowing was prudent overall.

The key principle to establish is that local authorities should go ahead only with those projects that promote Best Value, not those that result in them getting capital expenditure off balance sheet so they can avoid the DETR's controls. Social housing requires a framework that clearly separates out the strategic planning and landlord functions of local authorities. The Government is making good progress on this. But the framework should also establish a 'level playing field' between different options for the management of housing which thereby gives tenants a real choice over their landlord. If the Government is to achieve its goal of bringing all council housing up to a decent standard by 2010, much more has to be done to reach this real choice (Hilditch, 2001).

Recommendations

Implement as matter of priority the 'prudential' system for capital investment as envisaged in the Local Government Finance Green Paper (DETR 2000a).

Allow a far greater number of authorities to establish arms length housing companies as envisaged in the Housing Green Paper (DETR 2000b).

Ensure that there is a workable option in place for every housing authority to ensure that the target for 2010 is met.

Education

There has always been a wide range of partnerships in education involving the private and voluntary sectors in their various guises as employers, community stakeholders and providers of education or support services. The state school system has long relied upon a plurality of providers. Over recent years, however, PPPs have moved into more pivotal areas of the education system though, at least until very recently, this has generally been linked to under-performing schools and LEAs: the 'rescue model' (Chapter 3) has prevailed. In principle the introduction of greater diversity in the organisations who can run schools and work in partnership with the LEA could deliver some of the benefits that apply elsewhere in public services. It could allow LEAs and individual schools to tap into a wider array of skills and specialisms. Below we consider ways in which diversity may be extended. However, as was the case in relation to clinical services in health, we take a cautious approach to increasing the diversity of organisations that can manage or provide key services to schools. This is both because there is already considerable diversity in state schools and, perhaps more importantly, because we recognise that *if* greater diversity of schooling is introduced inappropriately it could undermine the role of governing bodies and have knock-on effects on the wider community of schools. If this were to happen it would contradict the criteria set out in Chapter 1: namely that PPPs should not undermine social equity or accountability.

The arguments for partnership in education are rarely clearly set out. When the Labour Government came into office in 1997 it emphasised its concern with driving up 'standards' or educational attainment in schools rather than spending time dealing with the 'structures' of educational provision. Although partnership approaches were seen as a pragmatic means of raising attainment they have repeatedly highlighted profound issues relating to the structures of educational provision – in particular the respective roles of the LEA, school governing bodies and school managers. Policy makers have also used various accounts of what it is that the private and voluntary sector will add to schools. Many education initiatives have been sold on the basis of drawing in private funding. Yet, in the context of publicly funded compulsory schooling this has always been a relatively weak rationale and, as the case study on Education Action Zones (EAZs) in Chapter 9 shows, in practice attempts to draw in private funding have often fallen short of expectations.

A more significant argument for partnerships in schooling relates to the possibility of drawing on the specialist skills of a wide variety of private and voluntary organisations in assisting schools and LEAs develop their strengths and address weaknesses. This has been a key feature of the National Grid for Learning (NGfL) that encourages schools to draw on a range of ICT providers in developing their capacity to use new technology both in teaching and in school management. Other partnerships may be of value in allowing heads and governing bodies to focus on their core activities by, for instance, passing responsibility for maintenance and administrative functions onto others. Partnership arrangements may also help in delegating real power to parents and governors by allowing them to make a judgement about the ethos and expertise of the organisations that provide key services within the school.

All partnership initiatives in education should further the policy objective of raising levels of educational attainment. However, it is a mistake to think of partnership initiatives as constituting a unified attempt to change educational policy. Education Action Zones (EAZs) are in many ways more closely linked to and should be considered alongside other area-based initiatives. Partnerships for delivering LEA services must be seen as part of a wider trend within local government to promote Best Value. PFI school deals have arisen in the context of PFI schemes more broadly.

Table 7.1, which draws together some of the main partnership initiatives that impact on schools, highlights the variety of roles that the private/voluntary sector can

Table 7.1 A typology of PPPs in education

	Impact of partnership initiative on schools	Role of private sector	Nature of public/private relations
Education Action Zones	Direct impact on schools in Zone but activities usually focus on specific pupils/curricular activities	Participates as a community stakeholder – expected to contribute towards zone funding, leadership and management	Binding agreement. Companies agree to sponsor and/or participate on Zone Forum
Independent – State School Partnerships	Direct impact on those pupils/ teachers involved – although not necessarily on all pupils or all curricular areas	Participates in variety of ways as part of the 'community of schools'	Range from binding agreement to less formalised joint activities
Education Business Partnership	Certain partnership activities (mentoring, work experience) have direct impact on pupils	Participates as future employer/community stakeholder	Local informal agreements, based on potential for mutual benefit
Private Finance Initiative	Influence on pupils is indirect – through consortium's ability to affect school environment. However some PFI deals also include training of teachers and pupils in IT	Service provider: primarily construction, asset management and ancillary services but also in some cases operation of networked IT service and provision of IT related training	Long term, high-value contract underwritten by partnership. Contracting parties are LEA and consortia, with binding agreement between LEA and Governing Bodies
LEA management and provision of core services	Company has responsibility for providing core, strategic services and impacts directly on some aspects of school management	Providing services including strategic management	Medium term, high-value contract underwritten by partnership
Management of Voluntary Aided/ Controlled & Foundation schools	Direct impact on school management: a private/ voluntary/religious organisation establishes a charitable foundation which, in most cases, owns the school building and land and nominates some members of the governing body.	Provider establishes charitable foundation to run school, nominate governors and provide strategic advice. (It may also contribute towards capital costs).	Occasionally a contract between LEA and provider organisation *or* an organisation may simply establish a Voluntary Aided or Foundation school if the application is accepted by the Local School Organisation Committee
City Technology Colleges and City Academies	Direct impact on school management: an individual, company or organisation may act as a 'sponsor' – setting up a charitable foundation to run a school. The sponsor contributes to the capital costs of the school and may own land and buildings. Funding comes directly from the DfEE rather than via the LEA.	Provides contribution to capital costs, owns school, establishes charitable foundation to run school	Agreement between DfEE and school sponsor.

play in partnership arrangements and the varying degrees to which PPPs impact on pupils' experience in schools. It distinguishes between contract-based partnerships and those initiatives (such as Education Business Partnerships) in which private sector participation is based upon informal agreement and motivated by a sense of corporate social responsibility or enlightened self-interest.

Here, we focus on the role of partnerships between sectors for the provision of core education services, both in schools and in delivering LEA services. We argue that the justification for the use of partnerships in the provision of core LEA services should be a desire for achieving Best Value rather than a punishment for public sector under-performance. Similarly, voluntary and private management of schools – so long as it is compatible with the requirements of accountability, equity and value-for-money – should not be used as an emergency measure, but as an option used at the discretion of schools to improve educational attainment and enhance local voice and choice. Once again, any such pilots need to be carefully monitored and evaluated before this approach could be adopted more widely.

Local Education Authority services

In the provision of LEA support services the case for diversity is fairly well established. In line with the rest of local government, LEAs have an obligation to seek Best Value in their provision of services. The Fair Funding regime allows schools to shop around for support services such as transport, though most schools currently buy them from the LEA and generally feel that they receive good value-for-money (Audit Commission, 2000). In relation to the provision of the LEA's core statutory responsibilities – special education needs, school improvement services, strategic management and access – where Best Value will also apply, the grounds for involving private and voluntary providers has, so far, been related to evidence of LEA under-performance.

Legislative restrictions on the use of partnerships have been one limiting factor. Currently, services involving 'the exercise of discretion' – such as administering applications for free school meals – can only be provided by another organisation on the basis that the current service is deemed to be inadequate. Another limiting factor has been political resistance – rooted in a perception that outsourcing core LEA services represents either privatisation or a move towards it and that this will necessarily weaken democratic accountability. In its enthusiasm for demonstrating intolerance of poor performance central government has not always been consistent in denying the charge that 'privatisation is the punishment for failure'. Nonetheless, the frequent claims that this is a step towards privatisation are inaccurate.

The key point is that LEAs retain their statutory responsibilities for ensuring the provision of services – contracting with private or voluntary partners for the delivery of those services in no way changes the LEAs' responsibilities, nor is it clear why accountability should suffer as a result of such partnering arrangements.[12] PPPs are more easily entered into in this area precisely because of the clarity of the purchaser-provider split, in contrast to the situation in schools explored below.

Until recently, there had been little encouragement of the majority of LEAs to consider engaging a variety of providers in carrying out their core duties. There now appears to be a growing recognition that the 'rescue only' approach towards partnerships cannot be reconciled with the principles of Best Value – leading to interest in exploring where and how successful LEAs could benefit from working, on a voluntary basis, with alternative providers (including other LEAs). As a result there is greater interest in developing new approaches to the partnering process and broadening the range of potential supplier organisations.

Up until March 2001 no LEAs involved in partnership arrangements had been inspected by OFSTED, leaving partnerships an untested improvement strategy (Audit Commission and OFSTED, 2001). Three LEAs – Tower Hamlets, Manchester and Barnsley – had improved very rapidly without the use of a PPP. However, in March 2001 OFSTED pointed to early indications of success in Islington where a particularly ambitious contract had been drawn up with a private provider (OFSTED, 2001a).[13] The model used appears to have helped clarify the role of elected members and put in place a set of challenging targets for the new provider (see Chapter 8).

The challenge will be for partnership arrangements to be responsive to the needs of each LEA. Developments in the contracting process should allow a diverse set of partnership arrangements to develop, increasing the scope for local innovation and learning. In the London Borough of Southwark, for example, a bidder was selected on the basis of their commitment to developing operational management arrangements that would evolve over time (Southwark Council, 2000). Rather than outsourcing specific services, the model used by Leeds LEA is the creation of a joint venture company with responsibility for delivering the majority of services to schools. Shared management is stated as a core goal of the arrangement with both the Council and the external partner equally represented on the JVC Board which is responsible for managing all the staff involved in education or administrative functions (Leeds City Council, 2000).

Progress in developing new partnership models has not been matched by efforts to facilitate successful LEAs providing services, or franchising successful models to other LEAs, though the DfEE has signalled support for moves in this direction (DfEE, 2000b, DfEE, 2001). As this Chapter has already argued, reform of the trading rules for local authorities would provide greater scope for LEAs to specialise and become recognised experts in particular services such as school improvement. New thinking is also needed about the level at which services are commissioned. At the moment there is an almost exclusive focus on individual LEAs. In some instances it may be preferable for smaller LEAs to join together to commission support services. Below the level of

LEAs it may sometimes be advantageous for clusters of schools – perhaps through an EAZ – to come together to jointly commission services.

The emerging diversity of PPP models, along with the evident capacity of some LEAs to turn themselves around without using PPPs, offers an interesting opportunity for serious evaluation of the effectiveness of different models of provision.

Recommendations

The Government should make it explicit that partnerships for delivering education services in no way alter the statutory responsibilities of LEAs. They do not amount to the privatisation of LEAs, which will continue to play an important role.

Partnerships for the delivery of LEA core services should not be seen as an emergency measure, but as a logical consequence of the Best Value process. All LEAs should consider the role that partnerships might play in increasing educational attainment. Restrictions on the use of partnerships outside of instances of under-performance should be removed. Government should make it clear that partnerships are not the only way of improving LEA performance.

The DfEE should commission an independent study of the performance of different types of partnering arrangements for LEA services, compared with LEAs that have

---

Diversity in state-funded schools

Although a range of types of schools already operate within the state-funded system, the Government has made clear its commitment to increasing this diversity (DfEE, 2001). Private, voluntary and religious bodies may become directly involved in school management in a number of ways. They may choose to act as a sponsor of a City Technology College or a City Academy (see Table 7.1). In this case an organisation or an individual forms an educational trust, owning or leasing the school/college building and, in the case of City Technology Colleges, nominating members of the governing body. It is likely that City Academies will be constituted in a similar way with a corresponding structure of governance. Their funding will come directly from the DfEE rather than the LEA though they can only be established if the LEA sees a need for a new school of this kind.

Alternatively any of the above non-public organisations can set up a charitable foundation to run a Foundation, Voluntary Aided or Voluntary Controlled school. Funding for these schools is received from the LEA. In all cases, these independent organisations are able to determine an ethos for the school and influence the running of the school nominating members of the governing body.

A wholly different model would consist of a governing body entering into a partnership (underpinned by contract) with a private or voluntary organisation to provide school management services. The provider may supply personnel to manage aspects of a school such as its finances, or it may offer consultancy services and management support to the head, or actually supply the key management team – the head, deputy, bursar, or heads of department.

There have been a small number of instances in which an LEA has contracted with a private or voluntary organisation to establish a Foundation or Voluntary Aided school, where the existing school is seen to be 'failing'. Possibly the best known example is the contract between Surrey LEA and the 3Es company to establish the King's College of Art and Technology – formerly King's Manor school. In 1998, following its OFSTED report, King's Manor was closed and re-established as a Voluntary Aided school. Surrey LEA invited tenders from organisations to act as the school's foundation body. The 3Es, which is an offshoot of another school (Kingshurst City Technology College in Solihull) won the contract to manage the school for five years from its reopening, with an option for a further five years. The 3Es established a charitable trust to hold the property of the school and to appoint foundation governors. The contract with 3Es includes a management fee and performance payments (based on increased pupil numbers) paid by the LEA, which are to be divided equally between the new school and Kingshurst.

From the point of view of the provider this model is attractive as it achieves significant control over the governance and management of the school. 3Es were able to nominate five out of the twenty-one members of the governing body, enabling them to influence more directly staff appointments and the overall operation of the school. The recent Schools Green Paper suggested changes to the law to allow an external sponsor to take responsibility for a 'weak or failing school' against a fixed term contract of five to seven years with renewal subject to performance (DfEE, 2001). This would build on the King's Manor model.

In principle allowing LEAs and governing bodies who so wish to explore new models for school management, drawing on voluntary and private sector skills where appropriate, is to be supported – though this is like to remain the exception rather than the norm. The potential advantages are that a degree of contestability should generate greater pressure for improvement and that the use of a range of providers should promote greater exploration of new ways of delivering services. Yet, in practice, current approaches to contracting for school management give cause for concern: they may not ensure clear enough structures of accountability. The key issue is the role of the school governing body, which has always been somewhat unclear. Government proposals to clarify their role are hotly contested. It is widely acknowledged that the most important function of the governing body is to appoint, monitor and support the performance of an effective headteacher. However, a private or voluntary organisation under contract to provide effective school services will, in most cases, also seek to control this key management decision. At the moment they do this through the transfer of a school to Voluntary Aided or Foundation status in order that the provider can nominate members of the governing board. The difficulty is that the role of the governors in schools is to act as representatives of the wider community. The danger that the governing body represents the interests of the provider organisation rather than those of the wider community is a real possibility in the Voluntary Aided and Foundation schools now being established. When the provider organisation is operating under a performance contract the potential for this conflict of interest is considerably increased.

A further concern with the applicability of this model is the erosion of the power of school governors it entails at a time when there is supposed to be a shift towards greater school autonomy. It is the LEA rather than schools that takes on direct responsibility for the often drawn out tendering and contracting process, in the context of school 'failure'. If the aim of fostering partnership approaches in school management relies on the extent to which LEAs are willing to take the lead, or if it applies only in cases of 'failure', it is not clear that the model will spread beyond a handful of schools.

If diversity in the nature of the organisations running schools is to become a choice for schools apart from 'failing' ones, then the shortcomings of the existing approach need to be addressed. Instead of using the Foundation or Voluntary Aided route for increasing the choice of educational providers alternative approaches are needed that allow new organisations to implement change within the school without weakening accountability mechanisms. Part of the logic of giving schools greater autonomy is that governing bodies should be responsible for entering into partnership agreements. However, most governing bodies do not have the skills or capacity for this and would need a great deal of independent advice and support.

Inevitably this is only likely to come from the LEA, which will therefore continue to play an important role. Indeed the role of the LEA as enabler and regulator of different models for school management is likely to need strengthening. Governing bodies are vulnerable entities and need to be able to rely on a supportive LEA. An LEA that thinks imaginatively about the possible use of partnership arrangements for delivering its own functions might also be well placed to think about how it can better support schools considering the potential role of new partners in school management.

There are a range of models that governing bodies might seek to employ, which differ in the extent to which they allow private/voluntary providers control over staffing and resource decisions. It should be stressed that in all instances we are assuming that the standard code of admissions applies and that funding streams should *not* be skewed towards schools with private/voluntary sector management. A level playing field should apply. Diversity must not be used as a backdoor way of skewing funding or changing admission procedures.

- Where a school faces specific, easily identifiable management weaknesses its governing body, on the basis of the independent support and advice received, may wish simply to tender for the provision of management support services. Existing staff would remain in place and under LEA or the governing body's employment.[14]

- There is the possibility of local schools coming together to purchase management support, with some personnel working across a cluster of schools but remaining in the public sector.

- A slightly stronger option would involve the governing body, if it had grounds for actually replacing existing school managers, contracting with a private or voluntary organisation to supply the headteacher and key management personnel. In this case, as in the case above, staff would not transfer to the provider's employment although the school manager may well seek to ensure that they are delegated responsibility for appointing staff.

- In the case of new schools (including City Academies, Voluntary or Foundation as well as Community schools), governing bodies may be appointed in the knowledge that management will be provided externally. The governing body, in this case, would be entirely independent of the provider organisation and would have the leverage to specify the broad educational outcomes being sought. It would be responsible for the conduct of the contracting process, and the selection and management of the provider (it would also be expected to consult widely with parents during this process). In this case, staff would be transferred.

- In the case of the few schools in which radical management change is required, the LEA should have the authority to suggest the establishment of a new governing body which would be charged with involving parents and stakeholders in the process of specifying contract terms, evaluating bids and selecting a new provider.

There are two main factors that may limit the spread of the most radical of these models – those involving partnerships with private or voluntary organisations who directly manage the school. First, we do not know how many governing bodies would actually want to enter into this type of contractual arrangement. Second, it is unclear how many private or voluntary providers would be willing to enter into arrangements that leave significant power in the hands of governing bodies that they do not control or influence in some way. The King's Manor model did not arrive by accident –

control over the governing body is seen by some providers, though not all, as an important feature of a workable model. Other providers, however, feel that control over the appointment of the head, rather than the governing body, is what matters.

The difficulty is that appointing the head is the most important function of the governing body. Unless this apparent impasse in school management is resolved, 'partnership schools' will only exist where the LEA effectively shuts a 'failing' school and starts again almost from scratch. Our view is that governing bodies should remain independent of private or voluntary providers. This is the best means of securing accountability. The problem with both governing bodies and providers seeking to control the appointment of the head might be solved through a system which obliges prospective providers to nominate their proposed head and management team who can then be interviewed by the governing body and parents. If the governing body is not impressed by the proposed management team they will speak to alternative providers. The real issue here concerns the wider question of whether school governing bodies do (or could) have the autonomy and the resources to act as the main 'purchasers' of education services. If so, the model we favour preserves accountability, ensures that governors still appoint the head and school managers but also allows educational providers to come forward with the team that they think is best placed to meet the needs of the school. Any pilots involving this model would need to be carefully monitored and evaluated before they are extended.

Recommendations

The Government needs to clarify the contractual relationship between an LEA and school governing bodies and the division of responsibilities between school governing bodies and the senior management in schools if partnering arrangements in schools are to go forward.

The model of enabling private or voluntary providers to establish Voluntary or Foundation Schools under contract with an LEA compromises the independent role of the governing body and should not be the primary way forward if private/voluntary providers are to be involved in school management.

Governing bodies should be provided with the support and resources necessary to contract for school management services where they consider this to be in the interests of the school. The LEA is in a good position to provide this support. The LEA will have to play a key regulatory role in ensuring that greater diversity in school management does not act to the detriment of the wider community of schools.

Improving the Private Finance Initiative in schools

As has already been made clear, school PFI projects should only proceed on the basis that they offer significant value-for-money and quality gains, not for accounting reasons. There also needs to be clarity about when the PFI is likely to be more or less appropriate – this is less likely to be the case for small refurbishments. Nonetheless, there are potential gains to schools from the PFI, particularly in relation to the release of head teachers from facilities and administrative management, as well as greater clarity about levels of expenditure on maintenance.

As with the health sector there is a question as to whether the PFI should be extended into new areas: particularly teaching and the curriculum. The Government's prospectus on City Academies did not appear to rule this out (DfEE, 2000c). If this were to happen curriculum delivery might be added to service procurement with the PFI payment mechanism based on educational outputs as well as asset availability. An advantage of this approach lies in the possible links between school design and operation. It would also avoid the problematic boundary issues created by the core/ancillary distinction within current school PFI schemes.

However, this approach sets up some difficult problems. First, the contracting relationship would for most schools be between the LEA and the contractor, creating a problematic three-way relationship that risks significantly reducing the role of the governing body. Secondly, to justify including the Design, Build and Operate functions together within a PFI arrangement, there would need to be a demonstrable link between the design of the building and service outcomes. Although head teachers do identify a link between the design of the school and pupil educational outcomes, this not yet been demonstrably proven (PricewaterhouseCoopers, 2000). Third, there would need to be strong mechanisms in place which allowed parents a powerful voice in the selection of the educational provider. Lastly, it is crucial that the school and LEA are not tied into a long contract with an educational provider. Contracts would need to be agreed which provide the LEA with the option of introducing a new private/voluntary provider every 5-7 years.

Once again the key issue is a structural one. The relationship between the LEA and the school governing body in relation to PFI contracts needs to be clarified if governing bodies are to have more confidence in going down the PFI route (Thompson, 2000). Schools need to know that they can hold the LEA to account if and when a PFI contract runs into problems. Once these issues are resolved the case for piloting more ambitious school PFI projects, which include new packages of services, will be greatly increased.

Recommendation

The DfEE should make value-for-money the only driver for the PFI in schools, with the accounting treatment of PFI projects decided after the contract has been signed.

Conclusion

This Chapter has considered the role that partnership arrangements could play in the key areas of health, education and local government services. It has drawn on the arguments set out in Chapter 6 in order to assess when and how partnerships can play a role in delivering core public services.

The models that emerge for PPPs in the delivery of services on behalf of LEAs provide a good example of a diversity of providers adopting different approaches to service improvement and competing on a potentially level playing field. However, in the provision of other local services such as social housing we are far from a level playing field. The Best Value approach to the provision of local services based on the local authority acting as strategic planner and purchaser and exploring the merits of a diverse range of public, private and voluntary providers is an attractive one in theory. Its focus on service improvement, user involvement and the encouragement of different models of provision and is laudable. However, it will fall down in practice unless it is underpinned always and everywhere by a level playing field in deciding the type of providers that should be selected and in the system through which capital is allocated.

Within the health service there has not been a consistent line on the rationale behind PPPs, whether it is access to private finance or value-for-money. In the provision of primary, intermediate and acute health care there are already a range of PPP models and new ideas are emerging for policy-makers to draw upon. Because there is a limited amount of evidence to go on, and the issues involved are so sensitive, we suggest a number of pilots which should be used to evaluate the effects of greater diversity in the provision of clinical services.

In education there are a range of models for the private and voluntary sector management of schools, but as yet limited evidence on the appetite of school governing bodies to go down any of these routes. They – and the interests they represent such as parents and the wider community – need to be adequately supported and their role should not be confused with that of the private or voluntary sector educational providers. Again the future development of PPPs will depend in no small measure upon resolving structural questions to do with the different role of LEAs, school governing bodies and school managers. In each area we think that – so long as it is premised upon a focus on quality, clear accountability systems, clear evidence and effective regulation – the shift towards a more diverse public service sector is to be welcomed.

Endnotes

1   By 2004 all PCGs are intended to have reached Trust status, at which point they operate as free-standing bodies, accountable to the Health Authority for commissioning care and taking responsibility for the provision of community health services. This should allow community care services to be 'managed' in a way that has not previously been possible, facilitating the attainment of high standards of service provision and improved mechanisms for increasing accountability to the local population.

2   The NHS Plan announced a new wave of PFI investment. Sixteen of the 29 schemes that have been approved in this latest wave of PFI projects include proposals to develop Diagnostic and Treatment Centres (DoH, 2001a). The Department of Health has suggested that there will be an extended role for the private sector and has 'not ruled anything out' (McGauran, 2001). However, it has stopped short of suggesting that private consortia would be eligible to operate all the clinical services.

3   This emphasis is reflected in the Department of Health's recent publication of plans to take forward the targets for investment in hospitals set out in the NHS Plan (DoH, 2001a).

4   Local Government Act (1999) Section 1 defines best value authorities as: (a) a local authority; (b) a National Park authority; (c) the Broads Authority; (d) a police authority; (e) a fire authority constituted by a combination scheme and a metropolitan county fire and civil defence authority; (f) the London Fire and Emergency Planning Authority; (g) a waste disposal authority; (h) a metropolitan county passenger transport authority; (i) Transport for London; (j) the London Development Agency (HMSO, 1999, Section 1).

5   There is an obvious problem where authorities are locked into long-term PPP contracts. Chapters 4-7 discuss the need to ensure break-out clauses from partnership contracts.

6   There are a number of important distinctions between Best Value (BV) and Compulsory Competitive Tendering (CCT). Under CCT discrete services were subjected to episodic market-testing that focused on reducing the cost of provision. CCT was characterised by a conflictual relationship between public sector commissioners and potential external providers and placed no emphasis on user involvement or consultation. The detailed prescription of the timing and form of competition led to unimaginative tendering and often frustrated rather than enhanced competition. In contrast, BV applies to all local authority services and is a process of on-going performance review that centres on improving standards. It aims to establish collaborative working practices between the service providers creating the conditions for increased engagement from the non-public sector (Martin, 2000).

7   The proportion of contracts won by 'direct service organisations' or DSOs between December 1991 and 1995 declined. Yet the proportion of contract *value* internally awarded remained at 75 per cent over this period (Local Government Management Board, 1995).

8   For example, IDeA (2000a) guidance states that 'retaining work in-house will only be justified where the authority can show it is competitive with the best alternative'. Authorities are called to revisit their standing orders on procurement and tendering to ensure that they are consistent with the provisions of the 1999 Local Government Act. However, at the moment 'authorities are free to decide how far, if at all, to separate client and contractor functions in their departmental structures' (CIPFA 1999c).

9   An example is the bundled school PFI project undertaken by Kirklees Council in which the Council's catering service providers won the relevant contract.

10   The conditions under which an authority is deemed to have 'effective control' over a joint venture company depend upon a number of different criteria being met. Broadly speaking the tests include the equity stake and proportion of directors held by the authority (at least 20 per cent of voting rights and/or the company directors being held by persons associated with the authority) and its business relationship with the JVC (for example, accounting for over 50 per cent of the company's turnover) (see DETR 2001b).

11   The limit on the value of goods and services provided to others would be calculated as a proportion of the authority's non-service specific income as shown in its consolidated revenue account for the previous financial year (DETR, 2001b).

12   See the Education and Employment Select Committee inquiry into private sector involvement in education (House of Commons, 2000) for an account of why accountability arrangements need not suffer.

13   OFSTED confused the issue by referring to the 'contracting out of the LEA's statutory functions'. It is necessary to repeat that an LEA cannot contract out its statutory functions: it can only contract with a provider to help it deliver its statutory functions.

14   In Foundation and Voluntary Aided schools the governing body employs the staff.

8. Making the public sector a better partner

The modernisation of government will require the public and private sectors to work together more effectively. The long-standing focus on cost minimisation – often at the expense of quality – also has to change. This Chapter considers how the partnership process needs to be organised if it is to result in genuine service improvement for citizens. It focuses on practical issues. It asks what skills and attitudes need to be developed, and what structures and regulations need to be in place if the potential of partnership is to be realised. It argues that government, together with the private sector, needs to reform both institutions and cultures. The public sector needs to improve its commissioning skills; forging partnerships with challenging performance targets rather than relying on short-term outsourcing contracts; learning to attract leading edge partners by building and shaping markets; working across departmental and authority boundaries in order to ensure that services are tailored to the needs of citizens and communities; and, crucially, by ensuring that all public service providers treat their employees fairly.

At the moment much of government is not set up to be an effective partner. It has a severe shortage of skills, those that it has are often unexploited, it finds it hard to learn from past mistakes, it is poor at picking quality partners and it is fiendishly difficult to get different bits of the public sector to work together to purchase services. Despite considerable progress there remains uncertainty about the type of employment conditions that the public sector should expect of those awarded public contracts. A lot needs to change. Government is the most important purchaser of goods and services in the economy yet, despite some improvements, in many ways it still acts like a novice.

None of this is to suggest that significant progress has not been made over recent years, it simply suggests how far there still is to travel. That there is a need for large-scale reform is hardly surprising. The skills and capabilities required by public managers will inevitably be very different in a world in which many services are provided through a diverse and overlapping public service sector rather than one in which managing in-house provision was the norm.

Skills and institutions

Guaranteeing high-quality services will require the public sector to attract and select between different options for delivery. It is vital therefore that the public sector is seen as being a credible client. This means sending consistent signals to the market place, encouraging new providers to come forward, being clear about the grounds on which partners are selected, and ensuring that public authorities have the right procedures in place to secure value-for-money.

The successful completion of a partnership arrangement for service delivery will require commercial negotiation, risk analysis and the application of management skills. The concentration of such expertise in the private sector poses a serious potential risk to the public sector. Not surprisingly one of the factors determining the success of PPP arrangements is the experience and expertise of the commissioning body. As Chapter 6 pointed out the Prisons Service and the Highways Agency are perhaps the best examples of public sector purchasing bodies. However, their experience is in sharp contrast with that of decentralised public bodies – such as NHS Trusts or schools – that undertake one-off capital projects. The latter may have little if any experience of the problems and pitfalls that can arise during a PPP deal and often have to buy in expensive advice.

The problem of a shortage of skills and experience exists across the public sector and local authorities are a good example of this.[1] Recruiting, training and retaining good staff in the field of project procurement and management is a great challenge. Remedying skill shortages will in part require the adoption of a concerted programme of training and development in procurement and contract management. It is vital that people with the necessary expertise are attracted into public service careers. This will be helped by addressing the low 'status' ascribed to procurement officers, and more generally by a greater flow of staff between the public, private and voluntary sectors.

Commissioning support provided by public institutions

Even if greatly improved training is made available it is unlikely that all public sector organisations with a commissioning remit – central departments, local authorities, other non-departmental agencies – will ever have the full complement of skills necessary for in-house 'intelligent commissioning'. The more ambitious commissioning becomes (with greater use for example of methods of involving service users) the more problematic this capacity deficit will be. Even with the development of greater internal expertise there will always be a need for access to externally provided specialist technical, legal and financial advice.[2]

Four organisations have been set up to play a part in the provision of skills and support. The Office of Government Commerce (OGC) is most involved in the wider policy process, setting the ground-rules and providing support for improving project procurement and contract management skills across central government in all forms of service delivery, not just PPPs. In order to do this it has set up a 'gateway review' process to facilitate the successful management of large, complex or novel projects (see Appendix 8.1). The Improvement and Development Agency (IDeA) is in many ways the counterpart of the OGC for local government in that its remit is to improve all forms of service delivery through the training of staff and the sharing of best practice. The Public Private Partnerships Programme (4Ps) was set up with a particular remit to support the development of PPPs in local government. Partnership UK (PUK) spans both local and central government and is tasked with offering 'hands-on' support to public sector bodies undertaking PPP projects, with a particular emphasis on new and innovative forms of partnership.

Key institutions in supporting public sector procurement

- *The Office of Government Commerce* was established in April 2000 to improve the efficiency and effectiveness of central government civic procurement. It provides a central resource of procurement skills to Departments and implements a 'gateway review' process. OGC chairs the Project Review Group and hence controls the allocation of PFI credits. It does not cover local government or the NHS except in respect of PPPs/PFI.
- *Partnerships UK* – itself a PPP – was launched in June 2000 and assists public bodies in developing large, complex, innovative, sensitive or high priority PPPs. It has its own resources to provide financial backing to projects as a 'development partner.' It works with the OGC on guidance and the standardisation of PPP contracts
- *The Improvement and Development Agency* was founded in 1999. It is controlled by the Local Government Association and supports local authorities in tackling the service improvement agenda by offering (amongst many other services) a range of help with procurement functions.
- *The Public Private Partnerships Programme* was established in 1996 to support local authorities in developing PPPs and PFI in particular by helping them in negotiations with Government and the private sector, disseminating information and providing a consultancy function. During 2001 it plans to work more closely with the IDeA.

Given their very recent establishment, most of these institutions have yet to develop a clear identity. The greatest challenge is faced by the OGC as its background and remit leave it open to the charge that it will not be neutral between PPPs and conventional forms of procurement. Establishing its credibility will demand a single-minded focus on securing the method of procurement that will deliver value-for-money for a particular project. It cannot be perceived to favour unduly the PFI/PPP route. In this sense it has to be seen to 'distance' itself from PUK which will continue to be a champion of PPPs.

The OGC and IDeA both face a great challenge in atracting and retaining the staff and expertise necessary if they are to offer a really comprehensive service. The IDeA in particular needs to fill the clear gap that is seen to exist in the co-ordination of skills and support for conventional procurement and non-PFI forms of partnership in local government.

Local authorities need to work together on the problem of procurement. Reforms from the centre can all too easily undermine the move towards authorities benefiting from greater strategic independence. Local authorities (and other public agencies) that have built up specific procurement expertise should be encouraged to share it with others embarking on a similar process. Effective procurement may also require change in the administrative structure of local authorities – in this vein proposals have been made for the implementation of a unified corporate framework in local government with a single system of quality assurance for procurement processes (IDeA/4Ps, 2000).

Beyond this there is a critical role for a boosted IDeA providing a comprehensive package of procurement support for local government (working closely with the private and third sectors as well as with all departments that have a role in local government procurement). This would involve it building on its existing functions in a number of ways:

- Work with the OGC to encourage local authorities to develop a 'gateway review process' for all major local government procurement projects.

- Provide information, guidance and advice on commissioning issues, including a menu of model contracts, commissioning procedures and contracting pitfalls to avoid. This could be brought together in a 'Procurement Guidance Manual' accessible through the web, co-ordinating the advice that is already disseminated by 4Ps, DETR, OGC, and PUK. All such guidance must make commercial sense and should be drawn up following consultation with the private and voluntary sectors.

- Allocate a fund used to encourage public/local authorities to share 'commissioning experts' with experience of PPP projects with other local authorities.

- Offer access to a register of legal advisers specialising in commissioning arrangements.

- Accredit organisations that offer procurement-training facilities and/or offer this service in-house.

- Act as a broker for secondment programmes between the public, private and third sectors.

- Support those authorities that are failing in their commissioning strategies (via 'troubleshooting teams') in order to prevent further action or intervention by the Secretary of State. Specific assistance would be offered on how to take action to encourage diversity in service provision following the issuing of a 'diversity target' (see Chapter 7).

- Conduct regular 'listening' exercises with the private and voluntary sector to ensure that their views are reflected in its work.

Finally, there is a gap in the present set of institutional arrangements – no one agency has a remit to help the NHS improve its general procurement and project management skills, yet the experience of both conventional procurement and PFI in health needs to be improved upon. There is a strong argument for the remit of the OGC, once its institutional capacity has developed, to be extended from PPPs to cover all forms of procurement in the NHS.

Sharing knowledge – a new information bank

A pre-requisite for a vibrant public service sector is the availability of comprehensive and authoritative data on the performance of key organisations from the private, voluntary and public sectors. In the local government market, in particular, councils want to know which private and voluntary providers deliver a good service and are committed to working in partnership, while public service providers want to know which councils are reliable clients. An information bank would provide public sector procurers with a reliable store of data on the track-record of alternative service providers and reinforce the incentive for all public service organisations to trade on their reputation.

We recognise that there is a lot of groundwork to be done before a new information bank could be established. The developments of common pre-qualification procedures for public sector contracts remain at an early stage and have not attracted a high take-up. There would also need to be a high degree of trust in the information that is used. OGC and IDeA should initiate progress towards such an information bank by discussing with private and voluntary organisations the type of information that might be required. Emphasis should be placed on providing accessible data that captures key elements of service quality, user satisfaction and flexibility in addition to standard information about the contract.

Increasing diversity – making and shaping markets

If public agencies are to draw on a diverse set of service providers they need to be competent at making and managing markets. Often public agencies have played too passive a role, doing little to encourage new and innovative voluntary or private sector providers to come forward. Though suitable practices will vary across different services, elements of best practice can be identified:

- Be clear about the scope of activities that are to be included within a project outline.

- Make clear that providers will be selected for their capacity to deliver value-for-money defined in terms of both cost and service quality.

- Provide 'positive signals' to potential providers – pinpointing in good time where there is an opportunity for providers to innovate rather than compete merely on price.

- Be pro-active in helping voluntary groups and smaller companies to engage in service provision and review whether there are aspects of the tendering process which will create barriers to entry for these organisations.

- Invite potential providers to comment on draft specifications and contracts.

- Co-ordinate the sharing of 'due diligence' costs by bidders in order to reduce the costs of bidding.

Increasing effectiveness – expediting the partnering process

It is often pointed out that a lack of investment in skills lies behind the public sector's poor track record in purchasing assets and services. One consequence is the gestation period it takes to complete large PPP projects. This varies across service areas – Figure 8.1 shows that the average time taken to move from the announcement of a project to contract closure for NHS PFI deals with a capital value greater than £25 million was 42 months for contracts signed prior to July 2000.[3] Figure 8.2 shows that the average time taken to complete PFI deals for a sample of 19 completed local government schemes was 26 months. On average authorities took 16 months to choose their preferred partner and a further ten months to negotiate closure of the contract (Audit Commission, 2001).

Specifying, advertising, negotiating and constructing complex capital and service projects will always take a considerable period of time. The extent to which the process of getting a PPP project approved adds to this gestation period is hard to assess because of a lack of comparative data on PPP and conventional capital projects. Prior research has indicated the degree to which conventional projects have been completed behind schedule.[4] It is also the case, however, that almost without fail

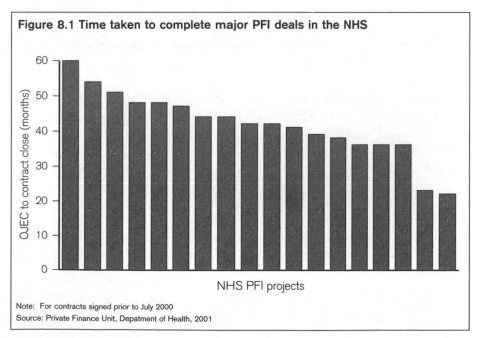

Figure 8.1 Time taken to complete major PFI deals in the NHS

OJEC to contract close (months)

NHS PFI projects

Note: For contracts signed prior to July 2000
Source: Private Finance Unit, Depatment of Health, 2001

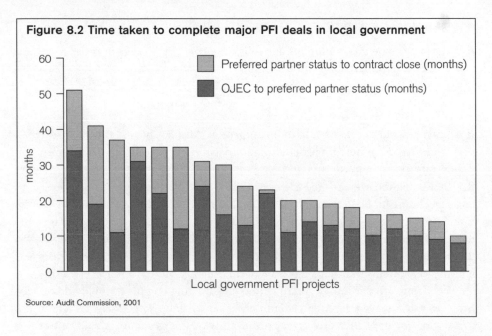

Figure 8.2 Time taken to complete major PFI deals in local government

Legend:
- Preferred partner status to contract close (months)
- OJEC to preferred partner status (months)

y-axis: months
x-axis: Local government PFI projects

Source: Audit Commission, 2001

large PPP projects take longer to compete than was initially anticipated. This is of great concern to government in that it contributes to the under-shooting of capital spending targets. It could also discourage some leading private sector players from entering (or remaining in) the PPP market: one PPP financial institution commented to us that the lengthy procurement process meant that being involved in an unsuccessful short-listed PFI bid could be 'career threatening' for the relevant managers. They suggested that aspirational managers were beginning to think about avoiding working in this field.

There are a number of reasons for these long time lags. Chapter 4 suggested that the framework for capital spending contributed to the problem by guiding public authorities towards the PFI route often in inappropriate circumstances. Research by the Audit Commission (2001) supports the view that a lack of commissioning skills will add to any delays. Submissions to the Commission also indicate that a lack of clarity in the initial contract specification together with reservations from the preferred bidder over aspects of the specification are key factors explaining why some procurement processes are so protracted. Other submissions argued that European procurement rules were unduly time consuming and cumbersome (discussed further below). Factors that may contribute towards a speedier procurement process include:

- the establishment of a project management structure that is integrated within wider policy and political decision making bodies

Figure 8.3 The mismatch of procurement procedures and the demands of modern local government

Local Authority responses to the statement: Procurement procedures in local authorities must be adapted to ensure partners meet the demands of modern local government

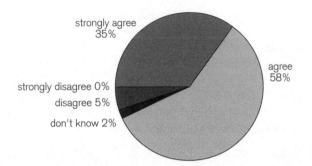

strongly agree 35%

agree 58%

strongly disagree 0%

disagree 5%

don't know 2%

Source: Responses of 167 Local Authorities to a postal survey of the Society of Local Authority Chief Executive (SOLACE) members, conducted in September 2000 by Zurich Municipal Management Services and SOLACE

- the avoidance of excessive detail at early stages in the procurement process

- a clear project plan with progress monitored against the plan on a regular basis

- clarity about methods for evaluating bids

- awareness of what financiers will want when they carry out due diligence

- involvement of auditors at every stage to prevent later delays

- the use of standard terms and guidance

There is widespread acknowledgement, particularly within local government, that without a genuine improvement in skills and support available to purchasing authorities dissatisfaction over the time taken for new projects to get off the ground is likely to persist. Figure 8.3 shows that an overwhelming majority (93 per cent) of those questioned in a recent survey agreed or strongly agreed with the statement that 'procurement procedures in local authorities must be adapted to ensure partners meet the demands of modern local government'.

A joint DETR/Local Government Association Review (chaired by Sir Ian Byatt) will soon be making recommendations for local government on ways of improving procurement and commissioning to deliver on the best value agenda. Over time, contract standardisation, the gateway review process (see Appendix 8.1), increased familiarity with the PFI system – together with reforms of the fiscal framework as set out in Chapter 4 – should improve the situation. Addressing the deficit in procurement and commissioning skills within public agencies should also be a unifying mission for OGC, IDeA, 4Ps and PUK.[4]

Recommendations

Across the public sector the status and career structures of procurement officers need to be enhanced.

The Office of Government Commerce needs to develop its own independent identity as a body focussed on securing the best method of procurement and managing the procurement process effectively. Whether or not it favours the PFI/PPP route over conventional methods of procurement for a given project should depend solely on value-for-money considerations.

The remit of the OGC should be formally extended to all forms of procurement and project management in the NHS.

Public agencies should be able to bid to become 'commissioning experts' jointly accredited by IDeA and OGC.

A new 'information bank' offering data on the performance of public service providers should be established by OGC together with IDeA.

Making partnerships work

An issue that arises in most discussions of PPPs is the distinction between a 'real' partnership and a straightforward contract between public and non-public sector agencies. Chapter 2 indicated some of the key distinctions, emphasising that partnerships involve risk-sharing and shared aspirations between the public and private sectors.

If PPPs are actually to bring about real gains in complex service areas this will require close forms of co-operation between the partners over the life of the contract. This will require much more than putting in place the right laws and regulations: 'hard' policy levers will not on their own be able to establish the attitudes and working practices that are necessary for partnerships to work. Nonetheless, the wider policy framework is important in as much as it provides an environment that can either help or hinder real partnering arrangements.

Quality

Partnerships must involve a clear focus on quality rather than public authorities simply selecting the cheapest bids. Most organisations, of course, wish to present themselves as being driven by the need to generate increases in quality but we have often found that the least-cost approach is the one taken by public authorities – regardless of the impact on service quality. This problem is clearly illustrated in a recent survey of local authorities' contracting policies for residential and nursing home care. Of the three-quarters of authorities that responded, 80 per cent stated that they did not explicitly differentiate among providers on the basis of quality (CCC, 2000). This result may be extreme but it is by no means unique. In the troubled PFI project intended to introduce Benefits Payment Cards, the purchasers, the Benefits Agency and Post Office Counters Ltd, ranked each preferred bidder's proposal on a range of criteria including the quality of their proposed technical solution, management arrangements and security against fraud. Yet in the end the procurement team selected the cheapest bid despite the fact that the provider (Pathway) ranked behind others on eight out of the eleven criteria (NAO, 2000a). In the first PFI hospital project, Dartford & Gravesham NHS Trust felt obliged to select United Healthcare as one of their two final bidders because they had submitted the lowest price bid. Yet its bid was felt to be less favourable than any of the others on scheme benefits; proposed risk transfer and overall quality of the consortium. Another bidder Trafalgar House, that was seen to have offered an excellent design but higher cost bid, was not selected to enter the final bidding round (NAO, 1999a). Examples of this type abound.

There is no single reason for this lack of a quality focus. Part of the problem, of course, is down to funding – public bodies with limited budgets will tend to choose the cheapest available option. Another factor is skills: focusing on the lowest bid is straightforward – choosing between different potential partners on the basis of their capability to improve service quality over the medium to long-term requires much finer judgements to be made. It may also be the case that the accountability framework contributes to the problem. Even if public managers had the resources, skills and inclination to go for a high-quality partnering approach they may still opt not to because of their concern that they could be publicly criticised by an auditing body for not selecting the most cost-effective model of provision (see Chapter 10). All of these issues need to be addressed if a quality focus is to become the norm.

Flexibility and continuous improvement

Finding ways of dealing with future uncertainty is a central challenge in any long-term partnership arrangement. Long-term contracts are always 'incomplete' in the sense that they cannot specify how the service provider should behave in every eventuality. As Chapter 2 pointed out this should result in precisely the risk-sharing and joint working that is a key component of partnerships.

Acknowledging the inevitability of uncertainty about future services does not diminish the need for clear output specifications at the beginning of a project. Indeed a shift away from input specifications to the outputs/outcomes of the service required will itself be an important safeguard against procuring assets which rapidly become obsolete. However, even in well-constructed contracts, in which key risks are clearly allocated to the appropriate party, considerable uncertainty will remain. In our deliberations we encountered very different views on the best strategy for dealing with this. At one extreme are those who seek to do everything possible to 'future-proof' contracts by writing highly extensive and elaborate provisions that seek to pre-empt all future contingencies, not least because of the demands made by financial investors in projects. We have heard many accounts of contracts larger than phone books. This approach can be highly expensive, do little to foster a shared sense of purpose between partners and ultimately be self-defeating as changes will be required during a long-term contract that are simply impossible to predict.

At the other extreme are those who argue that the scale of uncertainty inherent in any long-term service relationship renders traditional approaches to contracting redundant. A number of private sector firms argued that it would be desirable to move to an environment in which a public purchaser identifies a single strategic partner based on their capabilities, establishes desired outcomes jointly with them, and then – where necessary – agrees contractual terms. Public sector managers tend to express grave concerns about this approach because of the threat of contractor-dependency and the danger that a lack of competition will undermine value-for-money. Furthermore, the compatibility of this approach with the EU procurement rules needs to be carefully assessed.

EU procurement rules

One of the most commonly cited obstacles to partnering is the EC Procurement Directives which establish a framework of rules to regulate the awarding of contracts for supplies, works and certain services by public authorities. Currently when contracts exceed a given threshold, authorities are obliged to advertise for tenders in the Official Journal of the European Communities (OJEC) and adhere to a prescriptive tendering process.[5] The EU Directives regulate the nature of the dialogue that can occur between client and bidder during the tendering process. There is some scope for pre-tender dialogue and for using the 'negotiated procedure' – both represent important techniques for building trust and understanding about how best to meet desired outcomes within a fair and competitive tendering process. However, the rules governing these techniques could be more flexible and clearer. Purchasing authorities could then apply them with more confidence to PPP projects. The relevant EC directives are currently under review, which should provide an opportunity for the UK Government to push for these increases in flexibility.

Not surprisingly, we are attracted to an approach which falls somewhere in-between these two extremes. The need for the public sector to arrive at its own view of what the project should achieve (and corresponding output/outcome specifications) and then to encourage competition in the tendering process is absolute. Equally, however, there is a need to create institutions which help partner organisations to undertake regular reviews of services over the life of the contract. If the next generation of PPPs are to involve a greater element of service provision then there will need to be much more weight on the nature of these post-contractual governance arrangements.

The question of how to build in flexibility into partnership arrangements applies across the board but has particular salience for those public authorities subject to the Best Value regime who need to demonstrate 'continuous improvement' in their services. Achieving this over the lifetime of a PFI contract will not always prove straightforward. A number of mechanisms are currently being developed in this regard. One approach is to use demanding performance targets that require regular service improvements over time: these can take the form of annual improvement targets or, more ambitiously, *relative* performance targets which reward service providers for surpassing the quality achieved by providers in other 'similar' localities. Generally, however, the different partners will need to come together regularly in order to review how well the partnership is performing.

It is already the case that most PPP agreements include provisions that can be drawn upon to make periodic alterations in charges or service levels. Often, however, it is assumed that these procedures will be used very infrequently or as a measure of last resort. Delivering on continuous improvement will mean designing these 'change arrangements' in a way that allows them to be regularly invoked throughout the life of the contract. 'Partnership Boards' provide a forum within which the two sides of a partnership can meet (often with other key stakeholders) in order to discuss if and how services (and the partnership more generally) need to evolve over time. They are formal bodies that can be established by a contract or in a separate memorandum. For them to work effectively there needs to be a mutual commitment to regular contact between partner organisations as well as to joint problem solving. More widely, the senior management of public authorities need to be committed to making the relationship work over the life of the contract. Political leadership is needed to sustain the relationship as well as to set it up in the first place. As Case Study 8.1 shows, partnership boards tend to operate at a number of different levels spanning strategic and operational issues.

Appropriate performance targets and post-contractual governance arrangements are crucial but they should not distract purchasers from putting flexibility safeguards into contracts. These should include the right to secure changes in patterns of service provision; re-negotiate fees; market-test services at pre-arranged

---

Case Study 8.1 Partnership boards: Norfolk County Council & Capita

Capita have a contract to run IT and financial services for the council and have set up a 'strategic partnership board' (a voluntary association of members from the LA and the company). The board is the custodian of the relationship developed by the contract; monitors progress and performance; decides on changes in the scope of services to be provided (eg extending their scope) and agrees a three-year strategy and one-year business plan – reflecting the changing needs of the local authority and recognising the possible costs associated with changing requirements. The strategic partnership board is made up of Capita's Executive Chairman and 2-3 Divisional Directors along with the local authority's Chief Executive, three local authority Members and four Chief Officers. It meets every three to six months and is supported by two other partnership board 'layers' – one focusing on implementation issues and the other on day-to-day operational issues – that meet more frequently.

---

points in the contract; and, if their has been persistent contractual under-performance, to switch to an alternative service provider. All of this will be a challenge. In the past contracts have been agreed which make it very costly to alter contractual terms. If over the long-term, PPPs are to demonstrate that they can deliver continuous improvement whilst also being value-for-money then both public and private sectors will have to be committed to forging relationships (and contracts) which can accommodate flexibility. The expected cost of having to re-negotiate fees over the life of the contract should be included in the initial value-for-money calculation.

Finally, if there is a very high degree of uncertainty surrounding services – for example, due to rapid technological change or the expectation of political change – then it may be the case that long-term PPPs are simply not appropriate. The transaction costs incurred in securing a sufficient degree of flexibility may be so great as to make in-house provision, or shorter term contracting, a more attractive option.

Sharing gains

How to share some of the gains that may emerge over the life of a partnership relationship can be a source of controversy. One view is that gain-sharing mechanisms are irrelevant as bidders will simply alter their tender price to reflect the change in their expected returns that result from these provisions. While it is the case that there will be an impact on contract price, gain-sharing provisions can have a clear role to play in improving the performance and stability of the partnership. This is particularly the case where achieving revenue-generation or cost reduction relies on the active co-operation of the public sector and/or there is a high degree of uncertainty about the quality of the information provided by the public sector and hence the expected returns from a PPP. Generally gain sharing can help to:

- incentivise the private sector to look for efficiencies/or wider market opportunities while re-assuring public purchasers (and tax-payers) that they will also benefit.

- ensure that the tax-payer benefits from improvements in technology or other events that lead to windfall gains.

- help increase the political legitimacy of partnerships.

- represent an important way of building commitment, shared trust and a tangible expression that public and private sectors can benefit from a partnering relationship.

The nature of gain-sharing will vary across different types of partnership arrangement. Joint-ventures – in which both parties hold equity and receive dividends are one model. However, revenue-generating partnerships which are not based upon a JVC model, can also benefit from gain-sharing provisions within the contract (see Case Study 8.2 below).

Case Study 8.2 Profit-sharing: Siemens Business Services and National Savings

In 1999 Siemens Business Services (SBS), started to service all of National Savings' products for a period up to 15 years. Contractual provisions were designed to reduce the risk of SBS failing to deliver with it bearing the financial consequences of underperformance. Meanwhile other provisions ensured that National Savings would share in any successes; receiving half of the amount by which SBS's annual net profit margin exceeds expected profits (8.7 per cent a year over the life of the contract). Further profit sharing mechanisms were introduced in relation to the revenue flowing from the development of third party business (NAO, 2000d).

In relation to conventional PFI deals clear contractual provisions need to be introduced which ensure that any windfall gains from re-financing are shared (see Chapter 4). Some PFI projects have also introduced provisions through which schools gain a share of any efficiency savings made. For instance, the Special Purpose Vehicle involved in Victoria Dock Primary School deal in Hull, has agreed to re-invest some of the savings on the first year's facilities management costs into a 'community dividend', to assist with the school's environmental project.

Focusing on what matters

A key part of successful partnering arrangements is that both sides agree on the policy outputs or outcomes that are to be attained. Focusing on outputs or outcomes rather than 'fetishising inputs', as one submission to the Commission put it, is supposed to give the provider maximum scope to innovate. Conversely the more tightly that inputs are specified the greater the chance that PPPs will simply carry existing inefficiencies into the future.

It is now conventional to argue that PPP contracts should seek to incentivise the delivery of specific outputs: buildings that are available for use, hospitals with a specific number of beds, prisons that are able to accommodate their target number of inhabitants. For many contracts a genuine focus on outputs is attractive. Increasingly, however, the rhetoric, and sometimes the practice, of *outcome* based contracting is being used. Focusing on outcomes involves linking an element of contractual payments to the tangible benefits brought to users: finding a job, passing exams, or achieving improvements in standards of health. The desirability of contracting for outcomes in this way has already been acknowledged by the DfEE and the Department of Health.

Contracts to manage public services will inevitably lend themselves to the greater use of genuine outcome targets – educational attainment for LEAs or recidivism in the

---

Case Study 8.3 Outcome-based contracting: examples from four services

Prisons
A quarter of the places at Dovegate prison (see Case Study 6.1) due to open in 2001 will form a 'therapeutic community'. The significance of the proposed contract is that for the first time in a private prison, the contract includes a performance bonus that is linked to the reconviction rate of prisoners in this particular community after release. A bonus will be paid for those prisoners that have completed fifteen months of therapy treatment and do not re- offend within one year following release.

Education
Half of the annual management fee to be paid to the organisation contracted for LEA services in Islington, CEA, is dependent on 'educational outcomes'. For example, they can lose 12.5 per cent of their annual profit if the percentage of pupils attaining 5 or more GCSEs at grades A*-C does not improve from the original 26.5 per cent to 35 per cent in 2001, and to 39 per cent the following year.

Employment
Working Links, a joint venture owned by the Employment Service, Manpower and Cap Gemini Ernst and Young, operates 9 of the Government's 15 Employment Zones and is largely paid according to outcome-related targets. Working Links receives funds for designing and delivering an individually tailored plan to ensure that long-term unemployed clients are job ready, but in addition it receives £450 if they are placed in a job and at least £2200 if the job lasts for more than 13 weeks (and more if the person in question was out of work for over three years previously).

Highways
At the end of 2000, the Highways Agency invited four companies to tender for a PFI contract to upgrade the A1(M). The agency is exploring congestion-based mechanisms which would not attempt to differentiate between the various causes of congestion but would simply relate payments to the effect on the travelling public, providing strong incentives to build a road that rarely needs resurfacing and is designed to maximise safety (Highways Agency 2000).

prison service. The key question is how to incentivise the provider of a service to put effort into obtaining desired outcomes without transferring risks over which the service provider has little control. There are a number of examples of outcome-based contracting where these issues have been addressed in practice (see Case Study 8.3).

A citizen-focus

One way of encouraging providers to focus on the types of outcome desired by service users, and citizens more generally, is to link an element of the payment stream to measure of *user satisfaction*. As well as creating an incentive for service quality to increase in line with the public's expectations, this is also a useful way of encouraging providers to give proper attention to some of the intangible or 'softer' elements of provision which often get ignored by conventional performance indicators. Measures of user satisfaction should become the norm in public service contracts wherever there is an interface between the contractor and the ultimate user. This approach is not entirely new – it has already been experimented with in the housing and transport sectors.

Case Study 8.4 Prioritising user satisfaction: Copenhagen buses

In Copenhagen a 'quality measuring system' has been successfully developed in order to create financial incentives for private bus operators to improve service quality and ambience. Bonuses are given to the best operator (in 1998 this was almost seven per cent of the contract sum) according to a points system that gives twice the weighting to passenger satisfaction – measured through quarterly surveys – as to traditional 'objective' measurements. Under this system there has been a notable improvement in levels of customer satisfaction (Preston, 2001).

To make user feedback provisions commercially deliverable and acceptable to providers the following safeguards should be considered:

- User satisfaction methods should be as objective as possible, independently measured and verified, and the issues covered should be agreed by both parties.

- Linkage to payments should be sufficient to provide a genuine incentive but not so great as to transfer undue risk.[5]

- The contractor must have significant responsibility for delivering the outcome that is being evaluated.

Transparency

Organisations within a risk-sharing relationship will want to have full information and understanding about their partner's plans. In part this should come from close working relationships, say through the type of partnership board discussed above. However, there should also be full transparency in relation to the detailed financial flows between partners. Many of the public and private organisations we have received evidence from stated that 'open book accounting' is a vital way of ensuring this transparency. This aims to provide full visibility of costs and profit margins, allowing public authorities to monitor whether cost-padding is being used as a way of boosting profits. In principle this approach should reduce the potential for complaints of foul play and provide the basis for trust to emerge. In practice it seems that open book accounting is a necessary rather than sufficient condition for genuine transparency.[6] In particular, while it makes costs 'transparent' there is still the need to determine whether these represent the 'real' level of costs. This can be particularly difficult where the partnership involves a special purpose company whose reported costs simply reflect the charges levied by sub-contractors. Hence open book accounting should, wherever possible, be supplemented by cost benchmarking and/or other incentives for cost minimisation. In addition the degree of effort required by the public sector to implement open book accounting can be reduced, though not eliminated, by requiring the auditors of the PPP deal to check that the cost allocation principles used comply with those laid out in a schedule to the contract.

Joined-up partnerships

Services delivered through a PPP should be organised around the needs and requirements of citizens rather than being dictated by departmental boundaries. In theory one might expect that a typical PPP project would involve different public bodies commissioning services together – after all, the needs of citizens tend not to reflect the borders of single public agencies. The reality is quite different. To date PPPs have made little impact on cross-departmental working and have generally not contributed to services being bundled together in innovative ways. Currently four different models of 'cross-service PFI' can be identified (see Table 8.1). The shared feature is that a single project is used to deliver a service that transcends traditional boundaries between public agencies.

The explanation behind the lack of operational joined-up PPPs is not hard to find. To date, at least, the traditional grip of departmental structures and budgets – together with the complexity of the PPP process – has been tight enough to see off any moves to use PPPs to promote joined-up service provision. Funding for PPP projects flows from departmental budgets and bringing together different funding streams for a single project is not straightforward.

Over recent years Government has used a special 'joined-up' pot of £60m (£30m for 2000-1 and 2001-2) to encourage applications for PFI credits which transcend conventional administrative boundaries and deliver joined-up services. The response to the initiative has been poor. Partly this is due to the lack of advance warning offered to the private sector about the desire to see the pool of cross-agency PPPs grow (particularly in regeneration); though the quality of public agency responses has also

Table 8.1 Models of cross-service PFI

	Public agency	Central departmental funding	Example leading to joined-up service delivery
Single agency and department	Local Authority	One department	DETR funding a project to provide housing and a community centre.
Single agency and multiple department	Local Authority	Two plus departments	DfEE and DETR funding a project that combines education and community facilities (eg Speke Estate, Case Study 8.5)
Multiple agency and single department	Local Authority and public agency (or new legal entity)	One department	DETR funding for a Local Authority and Police Authority project that combines housing and a one-stop shop that delivers the majority of local services including policing.
Multiple agency and departments	Local Authority and public agency (or new legal entity)	Two plus departments	DETR, DfEE and DoH fund a project combining housing, schools and health centre (eg Woodberry Down, Case Study 9.2).

been disappointing. Another factor has been the project approval process for joined-up PPPs. The Treasury's Project Review Group (PRG) approves applications for all PFI credits and continues to provide a forum for departments to agree to co-fund a scheme and then manage it jointly. Over time it is likely that cross-service credits will

Case Study 8.5 Joined-up PPPs: the Speke Estate

The Speke Estate in Liverpool, nine miles from the City Centre with a population of 15,000, is recognised as one of the 11 most deprived communities in Liverpool and has been the focus of numerous regeneration initiatives. The 'Speke Forward Learning Centre' is the flagship scheme developed by the Speke Garston Partnership (a strategic partnership including community representatives). The centre is the first PFI project to have succeeded in obtaining funds from more than one department with the DETR and DfEE both involved.

The project includes a number of elements, all of which are to be located on the same site: a new secondary school containing a 'City Learning Centre' (a technology and performance space to be visited by other local schools); new community facilities (a library, youth and community centre, adult day care facility and two nurseries); a one-stop shop that can deal with up to 85 per cent of local authority enquiries; and a neighbourhood centre comprising new offices for South Liverpool Housing and Social Services.

be provided directly from the departments; in the meantime, the challenge is to create a smoother system between departments for the prioritisation and funding of cross-service PPPs.[7] For this to happen:

- Departments/agencies should be more open to these ideas and willing to rationalise or bend established processes to make cross-service projects viable.

- The private sector needs to be more pro-active in coming forward with suggestions on how services could be configured across agencies to suit the needs of individuals.

- DETR should take the lead in promoting joined-up PPPs and as a first step should undertake an evaluation of the problems inhibiting greater use of the 'joined-up pot' as well as taking the lead on simplifying the process for securing PFI credits for cross-service projects.

- PUK should develop its role in encouraging the private sector to come forward with proposals, and in ensuring that all cross-service bids have a single 'champion' who will act as a point of accountability and leadership for projects. It should also spread best practice for joined-up PPPs.

Joint commissioning by local authorities

Another area where there is great potential for more public-public collaboration to underpin improved PPPs is *joint commissioning by local authorities*. It is something of an under-statement to say that it is inefficient for all 467 local authorities to procure all their services independently; similarly it is highly unlikely that all of them will ever become expert service commissioners. This suggests the need to think much more boldly about the potential that exists for groups of authorities to commission services jointly, allowing pockets of expertise to emerge and the benefits of economies of scale and scope to be reaped. In some respects this does not break new ground. There is a long history of joint procurement of standardised commodities. What would be new, however, would be to extend joint commissioning into services.

Where local authorities are likely to have similar requirements across the board (for example, street lighting maintenance, payroll and other back office functions), 'bundling up' services across local authority boundaries has the potential to generate improved value-for-money. Fixed transaction costs can be shared and bulk-purchasing deals can be struck. For some authorities joint commissioning may create opportunities that simply would not be viable on their own. For example, call centres require an investment and critical mass of customers that would not be suitable for many district councils.

On the supply side, the larger contracts that joint commissioning produces may attract consortia that have the required experience and capital to deliver on large and complex projects. The development of large (sub) regional employers with the capacity to generate new investment and jobs may also be a powerful spur for joint commissioning in areas where government spending represents the lion's share of local economic activity.

Given the potential benefits, there is a need to address the impediments to more joint commissioning. A key concern is the loss of autonomy that this may imply for some authorities. This is not a trivial issue. At a time when central government is increasingly vocal in telling local authorities that their role should be commissioning as much as producing services, the idea of giving up control of the former is bound to be controversial. Some authorities may start to wonder what their core functions are. Nonetheless, this point can be overstated. Though joint commissioning will inevitably involve some loss of autonomy it is important to stress that many of the areas where there is the strongest case for 'bundling up' – payroll, call centres, street lighting – are not necessarily the most salient issues for local citizens.

Another related concern is that joint commissioning will impede local citizens' capacity to shape how services are delivered. Here the challenge is for groups of authorities to negotiate 'flexible contracts' with a single provider who agrees to alter aspects of service provision to meet the varying needs and preferences of different localities.

In order to overcome the barriers to joint commissioning, significant incentives will need to be applied to encourage pathfinder authorities to work together. If this results in savings and service improvements other authorities would be likely to follow suit. The Government Offices for the Regions should be given a central role in identifying and supporting this initiative – initially through the use of a new pump-priming fund.

Recommendations

Flexibility needs to be built into PPP contracts if they are to promote continuous improvement and value-for-money over time.

Partnership agreements should include a joint statement setting out the post-contractual governance arrangements, dispute resolution mechanisms, and processes for information sharing.

Wherever possible an appropriate measure of user satisfaction should be used to determine a portion of the payment made to providers. In order that this approach is compatible with Best Value, measures of satisfaction should be able to change over time.

Gain-sharing provisions should always be a feature of partnerships where achieving revenue-generation or cost reduction relies on active co-operation of the public sector and/or there is a high degree of uncertainty about the quality of the information provided by the public sector and hence the expected returns from a PPP.

As experience develops, outcome-based contracting should become a more prominent feature of PPPs, linking an element of contractual payments to the tangible benefits brought to service users.

Open book accounting should always be a feature of partnerships but, wherever possible, it should be supplemented by benchmarking and/or other incentives for cost minimisation.

Clearer guidance is needed on how local authorities can best sound out the market for service provision while complying with the European Public Procurement Rules.

Government Offices for the Regions should establish a fund to encourage joint commissioning by groups of local authorities.

PPPs and the workforce

It is widely recognised that PPPs will not receive public or political support if they are seen to impact unfairly on the workforce. At the same time a primary motivation for PPPs is the desire for increased value-for-money in the delivery of public services, defined in Chapter 4 as 'the optimal combination of whole life costs and quality to meet the user's requirements'. This definition is important because it makes the point that achieving value-for-money in a way that lowers the quality of the service is not acceptable.

In achieving value-for-money or implementing Best Value it is critical that public purchasers do not perceive that they have to choose the lowest cost option. Indeed, often this will prove short-sighted and fail to secure the desired quality of service. For example, trying to save on costs by hiring the cheapest cleaning contractor for a hospital can backfire if the result is a less efficient cleaning service with adverse clinical consequences. Ensuring that there is a well-motivated, trained, workforce capable of delivering a high quality service must therefore be a central part of the procurement process. Government should always seek to spread good employment practices.

Is there a problem?

In most public services, labour costs are a high proportion of total costs. There is an important distinction to be drawn between two ways of reducing unit labour costs.

Firstly, efficiency and productivity can be improved through the better management and utilisation of labour, including better training, though this might also involve tackling restrictive practices or reducing abnormally high levels of sickness and absence. Secondly, cost savings can be brought about through reductions in compensation and benefits, critically pay and pensions. This second type of cost saving does not represent a genuine improvement in overall productivity and is more like a transfer of value away from employees. Conversely, genuine efficiency and productivity gains through better utilisation of the workforce can be shared resulting in lower costs to the purchaser, some profits for the provider and potentially better terms and conditions for the workforce.

While workers who are transferred from the public to the private sector in PPPs usually enjoy protected terms and conditions – indeed in some sectors pay increases – it is also the case that in other sectors providers may hire *new* staff on terms and conditions that are less favourable than those of transferred workers. This results in the creation of a 'two-tier workforce' where different employees perform similar tasks in return for differing sets of terms and conditions. In cases where the Transfer of Undertakings (Protection of Employment) (TUPE) Regulations have applied to second and subsequent round transfers, the situation may be even more complicated with three, four or five sets of terms and conditions operating in a single workplace.

One argument is that multiple terms and conditions are inherently unfair and erode employee morale and commitment. There is particular concern that women and part-time workers suffer disproportionately from the effects of the two-tier workforce because they are over-represented in the affected sectors. It is also agreed that employers can experience increased administrative costs when operating multiple sets of terms and conditions. Against this, others point out that a two-tier workforce – in both the public and private sectors – is inevitable in the modern workplace. Restricting the freedom of employers to vary the terms and conditions of new recruits makes it hard for them to manage effectively.

Another issue that has received considerable attention is the treatment of pension provision in PPPs. While transferred staff have benefited from TUPE protection, this has often not extended to pension arrangements.

Evidence of the impact of PPPs on the workforce – prisons case study

Empirical evidence on the relative importance of improved efficiency and productivity and reduced terms and conditions in relation to labour cost savings in PPPs is scattered between individual public sector bodies and private firms that are reluctant to release it for reasons of commercial confidentiality. Recognising the lack of a robust evidence base the Office of Government Commerce at the end of 2000, perhaps belatedly, announced it would sponsor research into the issue.

One area where some reasonable data is available is the privately managed prison sector – that is conventionally constructed (non-PFI) prisons where the management has been privately contracted (Andrews, 2000). Costs per prisoner in four privately managed prisons in 1997-98 were 11 per cent lower on average than in comparable publicly managed prisons and staff costs accounted for all of this difference. The most important element of labour cost savings was reduced staff hours per prisoner, accounting for a third of the total. However, some of this appeared to reflect higher levels of crowding in privately managed prisons, rather than the increased use of labour saving technology, improved management systems or the efficient allocation of staff to key tasks.

Nevertheless, if the reduced level of staff per prisoner does not affect the quality of service delivery then it represents a significant efficiency gain. In the case of prisons, the evidence suggests that the quality of privately managed prisons – as measured by the Prison Service's Key Performance Indicators (KPI) is similar to that of publicly managed institutions. Further savings from lower levels of sickness absence do appear to reflect better management of labour.

However, of the total labour cost savings achieved by privately managed prisons, approximately two thirds appear to represent a reduction in the *aggregate* pay, benefits and conditions of the workforce. This figure needs to be interpreted carefully. In part it reflects the hiring of younger and therefore less expensive staff rather than reductions in pay and conditions of comparable staff. Pensions are, however, less generous in privately managed prisons.

It should be noted that in two of the four privately managed prisons used for the comparison above, the private contractor subsequently lost out to an in-house Prison Service team. This suggests that private management can be matched by a properly incentivised public sector. It is also necessary to be very cautious about drawing wider conclusions about the impact of PPPs from the prisons sector, which is widely seen as atypical of the wider public sector.

Cost savings from Compulsory Competitive Tendering (CCT) in local government services have been the subject of a number of investigations (for example Boyne, 1998). However, there is little robust data that distinguishes between productivity gains on the one hand and reductions in employee terms and conditions on the other. What evidence there is suggests that both types of cost saving have occurred (Escott and Whitfield, 1995). For example, in the case of cleaning, an Equal Opportunities Commission study found an average reduction in employment levels of 28 per cent and widespread reporting of increased intensity of work. At the same time there was evidence of cuts by contractors in wages, overtime, bonuses and paid leave. The most recent data comes from UNISON research which identifies numerous examples of the two tier workforce where new starters are employed on significantly worse terms and conditions than transferred workers (UNISON, 2000).

Policy developments

Over recent years the legal framework for employee protection has been subject to a number of revisions. In the UK, employee protection issues in PPPs have been addressed principally through the Transfer of Undertakings (Protection of Employment) Regulations (TUPE). The original TUPE regulations of 1981 implemented the EU Acquired Rights Directive of 1977 in the UK. The key provisions of TUPE as it currently stands are that wherever an undertaking, business or part of a business transfers to another employer:

● Employees' contractual terms and conditions transfer without reduction from employer to employer.

● Collective agreements also transfer.

● Rights to occupational pensions, invalidity and survivor benefits do not transfer.

● Transfer shall not in itself constitute grounds for dismissal. However, dismissals may take place after transfer for 'economic, technical or organisational reasons'.

● Employee representatives are to be informed and consulted about the transfer.

TUPE and the original EU Acquired Rights Directive have proved to be the subject of considerable controversy and case law. Legal disputes have concentrated particularly on the question of which activities count as a transfer and which do not. Indeed, TUPE was not conceived with PPPs in mind, and it is only as a result of legal challenge that its applicability in these cases has been established. Partly due to these developments the original 1977 Acquired Rights Directive was amended by a European Council Directive in 1998 and TUPE in 2000-01 was being revised in the light of this.

The Cabinet Office in 2000 published a statement of practice governing staff transfers in the public sector that applies directly to central government departments and agencies and is advisory for other areas of the public sector (Cabinet Office, 2000). This establishes that in most PPPs staff should transfer and TUPE should apply, except in 'genuinely exceptional circumstances', such as:

● where the activity is 'essentially a new or one off project';

● where the contracted service is significantly different from the service previously performed;

● where services or goods are 'essentially a commodity bought off the shelf';

● where the provision of services is ancillary to the provision of goods.

This guidance makes it clear that the public sector, as a good purchaser and employer, expects staff to transfer consistently when activities are outsourced and when contracts change hands. Of course, whether or not the guidance succeeds in practice in delivering the desired certainty depends on whether it is applied consistently and well. There is clearly some scope under the Statement of Practice for bidding firms or government departments to claim exclusion from the application of TUPE, particularly under the first two exceptional circumstances (above), allowing a possibility of exemption for projects that are fresh starts or particularly innovative.

Another important development has been the DETR's statutory guidance on the handling of workforce issues under contracting (DETR, 2001a). This clarifies that a range of workforce issues can be taken into account in local government contracting without authorities in any way falling foul of Best Value or the EU procurement directives. It reverses the provisions of the Local Government Act (1988) which prevented authorities from taking 'non-commercial' considerations into account when contracting and emphasises the extent to which public authorities can address concerns over the treatment of employees through appropriate selection criteria for bidders and contract specifications. This guidance, which came out of discussions of unions and employers, advocates a 'win-win' approach: that is, it argues that authorities can achieve better quality services through the improved treatment of staff.

Pensions

Pension, invalidity and survivor benefits were excluded from the original Acquired Rights Directive and TUPE regulations. The Treasury in 1999 published guidance for central government departments and agencies on how occupational pension arrangements were to be protected when staff transfer occurred. This aimed to offer 'transferring staff membership of a pension scheme which though not identical is "broadly comparable" to the public service pension scheme which they are leaving', defined in terms of the future accrual of pension benefits (HMT, 1999b). In early 2001 the guidance applied only to staff transfers from central government and the agencies, and was not compulsory for other parts of the public sector.

Cabinet Office guidelines outline a framework for the treatment of pension issues in relation to PPPs. However, the guidance in early 2001 was not compulsory outside central government agencies and the NHS. In addition the DETR has issued (non-statutory) guidance to local authorities which states that contractors should provide broadly comparable pensions or, alternatively, staff should stay in Local Government Pension Schemes under 'Admitted Body Status'.

Redundancies

It is clearly established in both the Acquired Rights Directive and also in the existing TUPE regulations that transfer of an undertaking shall not in itself constitute a reason for dismissal. However, dismissals may take place after transfer for 'economic, technical or organisational reasons'. Where productivity gains reduce required labour input service providers should be free to adjust the size of their workforce within the existing redundancy regulations.

Policy responses

There is widespread agreement that government should seek to promote good employment practices through its partnership agreements. Public money should not be spent on bad employers. However, the appropriate policy response for ensuring that this is the case is a matter of considerable contention. Before considering detailed policy options two overarching points need to be made. First, and most critically, the fair treatment of employees requires that public services are properly funded. Regulation on its own will never be able to compensate for the effects of a lack of resources. Second, high quality employment practices will require public authorities to have the skills and confidence to contract with high quality service providers rather than those who are simply offering the least-cost option. Ensuring that public authorities are properly resourced and have the skills necessary to make good employment standards a condition of the partnership agreement will generally be the most effective way of dealing with the concerns discussed above.

In addition to these general points a number of different and sometimes overlapping views exist about specific reforms that should be undertaken. One line of argument is that wherever possible staff providing services should remain within the public sector: there would then be no transfer of staff, the public sector would remain the direct employer and issues like TUPE and the two-tier workforce would not arise. In relation to asset-based PFI projects this would mean adopting a Design, Build and Finance (DBF) approach that excludes services. Though in some instances DBF may be an appropriate model we do not think this is the right way of thinking about addressing all employee protection issues. Given the centrality of measures such as Best Value and the Cabinet Office's Better Quality Services initiative to the whole modernising government agenda, and the emphasis they place on working in partnership, these workforce issues are likely to persist whether or not services are included within larger PFI projects. More generally, it is precisely in the area of the organisation of work that the private sector might make a significant contribution to the management of public services. A restricted DBF approach might signal a reduction in the likely scale and potential benefits of PPPs.

Another way of protecting existing public sector workers who might be transferred is to build on the current TUPE. It is already the case that government must update TUPE regulations in line with the new European Directive. It is considering whether it can take this opportunity to build more certainty into the application of TUPE to PPPs by introducing national measures that would go further than the Acquired Rights Directive. Pension provision in PPPs could also be addressed within the framework of TUPE by including pension benefits within the list of protected terms and conditions. This does not resolve the issue of how much flexibility employers should be allowed to exercise when replacing old pension entitlements with new arrangements: it would not be practical to require the provision of identical 'new for old' schemes in every case. However, enhancing employee protection of pensions through a revised set of TUPE guidelines is a sensible way forward. A guiding principle should be that new entitlements should be of equal value to the old entitlements.

An obvious criticism of relying exclusively on revising and strengthening TUPE is that it would not address concerns over the issue of the two-tier workforce. There are different ways in which these concerns over the treatment of future recruits may be addressed. One of these would be the adoption of a Voluntary Employment Standards Code of Practice. It would propose procedures and employment standards that would be expected to apply regardless of whether or not employees had transferred. The drafting and use of such a Code would seek to strike a balance between being excessively detailed, requiring too much monitoring and adjudication, and being excessively generalised and therefore ineffective. The guidelines could be drawn up by employer and trade unions (or employee representatives) under the guidance of the DTI. Providers of public services would be encouraged to apply the recommendations of the Code by allowing public authorities to take contractor compliance with the Code into account when choosing between bidders. Procurement decisions would still be made on the basis of value-for-money and the Code would be written in the spirit of the best value regime, which recognises that good employment practices lie at the heart of securing high quality public services.

Another way of addressing concerns over the two-tier workforce is to devise a new form of 'Fair Wages Resolution' (as operated in some form in the UK from 1891 to 1983). This would essentially extend the collectively bargained or 'going rates' of pay and conditions in the public sector to all providers and contractors of public services and operated in some form in the UK from 1891-1983. Such an approach, if enacted in law, would prevent employers from paying different rates to new starters because they would be covered by the same collective agreements as transferred staff. The implications of this approach are hard to establish not least because (as of spring 2001) a precisely defined account of how a fair wages resolution would apply to PPPs had not yet been set out. The standard employer response to calls for such a 'resolution' is that though firms recognise the need to provide the appropriate pay, conditions and opportunities to attract and retain suitable staff, they cannot be bound by collective agreements negotiated elsewhere.

The way forward

There are few other issues in the debate over PPPs that are so controversial. Public policy will continue to have the difficult job of reconciling the need to safeguard the rights of employees with the need to deliver value-for-money and innovation in public service delivery by allowing private partners to manage. In doing this it is important to recognise what regulation can and cannot achieve. The emergence of a two-tier workforce in terms of pensions is likely to occur across the economy as a whole, as employers' close generous final salary schemes to new employees and switch to arrangements where the value of pensions is determined by the success of individuals' own investments. Similarly, regulation on its own will never compensate for inadequate funding of services. Nonetheless, reforms are needed.

- The first priority is to make public purchasers more aware that the principles of Best Value and value-for-money do not imply going for the lowest-cost bid and that good management of the workforce is integral to the achievement of good quality public services. Public purchasers need to think about how they can ensure that workforce interests are properly taken account of in the contracts they agree with their partners. This would mean ensuring that contracting authorities are able to include issues such as health and safety, training, and equalities within contractual discussions.

- The second priority should be the consistent application of the Cabinet Office and DETR policy guidance and putting in place the revised TUPE regulations by Autumn 2001 to ensure that PPPs do not have an unfair impact on the pay and terms and conditions of transferring employees.

- The third priority must be to build a more convincing evidence base on the impact of PPPs on the workforce so that the debate does not go forward in an empirical vacuum. This evidence should consider whether the (relatively) recent Cabinet Office and DETR guidance are likely to make a significant impact on the handling of TUPE and the treatment of post-transfer recruits. If this more robust evidence-base reinforces the findings of the anecdotal evidence we already have – namely that in a number of sectors PPPs are having a deleterious impact on the pay and conditions of some post-transfer recruits – then we would be of the view that there is a policy problem that needs to be addressed. We would then want to consider ways of strengthening the regulatory framework – whether through a voluntary code or if need be through legislation. This possibility increases the need for those favouring increased protection to work on practical measures capable of generating support amongst good employers and government.

Several principles can be agreed upon at this point in time which should inform any future policy development:

- The public sector should encourage 'good' employment practices with public service providers following the spirit as well as the letter of the framework regulating employment.

- PPPs should not be used as a way of reducing the pay, terms and conditions of employees.

- Proposals for increasing protection should be driven by a desire to protect the interests of public service employees and to improve services rather than by an ideological opposition to PPPs.

Recommendations

Public purchasers need to be made aware that the principles of Best Value and value-for-money do not imply going for the lowest cost bid and that good management of the workforce is integral to the achievement of high quality public services.

The Cabinet Office and DETR policy guidance needs to be properly implemented.

Purchasers should always be allowed to make training, health and safety and equality features of PPP contracts.

Revised TUPE regulations need to be put in place by Autumn 2001.

A robust evidence base on the impact of PPPs on the workforce needs to be developed. If this reveals that PPPs are having a deleterious impact on the pay and conditions of post-transfer recruits then we would want to consider ways of strengthening the regulatory framework – whether through a voluntary code or if need be through legislation.

Conclusion

This Chapter started with the observation that Government's appetite for partnerships has not been matched by the capacity of public bodies to manage the partnership process successfully. It has examined some of the issues that government needs to address if it is to get the most out of partnerships – that is, for it to use PPPs as a means of improving the standards and responsiveness of services rather than as a way of lowering cost at the expense of quality. It is this focus on quality that is the thread that runs through our analysis of procurement skills and institutions, contracting styles, and employee issues.

Improving the skills and status of public managers involved in commissioning services must be at the centre of efforts to modernise government and to improve public management. Achieving this will depend in part on the organisations that have recently been created to support procurement being properly resourced. They also need to establish their own identity and self-confidence and champion the cause of skill development. More generally, the public sector needs to learn to become more adept at sharing the sources of expertise that already exists within its own ranks.

Another theme has been the pressing need to ensure that there is sufficient flexibility within long-term partnerships to deal with uncertainty and to allow services to evolve and adjust over time. Flexibility should not be secured at the expense of clear contracts and open competition. But it cannot be achieved by trying to write ever more detailed and complex specifications that seek to predict all future service requirements. We have stressed that successful partnerships are likely to be those in which effort has been spent in designing appropriate governance arrangements that can be used to manage key relationships over the life of a contract. We also pointed out the need to move towards a position where it is the norm, rather than the exception, for public authorities to commission services jointly: this will be a crucial step towards delivering partnerships that are designed around citizens' needs and expectations.

Our final theme concerned the role of employees in partnerships. Government should always seek to promote good employment practices not least because a demotivated workforce is unlikely to deliver quality services to the public. Despite the progress made on workforce issues over recent years significant concerns remain about the treatment of pensions and the terms and conditions of new recruits. We have stressed that the adequate funding of services, a focus on quality, and a far greater willingness on the part of purchasers to select providers with good track records on employment issues are important in ensuring all employees are treated fairly. The revised TUPE regulations must also be brought into play and the evidence-base on the impact of PPPs on the workforce significantly improved. If this shows that partnerships have an adverse impact on post-transfer recruits this suggests the need further to strengthen the regulatory framework.

Endnotes

1   Local government officers (including legal and finance personnel have tended to depend on conferences, publications and support from 4ps and external advisors to develop the skills and know-how they require for PFI/PPP projects (IDeA/4Ps,

2000). IDeA conducted a survey of all authorities which asked 'Has your authority planned or introduced any specialist training programmes for specific skills needed in Best Value for Members, Chief Officers, other managers, staff or Best Value Review teams?'. For all of the target groups, procurement training came out lowest of the five options – benchmarking, consultation, customer care, performance planning and target setting – except for Best Value Review teams where 'customer care' was lowest (IDeA, 2000).

2   It is worth stressing that the development of better procurement and project management skills is relevant to the success of all forms of procurement – not just PPPs – a view endorsed by the DETR and the Audit Commission and central to the DETR's Byatt Review of local government commissioning and procurement.

3   It is important to acknowledge that these data relate to 'first wave' NHS schemes.

4   See, for example, the National Audit Office review of major hospital building schemes completed in 1986-87 (NAO, 1989).

5   Another route through which government might expedite some types of procurement is by making more effective use of the potential of e-procurement. In theory, this should allow the public sector to reduce transaction costs, widen competition and greatly expedite the tendering process. In practice, e-procurement has yet to take-off and it is not clear how much of an impact it will have on the procurement of complex services rather than the purchasing of goods and commodities.

5   The threshold levels set depend on both the type of public sector body and what is being procured. In 2000-1 central government bodies had thresholds of approximately £94,000 for supplies and services and £3.6 million for works contracts. Other public sector contracting authorities had thresholds of £145,000 and £3.6 million respectively (IIMT, 1999c).

6   Where a 'reasonable' level makes the scale of the payment proportional to the importance of using this approach. Contracts that only link 0.1 per cent of payment cannot seriously hope to change behaviour.

7   It is also the case that open book accounting is very hard to achieve in small PPP deals.

8   From 2002-03 the DETR will have an unspecified proportion of its budget allocated for joined-up projects and all departments will have to include joined-up criteria in their framework for allocating PFI credits.

Appendix 8.1 The Gateway Review Process

From January 2001 the 'Gateway Process' will be mandatory for all new high-risk procurement projects and IT procurement of all sizes in central government, executive agencies and other non-departmental public bodies (OGC, 2001). OGC claim that the 16 Gateway Review Process Pilots has achieved 'value added benefits of five per cent for a cost significantly less than 0.1 per cent'. At present the Gateway Review Process does provide a best practice guide to local authorities, but given OGC's current remit the process was not developed with local authorities in mind and is only mandatory in respect to IT procurement.

The Review Process will provide projects with a degree of objective scrutiny by an independent team experienced in procurement. A Gateway Review is conducted over a period of 3-5 days and OGC has identified five critical points in the project life cycle – 'gates' – when a Review should take place. Three Reviews take place before contract award and the other two concentrate on service implementation and the confirmation of the operational benefits. This is illustrated in relation to the standard stages of the procurement process, as identified by the Gershon Report (1999), below:

Figure 8.4 The Gateway Review Process

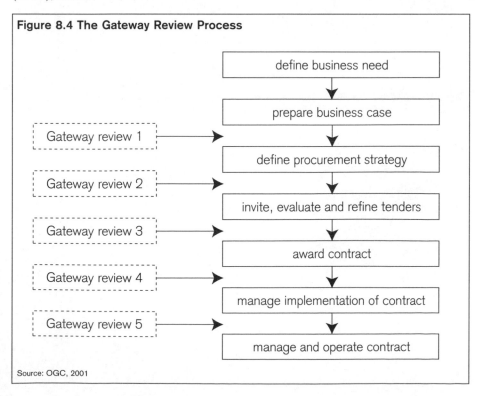

Source: OGC, 2001

The Review team of two to five people provide the project client with a report after each Gateway Review. On this basis the client decides whether to proceed (or implement recommended remedial actions). The process is set up to provide assurance and support for the Project clients, with OGC providing guidance and training.

IV:
Accountability

9. Communities and partnership

One of the features of many recent Government initiatives is the proliferation of efforts to involve citizens and communities in local decision-making on public services and regeneration strategies. The idea of community involvement is regularly invoked but rarely scrutinised. In this Chapter we examine why, when and how efforts should be made to ensure that PPPs are responsive to communities and reflect the needs of local people.

A first step is to establish whether the case for community engagement in PPPs is any different to that for traditionally delivered public services. The involvement of the community is an issue for all methods of service delivery; in-house, external and partnership. There are, however, three key reasons for believing that PPPs open up new possibilities for community engagement. First, by reconfiguring services and focusing on outcomes, PPPs create an opportunity for service planners and purchasers to reconsider traditional modes of governance and delivery. The more immediate the impact of PPPs on service users or front-line providers, the stronger the case for allowing those affected to be involved in shaping the nature of the partnership arrangement. The consequences of not doing this have been shown clearly in well-known PFI failures (for example, the Pimlico schools PFI project, see Chapter 4). Secondly, partnerships create new challenges for public accountability. Devolving authority over decision-making and public expenditure to non-elected partnerships creates the need for new and robust forms of accountability. Community engagement can help address the potential legitimacy deficit of some PPPs. Thirdly, PPPs offer an ambitious vision for local people themselves – and not just their representatives in public authorities or voluntary organisations – to be partners.

Throughout this Report emphasis has been placed on the contribution that PPPs can make to the realisation of desired outcomes: but this is only advantageous if these outcomes genuinely reflect the needs and expectations of citizens and service users. As the requirements of citizens rarely fit neatly into departmental silos, user involvement could itself act as a pressure for joined-up delivery. This could help overcome institutional inertia and reinforce measures taken at all levels of government – central, regional and local – to work in a cross-departmental way. Moreover, if the achievement of policy goals is dependent on the active co-operation of citizens then the case for community involvement is further bolstered. Examples of areas where service *users* are also service *producers* abound: residents' involvement in crime reduction projects, parents' role in improving educational attainment and citizens' participation in public health programmes.

'Community involvement' is a generic term applied to many different processes used to draw on the views and ideas of defined populations. This Chapter considers how the community can be given an effective voice in partnerships that include the public, private, voluntary and community sectors. This means that, as well as involving established representatives, the views of those citizens and interests whose opinions are less organised and harder to reach must also be heard.

Three ways in which citizens, civic groups and communities may be involved in local PPPs are explored in detail:

- Community involvement in partnerships delivering mainstream services.

- Community involvement (together with civic groups) in 'strategic' partnerships which set regeneration and other priorities for localities.

- Community involvement in the management and ownership of a neighbourhood's public assets (for example, council housing, community centres, public spaces).

Community involvement in PPPs for mainstream service delivery

In the traditional model of service delivery, the goals of user-empowerment and accountability are of little significance. It is thought to be sufficient that public purchasers of services are made answerable through the ballot box. However, even with a high turnout, voting is an extremely blunt method by which to give citizens influence over the provision of specific services. If there is to be genuine dialogue between the purchasers of public services and citizens, representative democracy must be supplemented by strategies for direct community engagement. The aim is to ensure that public agencies are purchasing the type of services that their citizens require and that these services are delivered to the specification that users demand. Far from undermining democracy, greater public input into service delivery may help reconnect government to its citizens.

There is plenty of evidence of the public's desire for decisions over services to be devolved to citizens, particularly over issues that affect them most directly (Rao and Young 1999; Edwards, 2001). The presumption in favour of using public involvement strategies should apply across all organisations delivering local services. While the focus here is primarily on services that are commissioned by local government, other public agencies – most notably the NHS – often lack effective methods of promoting community or user involvement. Hence the arguments made should also be of relevance in these areas.

The voice of the public as citizens, residents or service users should be heard at all the key stages of the commissioning process for services. Generally, however, the further 'up-stream' this occurs, the more significant and valuable it is likely to be. Though there are plenty of good examples of how local people can have a real role in shaping services, it is also the case that many instances of 'public involvement' have little or no impact on decision-making (Lowndes, 2001). A survey for the DETR found that only one third of local authorities considered public participation to have significant impact on final decision-making (Lowndes *et al*, 1998). The Audit Commission recently found that three-quarters of the 'best practice' authorities it surveyed failed to link the results of consultation with decision-making processes (Audit Commission, 1999b). If citizens are to have a real stake in partnerships then we need forms of community involvement which have some bite.

There are a number of points in the service delivery process at which communities could be given a say in partnership.

- *Strategy setting*. The Best Value framework already places a statutory duty on local authorities to consult with local residents, businesses and the users of local services (HMSO, 1999). Authorities should demonstrate the impact that these consultations have on the strategies that they adopt. There is also an expectation that councils will use public consultation to establish the demand for services before entering into a procurement project (DETR, 1999a). The purpose of consultation should be to establish whether, as well as how, a service should be provided.

- *Service commissioning*. Through partnerships funded by the Single Regeneration Budget, resident-led organisations can play an executive role in commissioning additional services for their locality. Local community groups can, for example, use regeneration funds to purchase additional mainstream services such as street maintenance or crime management services. There are more radical examples of community commissioning in other EU countries: for example in Denmark where groups of service users have a direct role in commissioning core services, such as social care (Greve, 2000).

- *Setting detailed service specifications*. Consultation over contractual specifications is already required for many PFI schemes (4Ps, 2000). The performance indicators and service delivery standards adopted to control and measure performance should be endorsed by all the main stakeholders, including service users such as tenants for housing schemes and school governors for schools. The Health and Social Care Bill (2000) places a duty on NHS organisations and all other bodies that provide care services to individuals (or purchase those services) to have arrangements for involving current and potential users of the service in decision-making (HMSO, 2000a). Yet the extent to which these consultation exercises will have a major impact on the nature of the service provided is still not clear. If these consultations are perceived to be tokenistic it will rapidly undermine their legitimacy.

- *Selection of service providers.* Service users and local citizens should have a powerful say in selecting the providers of key services. In relation to social housing there are well-established routes for community influence. Tenants can play a significant role in both examining procurement options and monitoring performance. Examples exist of tenants being involved in extensive discussions with a range of potential providers.[1] This type of activity should be more widespread and not unique to social housing. If, for instance, more schools are to enter into partnerships for the provision of management or other key functions (as discussed in Chapter 7) then parental involvement in the selection process is vital.

- *Managing contractual relationships.* Community representatives can be included as formal 'stakeholders' in partnership agreements. Some PPP contracts have created 'partnership boards' between purchaser and provider (see Chapter 8). These bodies can have contractually specified powers, including voting rights. They offer a vehicle through which the views of users can shape the way in which services evolve over the lifetime of a PPP. When partnership boards are created for PPPs that deliver key services directly to citizens, the expectation should be that a user representative will be included on the board. An example of this occurred in the Kirklees Schools PFI deal. The project is run as a joint venture company with the council holding a 30 per cent equity stake. The contract specifies that the 20 schools involved are able to nominate an 'observer' onto the partnership board. Though the observer does not have a formal voting right, he/she is able to represent the schools' interest by attending meetings and being privy to/participating in discussions; requesting information and reports; and raising items for discussion. Private sector companies that are likely to bid for future LEA service contracts have already signalled to the Commission their acceptance that teachers and governors should sit on partnership boards. Once again, it is critical that the public purchaser, in consultation with users, negotiates a contract that ensures that these partnership boards have real authority. If this does not occur, citizens and service users will rightly question the legitimacy and responsiveness of the PPP.

- *Ejection of poor service providers.* The views of citizens and service users should have a bearing on whether or not a provider retains a contract. This means thinking creatively about the types of mechanisms that citizens and service users have to hold failing providers to account or even 'eject' them. If there are pre-determined break points in a contract, at which providers can be re-appointed (or not), the expectation should be that users will have a say in this decision. Similarly, provisions that give public authorities the option to bring in new providers – for instance if there has been a failure to meet key performance indicators – offer an opportunity to involve local citizens. The scope for this approach in, for example, social housing is significant. Empowering tenants by giving them stronger hire and fire powers over their housing service providers, enabling them to trigger both a change in landlord and a change of manager, is being actively discussed and sometimes implemented (Hilditch, 2001). These approaches will *not* be applicable in every sector but could be adopted in other service areas, such as schools, where there is particularly close and regular contact between service providers and users.

Citizen voice could provide a powerful pressure for service improvement. As pointed out in Chapter 2, we think there is a strong case for ensuring a degree of contestability in public services: that is, allowing for the possibility that a new provider can replace an under-performing one. But there is no reason why it should always be the public authority that determines whether consideration should be given to switching providers: citizens should be brought into this decision. Contestability needs to be democratised. We acknowledge, however, that this approach does have its dangers. It risks placing excessive power in the hands of a small group of unrepresentative community activists. If providers feel that they may be ejected on the whim of a 'protest vote' they will be less inclined to bid for a contract or are likely to insist on a very high price to compensate for the additional risk. Nonetheless, so long as the process of user involvement is properly managed these difficulties do not seem to be insurmountable. Creative thinking is required on how best to make these ideas workable: the guiding principle should be agreeing clear procedures at the outset which are felt to be legitimate by purchaser, providers and users alike.

Improving the quality of community involvement

Elected representatives and local officials often express concern over the process of community involvement: questioning whether participants are really 'representative' of defined populations and raising concerns over whether the process may raise unrealistic expectations or undermine effective decision-making (DETR, 1998a). At all times there must be clarity over the scope and purpose of participation and a clear and transparent link between participation and decision-making processes. The credibility of community engagement also demands proper evaluation of its impact and feedback to citizens regarding the outcome of their involvement. Of course, 'best practice rules' should apply to both partnerships and public sector forms of provision.

Recommendations

The Cabinet Office and the Office of Government Commerce should provide joint guidance on how to conduct community consultation in PPP projects.

Local Strategic Partnerships could provide the appropriate forum for co-ordinating user involvement strategies across the public, private and voluntary sectors

Innovative forms of community involvement over decisions on the mode of service provision and the selection and ejection of service providers should be piloted by local authorities and other public bodies.

Public authorities should ensure that users have the same powers regardless of whether services are delivered through public, private or voluntary organisations.

The ability of service users to trigger a change in service providers may be particularly problematic within some long-term PFI/PPP contracts. Where it is considered desirable to ensure this level of user power, PFI contracts must have clearly designated break points at which user satisfaction can be gauged.

Strategic partnerships at the local level

It is widely recognised that sub-standard public services and poor quality and under utilised public assets are key problems in many disadvantaged areas, particularly in the most disadvantaged regions. Targeted area-based initiatives increasingly recognise the need to bring public sector agencies together and to introduce partnerships between these agencies and non-public sector groups if long-term improvement is to be achieved.

Regeneration policy is one area where partnerships abound. Current regeneration policies are the product of the evolution of urban policy over the post-war period. The history of partnership approaches to regeneration dates back to the 1977 Urban White Paper (Department of the Environment, 1977). Inner City Partnerships were formed in some UK cities in order to co-ordinate public sector responses to urban decline. In the 1980s the focus was predominately on physical regeneration adopting methods that marginalised local government and introduced top-down, private sector led programmes (Audit Commission, 1999a).

The limits of business involvement were soon apparent and led to a realisation in the early 1990s of the importance of working with local communities. This approach was reflected in the City Challenge and subsequent Single Regeneration Budget (SRB) initiatives where the involvement of the public, private and third sectors were a prerequisite for funding. As Table 9.1 shows, since the 1990s the concept of 'active citizenship' and the involvement of the community as well as public and private sector partners has been reflected in the criteria for regeneration funding streams (see also Westall *et al*, 2001). There has also been a decisive shift in focus from bricks and mortar to more complex social issues and recognition of the need to reduce reliance on centrally developed solutions and instead develop initiatives that reflect local realities.

Table 9.1 Outline of current key regeneration initiatives

	Single Regeneration Budget (SRB)	New Deal for Communities (NDC)	Neighbourhood Renewal Fund (NRF)
Start date	1994	1998	2001-2
Mission statement	Reduce gap between deprived and other areas	Tackle multiple deprivation in poorest neighbourhoods	Improve core public services in deprived neighbourhoods
Partnership	SRB funding requires schemes to be developed and implemented by local partnerships that include local business, the voluntary sector and local community	NDC is implemented through local strategy partnerships between local people, community and voluntary organisations, public agencies, local authorities and business	An operational 'Local Strategic Partnership' will be a condition for NRF funding
Geographical area covered	Ranges from a single housing estate to a whole region	Neighbourhoods of 1,000-4,000 households	LSPs will operate at least at the local authority level
Role of the community	Bids should include plans for 'capacity building' during the lifetime of the scheme (spending up to 10% of the grant on this). Partnerships can opt to have a 'year zero' (where no project spending occurs) to engage community	Encourages community-led partnerships: community is required to be fully represented in the partnership and involved in the identification of problems, development of the scheme and implementation	Each LSP will be eligible for £400,000 from the Community Empowerment Fund to help community engagement, administered through Government Offices for the Regions
Private sector	Bidders should maximise investment and non-financial support from the private sector	Financial sponsorship for initiatives and/or participation on partnership board	'Business brokers' will work to link the private sector to enterprise activity in deprived areas
Regional body to lead	Regional Development Agencies	Government Offices for the Regions	Government Offices for the Regions

Executive and advisory strategic partnerships

These 'strategic partnerships' all give local groups the opportunity to influence policy or priorities for a geographical area or policy issue. However, they differ greatly in their longevity and in the degree of influence they exercise. A distinction can be made between two categories of strategic partnerships: 'executive' and 'advisory'.

Executive partnerships determine priorities for an area and/or are at liberty to allocate public funds. Advisory partnerships influence public sector agencies that remain the accountable bodies and final arbiters of policy goals. Some of the partnerships involved in regeneration are temporary or time-limited. These could be characterised as 'shotgun partnerships' set up in order to access central funding streams, rather than 'bottom up' initiatives (Harding, 1998).

A plethora of other local partnerships have also appeared. Education Action Zones aim to improve educational attainment and cover a small number of secondary schools and their feeder primaries. The Zones' activities are overseen by Action Forums, with membership drawn from a wide range of local interests. Health Action Zones address health inequalities and are organised on a different scale covering a whole health authority area. Many elements of the New Deals for the unemployed are delivered by the Employment Service in various forms of partnership, as are Employment Zones (another form of active labour market policy) (Finn, 2001).

Engaging the partners

Strategic partnerships encounter a range of difficulties: high among them is securing effective private, voluntary sector and community involvement. This section summarises the case for including each sector and the challenges involved. One problem is common to all three: partnerships tend to lack clarity over the expectations made of each partner, what each stands to gain from their involvement, and how overall success will be gauged.[2]

The Community: citizens, residents, users

Partnerships often seek to engage members of the public directly by establishing mechanisms through which citizens, local residents or service users can express their views. However, while it is assumed that community engagement has a strong impact on the success of partnerships, the commitment to engagement is often merely rhetorical. Despite the goal of joint ownership of projects, partners rarely have equal control over a project. Lowndes (2001) highlights three potential pitfalls when trying to effectively involve citizens and their representatives in partnership arrangements:

- The misplaced assumption that disparate individuals can easily be represented by leaders of local organisations and associations. The use of 'official' representatives also increases the possibility of marginalising the interests of less powerful sub-groups.

- The possibility of tokenistic community representation, as a consequence of citizens' representatives having insufficient resources, and a lack of confidence and negotiating skills.

- The trading of concessions in order to reach 'consensus' can mean that the real goal of engagement is to 'buy off' those who articulate community demands.

The voluntary and community sectors

The benefits of incorporating voluntary and community groups in partnerships can be significant and include an improved understanding and advocacy of marginalised groups; an ethos of user involvement; and a capacity to innovate in response to social needs. There are, however, a variety of challenges around the engagement of these organisations in local regeneration partnerships. Westall (2000) identifies the following issues that need to be addressed:

- The involvement of the 'usual suspects' rather than the most appropriate players, largely because the costs of participation can be prohibitive;

- Influence by the voluntary and community sector is more likely to be over implementation issues rather than strategy, as the latter tends to be dominated by statutory partners;

- A power imbalance may arise when the local authorities fund the voluntary/community organisations in question;

- A history of misunderstanding between statutory agencies and the voluntary sector over the nature of their contributions.

The private sector

Many of the arguments for the engagement of the private sector in strategic partnerships echo those for its role in PPPs more generally. Businesses can bring commercial and managerial expertise, can offer valuable gifts in kind – from training facilities and mentoring to premises and office equipment – and can provide a way in to business networks. However, the engagement of the private sector 'up-stream' also implies that business (like 'the community' or 'the voluntary sector') is itself a legitimate stakeholder deserving inclusion within the partnership process. This lack of clarity over these different 'instrumental' and 'interest group' rationales is reflected in the very mixed picture of actual private engagement.

From the perspective of business, there are numerous reasons to consider involvement in partnerships. These might be *altruistic* (including philanthropy and a sense of corporate citizenship), *reputational* (the advantages of making these activities widely known), *commercial* and possibly *opportunistic* (the desire to secure attractive public sector service delivery contracts by demonstrating a commitment to an area). Finally, and perhaps most importantly, there may be a *civic* motivation: as a local stakeholder, business may desire a new role in local governance, having a say in the determination of relevant local policies and activities (Pike, 2000).

Despite the need for realism and sensitivity to business interests, many central government initiatives appear over-reliant on the commitment of the private sector to engage in strategic partnerships. This can be illustrated by the dearth of commercial backing for Education Action Zones (see Case Study 9.1 below) and the patchy record of corporate engagement in the New Deal for Community pathfinders, with business involvement in the most deprived areas proving to be particularly elusive (DETR, 1999b).

Low levels of business engagement can be explained by a number of factors including a lack of willingness to give up valuable time and cash. Most notably, businesses tend to be risk averse in this context and often prefer to participate in 'tried

---

Case Study 9.1 Engaging the private sector: Education Action Zones

Education Action Zones (EAZs) were introduced by the Government in 1997 and, by 2000, 73 EAZs covered 1400 schools in some of the most deprived areas of England. EAZs consist of clusters of schools working with a range of partners, normally including the LEA, voluntary sector representatives, health authorities, social services and businesses. Although LEAs were not excluded from leading the process, it was explicitly hoped that businesses, parents and community groups would take a leadership role in some of the zones.

Involvement in an EAZ was intended to benefit both schools and the private sector. Businesses were expected to bring additional funding as well as 'management expertise'. In return, they would learn from the multi-agency approach of EAZs; increase exposure to their products and services and influence the culture and direction of zone schools – making them more responsive to the needs of local firms. However, the primary motivation for the private sector was perceived to be altruism or enlightened self-interest (Hallgarten and Watling 2001).

Several evaluations of this initiative have highlighted that expectations of private sector involvement have not been met (Hallgarten and Watling, NAO, 2001b). Attracting funding proved problematic for many EAZs, particularly in the first round. The majority of contributions from the non-public sector have been in-kind rather than cash donations. The part played by business in the day-to-day management of zones has also undershot expectations, with no real examples of a business leading or managing a zone.

and tested' partnerships where the returns are more certain and where partnership failure will not reflect badly on them. This is reinforced by evidence that business is more likely to be attracted to partnerships whose primary purpose is to promote physical rather than social regeneration (Westall and Foley, 2001).

In addition to the problems of recruiting private sector partners, the quality of 'representation' of this sector is often unsatisfactory. Pike (2000) notes that business is frequently represented institutionally – for example, by Chambers of Commerce and in the past by Training and Enterprise Councils (TECs) – rather than by active members of companies. This creates a double problem for partnerships: they do not accrue the benefits of direct association with a business (in terms of skills and resources), nor do they necessarily have a recognised representative of the local business community (as Chambers are a self-selecting group). In 2001 TECs were replaced by the local Learning and Skills Councils which triggered concerns that private sector representation may decline further.

Overcoming the barriers to effective strategic partnerships

In addition to the challenge of getting the various different partners involved in strategic partnerships there are other wider policy issues that need to be addressed. In 1998 the Government rightly identified the problem of 'initiative-itis', the result of numerous government departments launching their own local and neighbourhood initiatives (SEU, 1998). Yet, at the same time the Social Exclusion Unit (SEU) highlighted the launch of a new initiative; the New Deal for Communities. By 2001 the final report of the SEU on neighbourhood renewal contained the same reference to 'initiative-itis', whilst simultaneously launching the Neighbourhood Renewal Fund and Community Empowerment Fund which are to be dependent on 'Local Strategic Partnerships' (SEU, 2001). Related to this problem is that of 'partnership fatigue' where the sheer scale of initiatives stretches the resources and patience of local authorities, private, voluntary and community organisations.

A further concern is the existence of multiple funding streams for strategic partnerships. These tend to be allocated on a competitive basis, according to different bidding criteria with varying procedures for evaluation. A number of organisations we heard from complained that this led to an unduly confusing and time-consuming system that excludes some of the most needy areas and diverts resources into expensive and possibly futile preparation of bids. Likewise, Audit Commission research into regeneration partnerships (1999a) notes that councils and their partners complain that a profusion of different schemes leads to perverse outcomes, fragmentation and short-term approaches to regeneration.

Local Strategic Partnerships (LSPs)

Some of these concerns lay behind the recent introduction of Local Strategic Partnerships (LSPs) whose initial aim was to rationalise partnership initiatives in any one locality (SEU, 2000).[4] LSPs will usually, although not necessarily, operate along local authority boundaries and will prepare a Local Neighbourhood Renewal Strategy and help set local Public Service Agreements. If no partnership exists to form the basis of the LSP, local authorities will lead this process. LSPs will be expected to include representatives from the public, private, voluntary and community sectors, involving some or all of the following groups: residents and community groups; voluntary organisations; faith communities; private sector and business organisations; local councillors; and a whole range of public sector organisations. LSPs could develop into umbrella bodies, encompassing a range of other partnerships – for instance, integrating their work with Health Action Zones (SEU, 2001). LSPs are intended to provide local co-ordination with priorities being set by all those who deliver or purchase different services together with those for whom the services are provided.

Welcome as LSPs are, there are a range of unanswered questions about their structure and remit. For instance, how will they 'work by consensus', given the large number of partners? What will 'equality' between LSP partners mean if local authorities have a pivotal role? And what is the rationale for private sector companies to engage with LSPs? If these issues can be properly addressed then LSPs should play a useful role in streamlining strategic partnerships and promoting co-ordination between public agencies.

Recommendations

The Government should make clear the presumption that – unless there are demonstrable local reasons for alternative arrangements – local authorities are the lead agency in Local Strategic Partnerships (LSPs).

LSPs and Health Action Zones (HAZs) should be integrated (SEU, 2001), but this should only be the start of the process of rationalising local partnerships. LSPs should be encouraged to bring together several local authorities where this is appropriate.

To deal with 'initiative-itis' and the 'proliferation' of partnerships there should be a moratorium on new funding streams for local partnership initiatives for at least three years. This will allow for the evaluation of current schemes before any new initiatives are launched.

The current situation of the Regional Development Agencies administering one funding stream – the SRB – while the Government Offices for the Regions allocate

New Deal for Community funding and the Neighbourhood Renewal Fund should be ended (as recommended by the PIU 2000). The Government Offices should be the sole regional bodies administering all forms of regeneration funding aimed at the local and neighbourhood level.

Funding streams need to reflect the time that it takes to create meaningful partnerships to avoid tokenistic representation.

Wherever possible the bidding and evaluation arrangements for regeneration schemes should be rationalised and made compatible. This would reduce the costs incurred in trying to utilise a range of funding mechanisms.

There should be greater clarity over what the private sector is expected to offer to, and what companies should stand to gain from, engagement in strategic partnerships. Public authorities should anticipate that the role of the private sector will be providing commercial and management skills rather than cash donations.

The Small Business Service (SBS) should take on a role of brokering opportunities for smaller companies, spreading best practice and illustrating the benefits of engagement.

Greater support should be provided to community representatives and organisations to ensure that they are in a position to take part in local partnerships. The Community Empowerment Fund is a positive step, but it should not just be used for community involvement in LSPs, it should be available for a wider range of partnerships (and therefore increased in size).

Community engagement through asset ownership and management

Here we focus on radical methods of giving communities a greater degree of control over local public services. The improvement of public assets – such as school buildings, council housing, health care centres, police stations, libraries, and leisure facilities – is another way in which local well-being can be enhanced. Beyond this, creative use of a neighbourhood's infrastructure can be used to address economic and social deprivation, for example, creating opportunities for local businesses and employment. This does not just apply to deprived communities. All communities are likely to be concerned with whether public assets are working to their full potential.

At the moment the drive to improve the physical quality of community assets is still largely executed through departmental funding mechanisms at both local and central levels. In relation to PFI, where 'bundling' of schemes across large areas has been required to provide economies of scale, this has been encouraged almost exclusively on a sectoral basis (see Chapter 7), schools being a prime example.

Comparatively little thought has been given to whether projects could be bundled across sectors on a *neighbourhood* basis.

Bundling by sector has clear disadvantages when set in a context of social policies directed towards neighbourhoods. It is likely to take decisions about the ownership and management of local facilities away from local communities and it militates against the use of small and medium-sized local contractors. It also tends to exclude small scale projects or ones which do not easily fit into a single department's remit. From a community perspective, it creates real difficulties in considering how best to maximise value from public assets (Ainger, 2000). This is not to say that the current trend towards bundling projects by sector should be stopped – it may well lead to significant value-for-money gains. But we do think there is a real need for the PPP policy community to think harder about how projects could be bundled together in a way which is of maximum benefit to local people and increases the say they have over local assets.

The conversion of public assets into 'community assets' has the potential to secure effective community engagement in regeneration partnerships. A number of vehicles already exist which could be built upon for this purpose. Development Trusts are perhaps the most widespread. These are independent, not-for-profit bodies, that hold assets such as land or buildings in trust (for example, on a long-term lease or ownership on the basis of a token payment). Most are seeking to build an asset base and generate income that will enable them to become financially independent and help them sustain their socially beneficial activities in the long-term (Development Trust Association, 2000).

Trusts are usually set up as companies limited by guarantee and are often registered charities. They tend to be formed as the result of grass roots community action, as part of an exit strategy for a regeneration programme or as the result of a commercial development. All have a community base, and adopt a 'self-help' approach to service provision. Their activities include building and managing workspace, providing sports and recreational facilities, running childcare centres, supporting small business and setting up community enterprises. Many of these activities are critical to regeneration efforts in an area. In short, Development Trusts provide a mechanism for allowing public assets to be used for community ends. Following the argument outlined below, they might be used as a template for a single neighbourhood commissioning body for PPPs.

'Community Trusts' and neighbourhood PPPs

The benefits of including representatives from the community, public, private and voluntary sectors in regeneration partnerships are potentially significant. However, such informal bodies sometimes fail to provide a sufficiently stable or accountable basis for public asset procurement or entering contractual arrangements with the private sector. Hence it would be beneficial to develop a legal entity, a 'Community Trust' which builds upon the idea of Development Trusts and provides a vehicle for the provision of asset-based services in a neighbourhood.

In order to work the Community Trust would need to have powers to:

- Take a strategic view of the fit between existing public sector assets and neighbourhood needs and develop a comprehensive plan for them.

- Take control of the property assets which were to be the subject of a PPP, PFI or other contract(s) that might originate from a variety of public authorities such as the local authority and local NHS Trust.

- Plan projects, negotiate, enter into and monitor the outcomes of contracts; and ensure that the assets provided the physical environment within which the statutory authorities could fulfil their obligations for service delivery.

- Offer a strong covenant that the private sector would be prepared to lend against.

- Act as a conduit for public revenue streams, including where appropriate PFI credits (Ainger, 2000).

The creation of such a Trust could provide a firm and accountable structure for the delivery of mainstream programmes. It could have an enhanced role as the single commissioning body for any relevant PFI/PPP project in the neighbourhood and could acquire the expertise – either in-house or externally sourced – to act as an 'intelligent client' in this regard. As a major property stockholder in an area, it would also have the capacity to use the assets it owned or controlled to reshape or influence the capital structure of the area to beneficial effect.

The PFI could be appropriate for some projects that involve a mix of assets and services (as in most SRB area projects) or projects that generate cash flows. An example of this approach evolved from the Housing Finance Corporation's project for the redevelopment of the run-down Woodberry Down Estate in Hackney, London (see Case Study 9.2 below). The aim was to address how local government organisation and funding could be structured to encourage cross-departmental working on asset and service delivery programmes – and how this could be integrated with programmes designed to empower local communities and involve residents (London Borough of Hackney, 1999).

The Woodberry Down project highlights a number of issues that need to be resolved in order to enable projects such as this to go ahead:

- As proposed, the 'Community Trust' would consider the well-being of the neighbourhood and its residents before any borough-wide or council policy, creating obvious problems for member organisations when priorities differ.

- The bodies charged with auditing public agencies differ between the health, education and housing sectors. These processes would have to be co-ordinated and joined-up in order allow such projects to go ahead.

- Separate departments are not adept at pooling their assets and revenues. This can frustrate the progress of cross-service PPPs.

Case Study 9.2: Community Trust Model: The Woodberry Down Estate

The *Woodberry Down Estate* project for cross-departmental asset management and service delivery, primarily combines housing, health, education and commercial retail assets (London Borough of Hackney 1999). The housing aspect of this is to be 40 per cent demolition and new build and 50 per cent refurbishment, replacing the old 2500 units of social housing with mixed tenure, low cost housing. The Woodberry Down Estate was highlighted by the DETR as being in the top five per cent of the most deprived estates in England. The new assets required are a nursery; a multipurpose centre (including library and police access); elderly person day centre; mental health support centre; management offices for tenants and leaseholders; multipurpose library; retail development; and sheltered housing.

The *Controlling Organisation* will bring together a number of organisations with assets and revenue streams relevant to the estate, and an interest in its successful regeneration – the health authority, LEA, local authority housing, Inner London Probation Service, police, resident's organisation, social services – all of which would transfer or pool their budgets in such a way as to ensure that the management of the estate and services is of maximum benefit to local people. It would be able to operate as a trading company and fulfil the tasks required of a 'single expert commissioning body'.

The controlling organisation will enter into contracts with service providers, whilst enabling local residents and community groups to have a strong influence over the choice of provider and scrutiny over the provider's performance.

The public agencies involved would grant a lease on the buildings for at least 30 years to the community based organisation and make legal arrangements for the integration of the asset owners and revenue providers.

Encouraging neighbourhood PPPs

To date, discussions of PPPs in relation to existing public assets have focused almost entirely on how their latent *commercial* potential could be better exploited (the wider markets initiative discussed in Chapter 5). In this Chapter we have considered how community groups, together with public authorities, could ensure that local assets are utilised to the maximum *social* advantage.

The idea of a 'Community Trust' as set out here has strong appeal. However, it raises a wide range of implementational and accountability issues. In taking forward one aspect of the Government's agenda – on neighbourhood regeneration – it cuts across another – the bundling of single sector PPP projects across localities. It also poses very difficult issues about the willingness and capacity of different public authorities to work together. Earlier chapters have already emphasised the potential for things to go wrong when the 'public' part of a PPP is complicated. But they also pointed out that joint-working across departmental and agency boundaries can often be the key to achieving genuine innovation. 'Community Trusts' provide an exciting way of testing out the extent to which public agencies are able and willing to join together at a very local level in order to allow local people to have more control over public assets and services.

Recommendations

Given the current lack of knowledge on how cross-departmental PPP projects work, pilot projects should be encouraged. The Neighbourhood Renewal Fund should be used to resource and incentivise Community Trusts. These pilots should be targeted on areas that have problems attracting private sector investment (for example, in regeneration schemes); and those that would benefit from a cross-departmental response to particular local problems (such as health, education and housing).

This would necessarily involve pilot public authorities at local, regional and national levels to work in cross-departmental partnerships and 'let go' of asset/revenue ownership rights in the interest of the local community. This process should be championed by PUK working closely with a few pioneering local authorities.

Local Strategic Partnerships should oversee the development of Community Trusts and neighbourhood PPPs in their area. Where Community Trusts are co-terminus (or virtually so) with other partnerships, the LSP should be empowered to bring these initiatives together.

Conclusion

Putting local citizens and civic groups at the heart of the debate on PPPs will help to redefine the relationship between the community and public space. This Chapter has set out a variety of ways through which the consent of local people can be obtained and their views and ideas adopted within partnership arrangements. It represents a challenge to the status quo and suggests the need for public authorities, public service providers and citizens themselves to adapt to new ways of working.

The effective development of 'strategic' partnerships to help improve public services or attain specific regeneration objectives needs to be predicated on public agencies themselves working more closely together: effective *public-public* partnerships are a prerequisite for effective PPPs. Equally, central government needs to stop talking about 'initiative-itis' and 'partnership fatigue' while launching more initiatives and partnerships. The importance of local government in securing the economic, social and environmental well-being of areas needs to be reaffirmed at the same time as local government demonstrates its commitment to letting go of power to local people. Citizens need to be willing and able to use their greater powers of voice in a measured way. Finally, public service providers from all sectors need to learn about and accommodate the diverse interests of local communities.

For too long proposals for enhancing community involvement in public services have lacked bite. If PPPs are really to mark a transformation in public service delivery it is essential that the vision of communities as the agents of partnership moves from lofty aspiration to concrete reality.

Endnotes

1   However, as the discussion of social housing in Chapter 8 pointed out, in many instances the current capital allocation system continues to deny tenants real choice over service providers.

2   Although linking strategic partnerships to initiatives to improvements in outcomes (health, education, employment etc.) has proven difficult, there is some evidence to suggest that bringing together regeneration initiatives can succeed in the delivering the policy goals intended. For instance, a study investigating the impact of an SRB project in Stepney, London, concluded that SRB funded housing renewal (re-housing and refurbishing) contributed to a considerable improvement in residents' health as well as better personal security and informal social networks (Ambrose, 2000).

3   The Local Government Association, whose 'New Commitment to Regeneration' provided a model for LSPs, argued that LSPs should primarily be concerned with the *mainstream* budgets and programmes of the public agencies involved; discretionary pots of funding for LSPs should be of secondary importance (LGA, 2000).

10. Making partnerships accountable

All partnerships give rise to important questions of accountability. PPPs deliver publicly funded services, they have implications for us as citizens as well as users, and we therefore need to be convinced that those charged with delivering them are accountable for what they do. So far in this Report we have put a heavy emphasis on value-for-money and quality as important determinants of whether or not partnerships should be adopted. These are necessary but not sufficient criteria: partnerships also need to be accountable if they are to be desirable.

The last Chapter explored one important component of accountability in its examination of how the interests of local communities and citizens could be better integrated into the process of establishing, monitoring and managing partnerships. This Chapter will argue, first, that accountability is essential for the success of PPPs; second, that accountability for the delivery of public services is already complex and is likely to remain so; third, that partnerships create some new accountability problems and accentuate some existing dilemmas; and finally, that PPPs can also help to improve accountability. Throughout we stress the limited nature of the debate on these issues, the urgent need for policy-makers and the 'PPP community' to start addressing them, and the extent of legal and political uncertainty on many of the questions raised.

Our starting point is the need for new thinking about forms of public accountability and how it is best delivered. The traditional model of accountability, which simply assumes that public services are delivered by public servants who are answerable to ministers, needs revising. The traditional alternative offered by 'privatisers' is to dispense with key forms of public accountability altogether. They seek instead to recast citizens as consumers, to prioritise the role of individual choice over collective deliberation, and to argue that contracts are the primary tools of accountability. In essence, they argue that models of accountability which exist within the private sector can and should be transposed to public services: all services should be judged on results; nothing else is needed.

We adopt a different and altogether more ambitious approach. Public accountability is a pre-condition for the legitimate use of public authority. It is the basis on which citizens are willing to delegate power to others to act on their behalf. It underpins government based on consent. Without proper accountability mechanisms organisations delivering services are not subject to democratic oversight and control, the rights of citizens are uncertain, and services are unlikely to reflect the needs of service users. Accountability is therefore an end as well as a means. For these reasons it needs to sit at the heart of discussions on the modernisation of public services – including the role of PPPs – rather than being introduced as an afterthought. The concept of public accountability[1] should apply to all publicly funded services –

regardless of whether or not they are delivered through public, private or voluntary organisations. Applying inadequate private sector modes of accountability on to the public service sector will not achieve this. But nor will a blind faith in the traditional mechanisms of ministerial responsibility and audit that have been used within the public sector. As forms of public-private working become more common, so too will hybrid forms of accountability that draw on the traditions of both public and private sectors.

In making our argument we maintain that public accountability has to satisfy three principles: transparency, responsibility, and responsiveness. *Transparency* means that organisations delivering public services are required to disclose key information, making their decisions open to public scrutiny. *Responsibility* means that there is clarity as to the organisation or individual that is answerable for particular decisions and courses of action. If responsibility is clear citizens will know where they should go for the purpose of redress if they are dissatisfied either with the service they have received as individual users, or more generally with the standard of the service they have authorised as citizens. Clarity between the roles of purchasers, providers and politicians in securing stated objectives helps identify who is responsible for what. This is the bedrock of any system of public accountability. *Responsiveness* means that services are able to adapt to reflect citizens' needs, priorities, and expectations and give quick redress to individuals when things go wrong: in this way accountability is a vital mechanism for improving service quality.

These three principles need to inform the different kinds of accountability which can be applied to public service provision.

- *Political accountability*: the designation of the appropriate level of democratic or representative body whether at an EU, national, devolved, local or neighbourhood level which has responsibility for commissioning and monitoring particular public services.

- *Legal and financial accountability*: the determination of those provisions of public law, contract law, and auditing and accounting procedures with which the decisions of ministers and their officials must comply.

- *Managerial accountability*: the setting of targets for performance, the provision of incentives, the specification of contracts, and the measurement of results to ensure that managers of particular services are responsible for the quality of services they deliver.

- *Citizen and user accountability*: the provision of information, forms of redress, and opportunities for consultation and participation both to the wider public and to particular groups of service users.

Accountability: the traditional approach

The modern state can be seen as a chain of relationships through which authority is delegated; in relation to central government, authority flows from citizens to MPs, MPs to ministers, ministers to civil servants, and civil servants to a variety of service providers. The chain is intended to create a clear line of responsibility. Citizens, MPs, ministers, and civil servants all in turn act as principals, to whom the level below is accountable; MPs are accountable to citizens, ministers to MPs, and civil servants to ministers. Citizens are the starting point of the chain, but they are also its end-point. Not only do citizens (ultimately) authorise and fund the provision of services, they are also the users of the services. Ministerial accountability (see below) is the dominant device through which citizens are supposed to hold those that act on their behalf responsible for their actions. It has become extremely opaque because of the long and complex chain of relationships that now make up the modern state.

The traditional model of accountability in the UK has been derived from a particular approach to public administration. This emphasises the divide between the public sector and the private sector and puts emphasis on political accountability – that of elected representatives to a legislature – as the most important form of accountability for the public services, supplemented by various forms of legal and financial accountability. This model has several key features in relation to central government:

- *Ministers are responsible*. Ministers report to Parliament and civil servants report to ministers. Ministers are at the apex of the hierarchy of offices in their departments. Each official reports to the official immediately above, and the most senior officials report to the minister.

- *Policy and administration are distinct functions*. The formulation of policy is the preserve of ministers who are drawn from Parliament and answerable to it. Implementation of the policy is the responsibility of the civil service.

- *Administration is organised bureaucratically*. The civil service is hierarchical, impersonal, and rule-governed, in order to maximise organisational efficiency. Every official has a clearly defined function to perform and each office works according to prescribed rules, and this minimises any departure from impartiality and objectivity in the work of each department.

- *Service providers (and assets) are publicly owned*. Both the inputs into services and the mechanisms through which services are actually delivered are controlled by government. This is supposed to ensure direct government control over service outcomes.

- *Decisions are open to public scrutiny.* The sector is 'public' because all work is supposed to be open to scrutiny and audit.

- *The norm of public service governs public administration.* Officials see themselves as public servants, acting in the public interest rather than for private gain, and acknowledge a public service mission.

Of course this stylised model portrays an ideal more than the reality. Critiques of it have pointed out that in practice the line between policy and administration was often blurred; administrative co-ordination was often flawed; decisions were often secret and not disclosed; and public officials sometimes pursued their own private agendas as well as the public interest. According to the critics many of these problems were exacerbated because the traditional model of accountability put a low premium on managerial accountability in relation to the performance of services. Public managers often would not be set clear performance objectives and even when they were they lacked the operational autonomy required for them to deliver on these goals. Central departments and politicians found it hard to resist the temptation to micro-manage service providers. Forms of citizen accountability often remained limited. Public information on services was often lacking and few channels existed for citizens to influence directly the planning, management and monitoring of services. Accountability became focused on compliance with procedures rather than on ensuring high quality results.

The growth of non-departmental public agencies which increased the expertise available to government and prevented central departments becoming overloaded has also challenged the ability of ministers to exercise any effective control over their areas of nominal responsibility. This process has greatly accelerated in the last twenty years with the adoption of the Next Steps agencies, the embrace of the 'new public management' (which has promoted the separation of many policy and implementation functions), the growth of alternative forms of service delivery and the greater stress that has been placed on collaborative working across different public, private and voluntary agencies. In this new world it is exceptionally hard to pinpoint exactly where ministerial responsibility really ends or begins.

Does this matter? Our view is that it does. Public accountability cannot be achieved without appropriate political and legal mechanisms to hold public authorities responsible. But it also needs effective forms of managerial accountability and citizen accountability which tend to be focused on outcomes not just procedures. Finding approaches to accountability which put a focus on delivering outcomes while also ensuring that citizens are treated in a non-arbitrary and non-discriminatory way is the key to revising existing accounting procedures. The question that we need to address is whether the use of partnerships makes this more or less difficult?

Does partnership pose new accountability dilemmas?

While PPPs do not raise entirely new accountability issues for public services, there are some particular issues associated with them that need to be addressed. It is also true that though they did not create the problems with traditional forms of accountability, the arrival of PPPs makes it even harder for the cloak of ministerial responsibility to hide increasing concerns about accountability in the modern extended state. In this respect the growth of partnerships accentuates and exposes existing accountability problems rather than creating new ones. But partnerships can also help identify new accountability solutions; not least because the distinction between the commissioning role of public authorities and the delivery role of providers can help to increase managerial accountability, generate transparency and ensure that public authorities are well-placed to ensure that services focus on the needs and expectations of citizens (Harden, 1992).

Political accountability

An overriding concern about the growth of PPPs is that this will shrink the realm of politics; the scope of 'operational' issues will increase and be delegated to private bodies which are not publicly accountable in the traditional sense. The greater use of long-term contracts for service provision, for example, is often thought to restrict the ability of elected politicians to make a difference. Partnerships are said to restrict the scope that exists for 'incremental policy-making' (Aronson, 1997). The danger is that citizens are unable to exercise one of their key rights, that of getting their elected representatives to act on their behalf to shape the decisions over how public services are provided and improved over time. These concerns are particularly acute if the public body responsible for managing the relationship with a private partner is *not* the same body that negotiated the contract in the first place (as happened with the PPP for London Underground). This is a recipe for confused accountability, the emergence of a blame culture between different public bodies, and public disenchantment.

A different challenge is posed by the growth of strategic partnerships, which offer the private and voluntary sector involvement in the *decision-making process* rather than service delivery. As Chapter 9 pointed out, often these partnerships are 'advisory' in nature and therefore tend not to raise such acute accountability issues. Sometimes, however, they are directly responsible for public funds, for instance when the 'responsible body' in a Single Regeneration Budget (SRB) partnership is not a public authority. As the use of these 'executive' strategic partnerships increases in importance, so will questions of their legitimacy: should non-elected bodies and individuals be permitted to exercise control over public funds and directly influence policy-making? The constitutional purist will see this an affront to the principle that elected officials accountable to Parliament or a local representative body should retain control over these matters.

These concerns invite a number of responses. First, any large project with fixed costs will result in tomorrow's politicians being constrained by yesterday's choices. PPPs are not exceptional in this regard, though they can accentuate the problem if they include binding contracts for service provision over the life of the project. The point here is that PPPs should be designed to incorporate flexibility – whether through the establishment of break-points at which services can be altered or the creation of decision-making bodies on which both partners are represented (see Chapter 8). If flexibility of this type is not achievable, or adds greatly to the cost of the project, then the partnership option is likely to be the wrong one. Second, instituting a clear demarcation of responsibility between policy-makers and service providers can assist elected politicians in focusing on representing their constituents rather than directly managing service organisations. Finally, it is all too easy to contrast the alleged complexity of the accountability relationships that emerge from partnerships with the clearer set of relationships that are said to exist when services are delivered by the public sector. When services are delivered by an in-house organisation different types of accountability problem exist: establishing political and managerial responsibility (and transparency) within hierarchical government organisations is far from straightforward. Accountability problems exist whether public services are governed through contracts or administrative hierarchies: the former can help generate clarity but may lead to a rigid approach based on formal provisions; the latter may allow for more flexibility but has tended to lead to public managers being held to account for inputs and process rather than delivering outcomes.

In relation to the concerns over private and voluntary sector involvement in the policy process, the constitutional pluralist would point out that the old model provided a form of political accountability which was increasingly fictional, and that the growing role of private, voluntary, and community groups helps energise policy-making. It can also facilitate both top-down and bottom-up forms of accountability – indicators of a more active and healthy civil society. Rather than seek to force these new governance forms into the old model of political accountability, the goal should be to support new decision-making bodies with public resources and public recognition so long as they are committed to acting transparently and to ensuring that their role and remit is clearly understood by the communities they work within.

Legal and financial accountability

A key concern with the growth of the public service sector is that is will undermine the notion that public accountability is ensured precisely because service providers must act according to statutory legislation and are subject to public law, audit and parliamentary scrutiny.[2] The private and voluntary sectors do not have to conform to the same rules and norms. They are, of course, legally accountable in the sense that providers are subject to company or charity law, codes of corporate governance, reporting requirements and auditing. It is also true that private and voluntary bodies involved in public service provision are subject to the private law governing contracts – they must meet the terms of their contracts, or suffer penalties. But the concern is that this represents a highly diluted form of accountability.

Public law and private enterprise

What is unclear is the extent to which this dichotomous approach towards legal accountability – which has public law and the public sector on one side, and private law and the private sector on the other, is starting to break down. This uncertainty stems from different views over the extent to which public law does now, and should in the future, apply to private and voluntary sector providers working within the public service sector.

One view favours limiting the scope of public law; maintaining the presumption in favour of using private law to govern the relationship between government and providers. Doing anything else would invite judicial intervention into the affairs of private and voluntary organisations and start a process through which the 'frontiers of the state' roll forward (Oliver, 2000). Defenders of this view point out that key public law measures such as judicial review can still apply to the public authority's decision to *enter into* a contract but not directly to the activities of the private service provider. It should be the responsibility of the public authority, rather than the courts, to ensure that contracts include provisions that ensure adequate performance and protection of rights. Support for this view can be found in recent cases which have suggested that judicial review does not apply to bodies which derive their authority from contracting with a public authority (for instance a residential care home and a local authority).[3]

The alternative view is that if the same system of public accountability is to apply regardless of who is delivering a service then public law needs to extend beyond the parameters of the public sector into the wider arena of public service organisations. All organisations wielding discretionary power should be subject to the same general principles of law (for example, to act with legality, fairness, and rationality) regardless of whether they are formally public or private bodies. If this is not the case then the growth of PPPs will diminish the domain in which basic constitutional protections apply. Supporters of this view point out that increasingly the test used in these matters is not whether or not an organisation is 'public' but whether it is performing a 'public function' (De Smith *et al*, 1995).[4]

There are a number of clear examples of public law being extended in this way:

- In some instances the courts have decided that judicial review *can* be extended to the activities of private bodies operating in the public services. For instance,

City Technology Colleges – which, unlike community schools, are legally independent entities (see Chapter 7) – have been subject to judicial review.[5] This is on the basis that they are created with the Secretary of State's approval, they are publicly funded, and if they were not subject to judicial review then parents with a grievance would be left without a legal remedy.[6]

- The Human Rights Act (HRA) which came into force in 2000 applies to bodies 'whose functions are functions of a public nature' and requires them to act in a way which is compatible the European Convention on Human Rights. It is important to stress that the HRA only applies to the *public functions* of these organisations: thus a company running a prison would be required to comply with the Convention in relation to its treatment of prisoners, but not in relation to any security work it carried out for a private contractor.[7]

- The Freedom of Information Act which will come into force in 2002 gives the Secretary of State a discretionary power to designate as 'public authorities' any organisation which appears to exercise functions of a public nature (discussed below).

- The European Commission's approach towards what it calls 'services of general interest' is consistent with this interpretation of the wider reach of public law. It has argued that: 'It is all too easy to treat public sector and public service as synonymous and fail to distinguish the legal status of a service provider from the nature of the service being provided... European policy is concerned with the general interest, with what services are provided and on what terms, not with the status of the body providing them'.[8] On a narrower point, the European Court of Justice has held that the 'direct effect' of directives could apply to a body, whatever its legal status, which is responsible for providing a public service under the control of the State. This has, for instance, meant that the privatised company British Gas has been construed as a public authority (Foster *v* British Gas 1990). It should be pointed out that, though significant, this ruling has no direct implications for the application of judicial review under national law (as is sometimes contended).

What this discussion reveals is the extent to which there is no settled legal doctrine on the precise application of public law or judicial review to private bodies performing a public function (or for that matter the common law definition of 'public function'). As the notion of the public service sector becomes more established so these issues will become more important and new rules are likely to emerge.

Accountability avoidance

A second concern is that by introducing a range of service providers from outside the public sector it may be easier for public service organisations to shirk responsibility that would clearly belong with them if there was a single public sector provider. An example of this occurred in Australia when an employee of a private company operating under contract for the Post Office allegedly damaged a pensioner's post box. Australia Post claimed that they were not liable for the damage, similarly the post company denied responsibility. In the end the pensioner who could not afford to sue the company successfully used the Ombudsman to gain compensation from Australia Post. One solution to this type of problem is to ensure either that the contract with the private supplier is drawn clearly enough so that the private company has to accept responsibility and to insist upon simple and accessible grievance procedures; another would be to identify clearly the public authority as the responsible body.[9] It is vital, however, that the public should know where ultimate legal responsibility is lodged.

Unfortunately this is not always the case. The difficulty is that because the legal environment has evolved in an *ad hoc* way the position relating to the responsibility of public authorities varies considerably (Newdick, 2000). Under the De-regulation and Contracting-Out Act 1994 public authorities are identified as the bodies that will be held liable for a failing service provided by a third party.[10] Responsibility is therefore clear (though this calls into question the extent to which risk is genuinely being transferred to private providers). This approach allows an aggrieved citizen to take action against a public authority who in turn should seek compensation from the provider according to contractual terms. However, this Act only applies to particular services; in other situations a different legal regime will apply.

Related to this is the possibility of private sector bankruptcy making it hard for the public sector to ever transfer real responsibility to private partners.[11] Regardless of how a service is provided ministers will be keen to ensure continuity of provision and are likely to feel that, whatever the formal provisions of a contract, they still carry 'despatch box risk'. In some instances, this may lead them to take measures to avoid the possibility of a PPP going bankrupt. This is particularly likely to be the case where there is a limited pool of alternative providers or where government itself does not retain an in-house capacity. In these instances private providers may alter their course of behaviour on the basis that government will be likely to prop them up if things go wrong.

Averting these potential problems requires clearly specified contracts that, as far as possible, assign legal responsibility between the partners, makes clear how under-performing providers will be replaced, and establish systems of arbitration which allow for disputes over responsibility to be speedily resolved. It also suggests that government should be confident about the financial security of its partners.

Related to this are concerns over financial accountability. Public accountability means making key decisions about the use of public resources in an open way and allowing others to scrutinise these decisions. In relation to PPPs this raises the issue of the transparency of the methodology used to develop a Public Sector Comparator (PSC) constructed to provide a benchmark against which to assess whether or not a proposed partnership offers value-for-money. At the very least there should be no more cases like the National Air Traffic System (NATS) where no PSC was constructed. Moreover, as discussed in Chapter 4, the PSC should be regularly discussed throughout any negotiation process and should be fully disclosed at the appropriate time. In very large projects it may be wise to allow for a final verification of the proposed contract by an independent outside body. In the case of a local authority contract, that body would report directly to council members. However, transparency should extend beyond the formation of PSCs. A key issue is that audit bodies should have access to all relevant financial and performance data to allow them to make an independent assessments of partnerships.

Managerial accountability

One of the potential advantages of partnerships is the additional clarity that specifying desired outcomes or outputs and allocating responsibilities can bring to service delivery. However, as Chapter 2 pointed out, a common attribute of partnerships is that it is impossible to specify fully the way in which the relationship and the services it produces will evolve. As circumstances change, so the partners to long-term contracts will need to fill in the gaps of the original contract, revise outdated provisions, and challenge themselves to come up with new types of provision. Regardless of how well a partnership contract is written it cannot be the only mechanism through which accountability is achieved: as John Stewart put it 'government cannot be reduced to a series of contracts' (Stewart, 1993).

Indeed, imposing responsibility on a single agency where this is inappropriate will not enhance accountability: there will be many instances where responsibility for delivering outcomes has to be shared. Often an under-performing service will result from a combination of poorly specified contracts, poor delivery by providers, and poor contract management by both parties (this appears to be the case in relation to the performance of housing benefit contracts in London and elsewhere). Shared responsibility will be made more explicit where mechanisms are created to allow public authorities to agree to changes with providers in the nature of services over the life of a contract. The development of these governance mechanisms, such as the partnerships boards discussed in Chapter 8, can play a crucial role in ensuring that the public interest is preserved but they inevitably lead to a degree of fuzziness in the allocation of responsibility between partners. The challenge then is to ensure that any such body has a clear remit and membership, operates transparently and is subject to scrutiny.

Another issue concerns the extent to which current forms of management accountability put an undue emphasis on rule compliance, box-ticking and mistake-avoidance and in doing so undermine one of the rationales for adopting partnerships: innovation in delivering services. If providers are to be innovators, they have to take some risks, not all of which will turn out well. This suggests the need for clarity on the types of risk that are acceptable and the impact that accountability procedures have on willingness to innovate.

In some areas of public services – for instance where safety concerns are paramount – regulatory and accountability procedures must be stringent and a precautionary approach must prevail (though even here we would want service providers to have incentives to innovate in order to improve safety procedures). In other areas it will be more appropriate to ensure that accountability procedures do not unduly incline providers towards avoiding any course of action with which there is a degree of risk. Getting the proper balance in accountability is a key issue for PPPs and more broadly for joined-up governance.

This problem is easily stated, but not so easily solved. It is certainly the case that the Public Audit Forum (PAF) – which brings together the National Audit Office, the Audit Commission and the Scottish and Northern Irish auditing bodies – needs to step up its work on the impact of accountability mechanisms on innovation. In addition departments and public authorities should act upon PAF's guidelines for encouraging 'well-thought through' risk-taking (PAF, 1999). Striking the right balance on accountability and innovation will rely upon learning lessons from previous partnerships as well as developing governance structures that can fill the gap between contractual provisions and the formal mechanisms of accountability represented by Parliament, audit and the courts. There are no easy solutions here, and mistakes will continue to be made. What is vital is that there should be maximum transparency to ensure full and open debate of the issues in each case, so that appropriate lessons can be learned and better guidelines adopted.

Citizen and user accountability

Some aspects of PPPs could help to enhance transparency in relation to public services while others may impede this. The benign side of PPPs relates to the detailed specification of the terms of the contract. Once the contract has been agreed, then the service standards should be published, accessible to everyone in the public domain, including the users of the service. Service users and managers should all be aware of the level of service that is expected. In some instances this performance management regime will result in private providers being obliged to meet (and report on) a wider range of performance targets than do their public sector counterparts.[12] The emergence of a diversity of providers should also allow for the production of comparative performance data; more effective forms of benchmarking across different types of public service organisation; and ultimately, under-performing providers to be replaced by a more attractive alternative.

The more problematic side is that it is very difficult to make the phase of negotiating the contracts fully transparent, because there will be rival bids, and much of the information in those bids is likely to be deemed commercially sensitive. Commercial confidentiality can be used as an excuse for minimising the transparency. We are keen to ensure that the Cabinet Offices guidelines on contracting, which state that 'commercial confidentiality should not be used as a cloak to deny the public's right to know', are put into practice (Cabinet Office, 1997). Evidence we received from a number of trade unions suggested serious concerns about the misuse of commercial confidentiality clauses. On a more positive note the disclosure arrangements that have been introduced for PFI projects in the NHS – where Strategic Outline Cases for projects have to be published and released to key stakeholders within a month of approval – appear to be a step in the right direction.

The provisions of the Freedom of Information Act (which comes into force in 2002) are relevant here. The aim of the Act is to provide citizens with the right to obtain information from public authorities. The draft applies to designated public authorities and will give the Secretary of State discretion to designate any group who appears to 'exercise functions of a public nature or is providing under a contract made with a public authority any service whose provision is a function of that authority'.[13] If the notion of a 'public function', as discussed above, is applied, then public service providers should fall under the Freedom of Information Act. However, whether or not this is the case will be up to the discretion of the Secretary of State – which does not provide a sound basis for guaranteeing citizens' access to information from key service providers.

Finally, we need to ensure that we avoid the experience of some other countries where the growth of contracting has on occasion led to a levelling down towards standards of disclosure used in the private sector rather than a levelling up to those of the public sector. For instance, in Australia state-owned public enterprises have been exempted from the Freedom of Information regime on the basis that this provides equality of treatment with private sector competitors (Aronson, 1997). The requirement should rather be that the public service sector converges on the highest available standards.

Making partnerships accountable: the way forward

Our starting point is that all public service providers – regardless of their legal status – should be subject to the same standards of accountability. We agree with those who say that providing public service is a 'privilege' that brings with it responsibilities (Straw,

2000). It would be perverse, therefore, if governments could use partnerships as a way of weakening public accountability obligations such as compliance with key statutory provisions aimed at improving the rights of citizens in relation to public authorities and service providers. Instead, what is needed is acceptance of a new framework for public accountability which enshrines the highest standards and the best practice that currently exist. Proposals for developing such a framework to make PPPs accountable are best bundled together under the three principles of accountability we have identified – transparency, responsibility, and responsiveness.

Transparency

A level playing field should apply in relation to standards of disclosure from all public service providers, regardless of the sector from which they are drawn. Public audit bodies should be confident that they can access the necessary information for conducting proper value-for-money studies of how effectively public money is being used by all public service providers. In order to ensure access public auditing bodies must have a statutory right to access information on public contracts over and above a certain size.[14] It is important, however, that this right is discharged in a responsible and measured way. Accountability is not cost-free: it involves time and resources. Hence guidelines should be negotiated between audit bodies and representatives of private and voluntary providers.

The Freedom of Information Act needs to be applied in an inclusive way which covers public service providers and is not dependent upon the discretion of the Secretary of the State. The Act does not specify any timeframe for the Secretary of State to decide which providers should be covered by the Act – so it could be years before private companies are included as providers delivering public services under a PPP/PFI contract. Similarly, to ensure that commercial confidentiality does not restrict transparency the current framework that applies in the NHS for disclosure on PFI deals should be extended to other public authorities.

Recommendations

Private and voluntary providers must accept that higher standards of disclosure and transparency apply in the public service sector than in the rest of the economy.

Performance data on services provided through partnerships should always be made publicly available.

The methodology behind the construction of a Public Sector Comparator should be disclosed.

The mandatory framework for disclosing information that currently exists in the NHS should be extended to all PFI projects. PFI projects should always stipulate the stage in the process at which information will be made publicly available.

The National Audit Office should have statutory powers to access information on private providers relating to public contracts above a certain size.

The role of Parliamentary committees, both in the Commons and House of Lords, in scrutinising the activities of PPPs should be developed.[18]

At the local level the new forms of scrutiny committee (emerging following the Local Government 2000 Act) should be used to examine the performance of local PPPs.

Responsibility

If responsibility can be side-stepped then the whole notion of the public service sector will be compromised. Particular problems can arise when more than one public purchaser is involved in a contract and the relationship between them is unclear. Furthermore, having one public body negotiate a contract when a different body will be responsible for managing that contract – as happened with the PPP for London Underground – is a recipe for trouble. Another way in which individuals or organisations could be held responsible is through the application of public law to PPPs. Moving to a situation in which public service providers have to reflect the full rights of individuals as citizens as well as service users will be challenging. However, steps in this direction have already been taken: the Human Rights Act provides an example of how the domain of public law can and should encompass a wider public service sector.

Recommendations

The responsibility of the different bodies in a partnership should always be made explicit in the contract. Public authorities are always responsible for ensuring that citizens will not suffer as a result of contractual deficiencies.

Often it will be appropriate for the public body to be the legally responsible authority for citizens' grievances. If so contracts must be designed in such a way as to ensure that public authorities can claim against providers for failure to perform their duties.

The status and areas of competence of decision-making bodies set up within PPP contracts (such as 'partnership boards') should always be made explicit.

Contracts need to set out clearly the actions that public purchasers can take to enforce agreed terms – this is particularly relevant when there is more than one public body involved in purchasing services.

The public body that will be held to account legally and politically for managing a contract should always be the body that establishes that contract in the first place.

The application of judicial review to service providers who are not in the public sector needs to be clarified. The test for whether public law should be applied should be the nature of the function being performed by a public service organisation rather than its legal structure.

Responsiveness

The principle of responsiveness is at the heart of the modernising agenda for public services. Most of the means for achieving a responsive system of public services have been discussed elsewhere. Chapter 8 discussed how partnership arrangements need to be structured so as to ensure continuous improvement and Chapter 9 set out the different ways in which citizens and service users can be involved in the commissioning, monitoring, and governance of partnership arrangements. Our approach is based on the view that accountability mechanisms are an important quality-control mechanism. They are early warning systems for when things go wrong. Putting responsiveness into action means developing mechanisms by which the opinions of citizens can first shape the configuration of services and then act as a spur for continuous improvement. It also means having clear incentives for high levels of performance and speedy compensation for unacceptable levels of provision.

Recommendations

All PPPs contracts should clearly set out the grievance procedures through which individual citizens have redress.

The Public Audit Forum should undertake a 'lessons learnt' study of the impact of auditing practices on the level of innovation in PPP projects.

Conclusion

This Chapter has set out how public accountability can be applied to the wider public service sector. It has argued that involvement of private and voluntary providers in public services need not and should not lead to a dilution of public accountability and has set out a number of reforms which will help ensure that this is the case. It has also acknowledged that, on the one hand, traditional approaches to accountability – which were already problematic – may be further stretched by some PPPs; whilst on the other, partnerships can be a powerful device for bringing greater clarity to different roles and responsibilities, improving transparency and enhancing responsiveness to service users.

The accountability agenda we have developed in relation to the public service sector is very different from the privatisers' agenda that was explored in Chapter 1. Their aspiration was to develop a new market model of citizenship and accountability in which individuals would discipline service providers through their own choices in the marketplace. This approach has traditionally been counterposed to a constitutional and democratic model of citizenship and accountability which relies upon the application of rules and norms of public law and administration.

In the past these two approaches have been set out as mutually exclusive. It has been assumed that if services are provided through contract then the relevant form of accountability will be based upon 'exit' strategies, whereas public sector forms of provision will be held accountable through direct public ownership and democratic 'voice'.

This traditional polarisation is no longer adequate. As hybrid forms of public service organisation become more common, so the need for hybrid models of accountability will grow. One example of this was set out in Chapter 9 where we discussed the potential of 'democratic contestability' – which involves service users exercising their voice to shape, prod and ultimately evict inadequate service providers. At the same time providers will be encouraged by financial pressures, and/or the watchful eye of governing bodies, to deliver high quality services.

Another development is the move towards the use of partnership boards as a means through which public sector representatives play a role in monitoring performance and proposing new forms of provision, while also acting as guardian of the public interest. Yet another example comes in the form of the growing extension of public law principles to private bodies – a clear example of the norms of the public domain shaping behaviour in the wider public service sector. The fact that providers can ultimately be indirectly held to account by public purchasers deciding to purchase services from elsewhere should not preclude citizens themselves from directly being able to influence services.

In all these ways the shift towards pluralism in procurement and/or provision which PPPs represent can go hand in hand with more diverse and effective forms of accountability.

Endnotes

1   Accountability is a term used in several different ways, but at its heart is a relationship between a *principal* who commissions a service and an *agent* who carries it out. For public services in modern democracies the principals are citizens who require a public service. Through their representatives in Parliament (or local government or indeed a neighbourhood level association) they authorise the service and the funding for it. An agency is created to deliver that service. At the national level that agency is accountable to Parliament for the quality of the service and how the funds provided have been spent. Agents are 'held to account' by being required to render *in public* an account of their actions and also by providing redress or suffering penalties when mistakes are made. In this way agents are made to accept responsibility both for how well they have carried out the original instructions of their principal and also for the outcomes of their actions. The purpose of procedures for accountability is to ensure that as far as possible the distance between the interests of principals and agents is as small as possible, so that the outcomes broadly conform with the original expectations and intentions of the principal.

2   See Freedland (1998) for a discussion of this. He contends that the shift away from the traditional citizen-state relationship in public services has created a 'crisis in legal analysis'.

3   See Servite (2001). In this case it was held that judicial review did not apply to a residential care home as the source of the private body's powers derived from contract rather than statute. The relationship between the service provider and the council was held to be purely commercial – and as a result any dispute would have to be resolved by private law.

4   Much of the debate of this point stems from *Datafin* (1987).

5   See Brunyate and Hunt (1989). Also see Hunt (1997) for discussion.

6   Against this, the courts have recently held that judicial review could not be applied to the decision of a private provider of residential accommodation (working under contract to Wandsworth council) to close the home they operate.

7   The rights covered by the European Convention on Human Rights are wide ranging, extending from a responsibility on the company to protect life, to provide a fair hearing and avoid degrading treatment, to protection of the rights to privacy, freedom of speech and enjoyment of property. Any individual who believes that the company has infringed their rights under the Convention can initiate proceedings against the company in court and, if successful, obtain a range of remedies including financial compensation. The individual can also rely on the Convention in the course of any other proceedings involving the company, such as a negligence action.

8   European Commission (1996) It should be pointed that these services of general interest are different to some of those considered in this Report in that they focus on postal services, telecommunications and other utilities.

9   Australian Industry Commission (1996). Some public authorities, such as the state of Western Australia have decided that they should always remain fully responsible for a service regardless of the nature of the provider.

10   S. 72 (2) of the 1994 Act. Similarly the European Ombudsman has stated that the Commission remains responsible for the quality of administration carried out by outside bodies under contract: see case 630/6.6.96/CJ/UK/IJH, European Ombudsman's 1997 Annual Report.

11   Though see Chapter 5 for a discussion of 'public sector bankruptcy'.

12   This is the case for private companies operating prisons. They are required to meet detailed performance targets, specified in each contract, in addition to those performance targets that are common to both public and private sectors, for example Key Performance Indicators.

13   Freedom of Information Act s5 (HMSO, 2000c)

14   This is line with the findings of the recent Sharman Report (2001).

15   This was proposed in a CPPP submission (Bogdanor, 2001).

V:
Conclusion

11. Partnership 2010

This Report seeks to extricate public private partnerships from an ideological morass. Throughout our goal has been to identify if, when and how partnerships can help deliver publicly funded services and achieve progressive policy outcomes. The fact that a group of people on the centre-left think partnerships have a significant role to play in our public services may be noteworthy in the UK but would generate little comment in many other countries. Once again, it is worth recalling that many of the societies that see a diverse set of public service providers as a natural state of affairs have levels of public investment and social provision that those on the centre-left in the UK can only envy.

The Report identifies the weak and the strong arguments for partnerships, explores where they are working and where they are not, examines where they should go next and the new challenges they must meet. Though we think partnership has a role to play it must not be presented as a panacea for the problems within our public services. Partnership will be one of many approaches to public service reform. Hence our emphasis has been on realistic next steps rather than grand blueprints. But in concluding our Report we want to describe a destination which all those who believe PPPs have a role to play in improving our public services should want to reach. Assuming – and it is a big assumption – that we have a decade of progressive government, continuing a steady but sustainable increase in public investment, that is willing to think boldly about the ways in which PPPs might evolve, what would be the characteristics of partnerships in 2010?

Quality rather than cost-cutting

The association between private or voluntary provision of public services and cost-cutting will have ended. Partnerships will not be something that politicians do to make cost-savings during an economic down-turn or when departmental budgets are reduced. They will be an established way of providing high quality services. The contribution that expertise and investment from outside the public sector can make to innovation and responsiveness will be widely recognised across the political spectrum and not be a source of contention. The private and voluntary sector will seek to maintain this consensus by promoting best practice and guarding its reputation for quality.

A grown up debate

Rather than the private sector believing its interests lie in public sector retrenchment, its role in delivery will see it joining forces with those arguing for sustained investment in high quality universal public services. It will work with, not against, government.

The tendency that has existed in the UK to link diversity in provision to privatisation and the rolling back of government will have been broken: partnership will no longer be seen as privatisation by stealth. There will be clarity over when and why partnerships have a role. Politicians will no longer push the argument that PPPs are simply a device to increase investment off-balance-sheet. Nor will they imply that it is fine for the private sector to be involved in public services so long as they do not make a profit. Partnership will not be pushed into areas where there is not evidence that they perform for ideological reasons. Decisions to use PPPs will be reversed if there is evidence that the public sector is the better option. There will be a recognition that though partnerships can work well they can also fail (as they sometimes will) or be out-performed by in-house provision. The tendency to pick one best model of partnership for public enterprise and promote it at the expense of others will have been replaced by a willingness to have a public discussion about the strengths and weaknesses of different approaches.

A self-confident and discerning public sector

Public mangers will have the experience and confidence to allow more innovative partnership models to emerge. Those managers destined for the top of their profession will have been involved in both commissioning and providing services. More broadly, public service career paths will have emerged in which aspirational managers move between public, private and voluntary sectors. The cultural and professional walls that separate the different sectors will have become porous.

Public authorities will become more agile at commissioning services across departmental and geographical boundaries, shaping them instead around the life styles of citizens and the needs of localities. The standardisation and uniformity of models and contracts used in the early years of PPPs will give way to a greater capacity and willingness of public authorities to adopt flexible models tailored to local circumstances. Public managers will have real discretion. The PPP/PFI process will not be used as a covert way of centralising decisions on capital investment. Nor will central government set up area-based partnerships as a means of by-passing local government.

Government will have mastered the skill of creating strong links with a diverse set of public service organisations rather than being dependent upon a few usual suspects for the provision of services. Indeed, it will be vigilant in ensuring that localities or public authorities never become dependent on single firms: Britain will not be made up of a string of 'one company towns'. Public authorities will make sure that they are not locked into contracts with single providers from which they cannot escape. They will be confident that they can fulfil their role as guardian of the public interest through the establishment of effective governance bodies within PPPs. The public sector will remain in control. The regulatory landscape will evolve and common systems will apply across the whole public service sector ensuring that all providers working under public contract have to meet high standards. These changes will have convinced public authorities that they no longer have to specify the inputs into a contract in order to secure accountability and high quality outcomes.

The public sector will itself be a world-class provider across many service areas, not least because of the spur it will have received from the wider array of private and voluntary providers that have emerged. Government will be much better at sharing information and using its collective muscle to spread good practice and drive out those who under-perform. It will be a demanding partner. As the most significant and sophisticated purchaser of services in the economy government will be intolerant of poor quality. Leading-edge private and voluntary organisations will be keen to have their brand associated with the public sector.

A diverse and responsible set of private and third sector partners

Public sector commissioners will face a rich and diverse menu of partnership options which span a range of public, private and voluntary organisations. All providers will be familiar with and accepting of the forms of accountability and disclosure that working in the public service sector involves. A feature of these relationships will be the development of providers whose reputation is premised upon quality and a commitment to a public service ethos. Clear contracts will still be necessary – and they will be rewarded on a competitive basis – but all parties will be more able and willing to work closely together. Trust and reputation rather than ever more detailed legal provisions will be the driver of this more collaborative approach. Long-term partnerships will involve powerful governance bodies that allow the relationship between public and private sectors to evolve flexibly over time. Alliances of leading edge organisations will come to government with proposals on how public services can be improved. The market place for partnerships will be welcoming to new entrants, particularly those from the community sector. The increasing use of joint-ventures and long-term strategic agreements will, at least at the edges, blur the boundaries between the public, private and voluntary sectors. New legal vehicles will emerge – something between the plc, trusts, and public bodies – which are better placed to accommodate the hybrid organisational forms that are emerging within the public service sector.

Good employment

Employees will be confident about how they will be treated by private providers. Public money will not be spent on providers who treat employees badly. Partnerships will not be used as a way of reducing pay and terms or conditions. This will be achieved through public authorities focusing on quality, being selective about who they contract with and, if need be, through changes in the law. Public service provider organisations will lead the way in progressive employment practices ranging from family friendly working to employee share ownership. Public service workers will define themselves less by the legal form of the organisation they happen to work for and more by the type of service they provide.

Putting the 'public' into public private partnerships

Partnerships will not seen as an obstacle to citizen participation in decision-making. The reverse will be the case: PPPs will pushing forward the frontiers of citizen accountability. Partnership proposals will be based upon the consent of local people. Public assets will be managed creatively to maximise their social value to citizens. It will be the norm rather than the exception for communities and citizens to be involved in the governance of their public services and spaces. Commissioning practices will ensure that contracts are based upon the outcomes that communities themselves have chosen. Citizens will have a louder voice in selecting, advising, monitoring and if need be firing service providers. More generally, citizens will receive full access to information on the nature of providers, the level of services they will receive, and be sure of the forms of redress they can rely on. High levels of public accountability will apply evenly across the whole public service sector.

The way ahead

Is this destination ever likely to be reached? Many would say not. We could be accused of having an unrealistic vision – detached from political reality and impossible to implement. The reason we disagree is because so much of what we describe already exists in one form or another in other countries or in microcosm in the UK. We also believe that this is a vision in tune with the feelings of the great majority of people in the UK who remain supportive of universal services but anxious that their quality and responsiveness improve.

It is true, of course, that that any number of factors could prevent this destination from being reached. It will require a commitment to sustainable increases in public funding, a desire to make the case for partnership, a willingness to admit the flaws of some recent models of PPPs and a determination to make a reality of the rhetoric of evidence based policy. It will also require action to be taken now. High quality and popular universal public services need to be a defining feature of Britain in 2010: the sooner we get partnerships right, the more likely this is to be the case.

Abbreviations

AC	Audit Commission
ACD	Appeal Court Division
BBC	British Broadcasting Corporation
BNFL	British Nuclear Fuels Limited
BV	Best Value
BVPP	Best Value Performance Plan
BVR	Best Value Review
CCT	Compulsory Competitive Tendering
CIPFA	The Chartered Institute of Public Finance and Consultancy
CMLR	Common Market Law Review
CTC	City Technology College
CTRL	Channel Tunnel Rail Link
DBF	Design Build Finance
DBFO	Design Build Finance Operate
DBGO	Design Build Guarantee Operate
DERA	Defence and Evaluation Research Agency
DETR	Department of the Environment, Transport and the Regions
DfEE	Department for Education and Employment
DoH	Department for Health
DSS	Department for Social Security
DTI	Department for Trade and Industry
EAZ	Education Action Zones
EIB	European Investment Bank
FCE	Finished Consultancy Episodes
GGNB	General Government Net Borrowing
GORs	Government Office for the Regions
HA	Health Authority
HAZ	Health Action Zones
HiMP	Health Improvement Programme
HMP	Her Majesty's Prison
HMSO	Her Majesty's Stationery Office
HMT	Her Majesty's Treasury
HRA	Human Rights Act
ICT	Information Communication Technology
IDeA	Improvement and Development Agency
IHA	Independent Healthcare Association
ISP	Intregrated Service Provider
JVC	Joint Venture Company
KPI	Key Performance Indicator
LA	Local Authority
LEA	Local Education Authority
LMS	Local Management of Schools

LSP	Local Strategic Partnership
LU	London Underground
MRI	Magnetic Resonance Imaging
NAO	National Audit Office
NATS	National Air Traffic System
NCVO	National Council for Voluntary Organisations
NDC	New Deal for Communities
NGfL	National Grid for Learning
NHS	National Health Service
NRF	Neighbourhood Renewal Fund
OGC	Office for Government Commerce
OJEC	Official Journal of the European Communities
PAF	Public Audit Forum
PCG	Primary Care Group
PCT	Primary Care Trust
PFI	Private Finance Initiative
PLC	Public Limited Company
PPP	Public Private Partnership
PRG	Project Review Group
PSA	Public Service Agreements
PSC	Public Sector Comparator
PSNB	Public Sector Net Borrowing
PSRE	Public Sector Research Establishment
PUK	Partnerships UK
QBD	Queen's Bench Division
RAMIS	Resource Accounting and Management Information Service
RAB	Resource Accounting and Budgeting
RDAs	Regional Development Agencies
RSL	Registered Social Landlords
SBS	Small Business Services
SEN	Special Educational Needs
SEU	Social Exclusion Unit
SOLACE	Society of Local Authority Chief Executives
SPV	Special Purpose Vehicle
SRB	Single Regeneration Budget
TEC	Training and Enterprise Council
TfL	Transport for London
TUPE	Transfer of Undertakings (Protection of Employment)
VA	Voluntary Aided
4Ps	Public Private Partnership Programme

Glossary

Accountability: The ability of the public (state and citizens) to hold to account those exercising public authority over standards and the use of public funds in delivery of services.

Best Value (BV): The duty conferred on local authorities in the Local Government Act 1999 to secure 'continuous improvement' in the way that they exercise their functions, having due regard to a combination of economy, efficiency and effectiveness.

Commissioning: The complete process performed by a public agency to decide and implement a strategy for the delivery of services; encompassing the specification of outcomes or outputs, the procurement of services and ongoing monitoring and management.

Community: A subset of the 'general public' – a heterogeneous group of people – bound together by geographical proximity and/or convergent interests. It is a generic term for local *stakeholders*, usually those living in an area smaller than a local authority.

Community Trust: A distinct legal entity, established to unify the management of community assets that are usually held by a range of public authorities and to act as a single, expert body – *commissioning* services on behalf of a community.

Compulsory Competitive Tendering (CCT): The legal requirement on local authorities – introduced incrementally in the UK from 1980 and abolished in 1999 – to engage in competitive tendering (a type of market testing) in accordance with statutory procedures before carrying out certain defined activities in-house.

Contestability: The process through which service providers enhance their quality and efficiency as a result of pressure from potential alternative providers in any sector.

Contracting out: An 'outsourcing' arrangement whereby a public agency enters into a contract with an external supplier, for the provision of goods and/or services.

Conventionally financed: A conventionally financed public contract is one in which a public agency secures the finance directly and pays the contractor as works are progressed.

Core activities: Those operational elements of an organisation, that involve making key decisions (setting service strategy) and/or the delivery of services, integral to the overall performance of the organisation.

Design, Build Finance (DBF): A form of *PFI* that involves the procurement of an asset using private finance, without private sector operation of the associated services.

Design, Build, Finance and Operate (DBFO): The dominant form of the Private Finance Initiative (PFI) in which the service provider is responsible for the design, construction, financing and 'operation' of an asset. Operation refers to the provision of some or all of the services related to the asset's use.

Design, Build, Guarantee, Operate (DBGO): A *PPP* model in which a financial institution guarantees the completion of the project on time and to budget. The private providers of the project retain the design, construction and deliver some or all of the operational elements.

Design, Build, Operate (DBO): A form of PPP, in which the public sector provides finance for a capital investment project but the providers of the project retain the design, construction and deliver some or all of the operational elements.

Diagnostic and Treatment Centres: New healthcare facilities aimed at providing same-day testing and diagnosis, and performing dedicated elective surgery, in order to reduce NHS waiting times.

Governance: The structure of management and decision making within an organisation.

Joint Venture (JV): A distinct legal form of PPP arrangement involving public and private bodies assuming some form of equity stake in a PPP.

Joined-up: The transcending of departmental and/or relevant service boundaries in order to get more effective provision to meet user requirements.

Level playing field: Occurs when no one method of service provision or type of service provider has an inherent (dis)advantage over others as a result of barriers which impede objective selection between potential providers.

Market testing: Competition for the purpose of comparing the viability (in terms of cost and/or quality) of in-house work with that of alternative external contractors.

Not-for-profit-bodies: The collective term for organisations whose operations do not generate profit for their owners; including trusts, industrial and provident societies, and voluntary bodies.

Outcomes: The consequences of service delivery in terms of its contribution to broad policy goals, without stipulation of how such results are to be realised. This normally involves private sector provision of *DBFO*.

Outputs: The delivery of a component of a service, tightly defined and/or tangible so as to allow for target setting and accurate monitoring.

Private Finance Initiative (PFI): Arrangement whereby a consortium of private sector partners come together to provide an asset-based public service under contract to a public body.

Privatisation: The full transfer of assets from government to the private sector.

Procurement: The component of the *commissioning* process that deals specifically with purchasing a service from a provider. This occurs once decisions have been taken over what outcomes or outputs are to be secured and involves the negotiation of contracts.

Public enterprise: A revenue generating enterprise that is at least in part publicly owned, controlled and operated.

Public Private Partnership (PPP): A risk-sharing relationship based upon a shared aspiration between the public sector and one or more partners from the private and/or voluntary sectors to deliver a publicly agreed *outcome* and/or public service.

Public sector: Refers to public agencies and enterprises, that are state financed, owned and controlled.

Public Sector Comparator (PSC): A benchmark to assess the *value-for-money* of *conventionally financed* procurement in comparison with a privately financed scheme for delivering a *publicly funded* service.

Publicly funded: Publicly funded services, via any service provider, are paid for by the state rather than through revenues from user charges.

Purchaser-provider split: The separation of the organisation responsible for delivering a service from that responsible for determining what type of service should be provided.

Risk allocation: The allocation of the responsibility to bear the financial consequences of failure to deliver the agreed project specifications, ideally devolved to the party best able to 'manage' that risk.

Service providers: Companies or organisations providing services.

Special Purpose Vehicle (SPV): An organisation that can be established as a distinct legal entity to bring together the companies involved in a *PPP* in order to manage the project and share the risks and rewards.

Stakeholder: Individuals or groups on whom decisions taken (outside their full control) will have a direct impact.

Strategic partnership: A cross-sectoral partnership that can influence policy or set priorities for a geographical area. 'Executive' strategic partnerships determine priorities and/or are at liberty to allocate public funds. 'Advisory' strategic partnerships influence public agencies who remain the accountable bodies.

Transfer of Undertakings and Protection of Employment (TUPE): Regulations introduced in 1981 with the aim of safeguarding the rights of employees on their transfer to another employer, for example when their work is 'contracted out' to an external service provider.

Value-for-money (VFM): The optimum combination of whole life costs and quality in order to meet users' requirements

Voluntary sector: An umbrella term adopted for the wider non-profit 'third' sector including co-operatives, mutuals, charities and social enterprises.

References

6 P and Kendall J (1997) 'Introduction' in 6 P and Kendall J (eds) *The Contract Culture in Public Services* Ashgate: Vermont, US

Ainger B (2000) 'Neighbourhood PPPs: Using the community's assets better' in *New Economy* 7.3 September 2000, IPPR

Ambrose P (2000) *A drop in the ocean: The health gain from the Central Stepney SRB in the context of national health inequalities* Health and Social Policy Research Centre, University of Brighton

Andrews C (2000) *Contracted and publicly-managed prisons: cost and staffing comparisons 1997–98* London: HM Prison Service

Aronson M (1997) 'A Public Lawyer's Response to Privatisation and Outsourcing' in Taggart M (ed) *The Province of Administrative Law* Oxford: Hart Publishing

Arthur Andersen and Enterprise LSE (2000) *Value for Money Drivers in the Private Finance Initiative: A Report commissioned by Arthur Anderson and Enterprise LSE* London: HM Treasury Taskforce

Audit Commission (2001) *Nothing ventured, nothing gained: the management of procurement under the private finance initiative* London: Audit Commission

Audit Commission (2000) *Money Matters: School funding and resource management* London: Audit Commission www.audit-commission.gov.uk/ac2/NR/LocalA/brmonmat.htm

Audit Commission (1999a) *A Life's Work: Local Authorities, Economic Development and Economic Regeneration* London: Audit Commission

Audit Commission (1999b) *Listen Up! Effective Community Consultation* London: Audit Commission www.audit-commission.gov.uk/ac2/NR/LocalA/mpeffect.pdf

Audit Commission (1997a) *The Coming of Age: Improving Care Services for Older People* London: Audit Commission

Audit Commission (1997b) *Capital Gains: Improving the Local Government Capital Expenditure System* London: Audit Commission

Audit Commission (1997a) *Take your Choice* London: Audit Commission

Audit Commission and Office for Standards in Education (OFSTED) (2001) *LEA Support for School Improvement* London: The Stationary Office

Auditor General Western Australia (1997) *Performance Examination. Private Care for Public Patients – The Joondalup Health Campus Report* No 9, November 1997

Australian Industry Commission (1996) *Competitive Tendering and Contracting by Public Sector Companies* Canberra: AIC

Bartlett W and Le Grand J (1994) *Costs and trusts* Bristol: School for Advanced Urban Studies, University of Bristol

Barr N (1993) *The economics of the welfare state* Oxford: Oxford University Press

Bartlett W, Roberts J and Le Grand J (eds) (1998) *A Revolution in Social Policy: lessons from developments of quasi-markets in the 1990s* Bristol: Policy Press

Billis D and Glennester H (1998) 'Human Services and the Voluntary Sector: Towards a Theory of Comparative Advantage' *Journal of Social Policy* 27.1

Bishop M, Kay J and Mayer C (eds) (1995) *The Regulatory Challenge* Oxford: Oxford University Press

Bogdanor V (2001) *The Doctrine of Ministerial Accountability* IPPR www.ippr.org

Bowen D and Charlton E (2000) 'The magic of online trading' in *Financial Times – Understanding e-procurement* Winter 2000 www.ft.com/eprocurement/

Boyle S and Harrison A (2000) 'PFI and Health: The story so far' in Kelly G and Robinson P (eds) *A Healthy Partnership: The future of public private partnerships in the health service* London: IPPR

Boyle S and Harrison T (2001) 'PFI in perspective' *Public Finance* 9-15 March 2001

Boyne G (1998) 'Competitive tendering in local government: a review of theory and evidence' *Public Administration* 76, Winter 1998

Broadbent J, Haslam C and Laughlin R (2000) 'The origins and operation of the Private Finance Initiative' in Robinson P *et al The Private Finance Initiative: Saviour, Villain or Irrelevance?* London: IPPR

Brooks R (2000) *Including the Affluent* mimeo London: IPPR

Brown G (2001) *Civic Society in Modern Britain* Speech to National Council for Voluntary Organisations Annual Conference, July 2001

Brunyate (1989) R v Governors of Haberdashers' Aske's Hatcham College Trust, *ex parte* Brunyate and Hunt, 7 March 1989 *The Times*

Burchardt T (1997) *Boundaries between Public and Private Welfare: A Typology and Map of Services* London: Centre for Analysis of Social Exclusion

Burchardt T and Hills J (1996) *Private Welfare Insurance and Social Security: pushing the Boundaries* York: Joseph Rowntree Trust

Cabinet Office (1997) *Better Quality Services: A Handbook for Senior Managers* London: Cabinet Office www.cabinetoffice.gov.uk/servicefirst/index/publications

Cabinet Office (1999) *White Paper: Modernising Government* London: The Stationery Office

Cabinet Office (2000) *Staff Transfers in the Public Sector – Statement of Practice* London: The Stationery Office www.cabinet-office.gov.uk/civilservice/2000/tupe

Cambridge Education Associates *Support Services for Schools August 1999* (unpublished)

CBI/NLGN (2000) Evidence to the DETR/LGA sponsored Review of Local Government Commissioning and Procurement submitted to the Local Government Procurement Taskforce in December 2000 (unpublished)

Centre for Public Services (CPS) (2000) *The Contract Capital of the North? The future of council services in Middlesbrough A briefing report for Middlesbrough UNISON* www.unison.org.uk/resources/ or www.centre.public.org.uk/briefings/

Charlesworth J, Clarke J and Cochrane A (1996) 'Tangled Webs? Managing Local Mixed Economies of Care' *Public Administration* 74, Spring 1996

CIPFA (2000) *Personal Social Services Statistics 1998-99 Actuals* London: CIPFA

CIPFA (1999a) *Probation Service Statistics 1999-2000 Estimates and 97-98 Actuals* London: CIPFA

CIPFA (1999b) *Police Statistics 1998-99 Actuals* London: CIPFA

CIPFA (1999c) *Commissioning Local Authority Work and Services: Code of Practice* London: CIPFA

CIPFA (1999d) *Education Statistics 1998-99 Estimates* London: CIPFA

Commission on Public Private Partnerships (2000) *Summary of responses to Call for Evidence, Consultation on Public Private Partnerships* London: IPPR

Commonwealth Department of Finance (1995) *Examining Contestability in the APS* Discussion Paper 3

Continuing Care Conference (2000) *Local Authority Contracting Policies for Residential and Nursing Home Care* A report of independent research prepared for the Consumer Issues Group of the Continuing Care Conference

Corben P (1997) *Port Macquarie Base Hospital – Peer Review Network Draft Report 1995-96*

Corry D, Le Grand J and Radcliffe R (1997) *Public/Private Partnerships: a marriage of convenience or a permanent commitment* London: IPPR

Datafin (1987) R v Panel on Takeovers and Mergers, *ex parte* Datafin plc, QBD 815

Davies H (1992) *Fighting Leviathan: Building social markets that work* London: Social Market Foundation

De Smith S, Woolf L and Jowell J (1995) *Judicial review of administrative action* London: Sweet and Maxwell

Deakin S and Michie J (eds) (1997) *Contracts, Co-operation, and Competition: studies in economics, management, and law* Oxford: Oxford University Press

Department for Education and Employment (2001) *Schools: Building On Success* London: Department for Education and Employment

Department for Education and Employment (2000a) *Departmental Report 1999-2000* London: The Stationery Office

Department for Education and Employment (2000b) *The role of the Local Education Authority in school education* London: Department for Education and Employment

Department for Education and Employment (2000c) *City Academies – schools to make a difference: A prospectus for sponsors and other partners* London: Department for Education and Employment

Department of the Environment, Transport and the Regions (2001a) *Best Value and Procurement – Handling of workforce matters in contracting: A consultation paper on draft guidance* London: Department of the Environment, Transport and the Regions www.local-regions.detr.gov.uk/consult/bv/proc/index.htm

Department of the Environment, Transport and the Regions (2001b) *Working with others to achieve Best Value, Section 16 of the Local Government Act 1999, A Consultation Paper* London: Department of the Environment, Transport and the Regions

Department of the Environment, Transport and the Regions (2000a) *Green Paper: Local Government Finance* London: The Stationery Office

Department of the Environment, Transport and the Regions (2000b) *Green Paper: Quality and Choice – a decent home for all* London: Department of the Environment, Transport and the Regions

Department of the Environment, Transport and the Regions (1999a) *Local Government Act 1999: Part 1 Best Value in Circular 10/99* London: Department of the Environment, Transport and the Regions www.press.detr.gov.uk/9912/downloads/1208/bv.pdf

Department of the Environment, Transport and the Regions (1999b) *New Deal for Communities – Learning Lessons: Pathfinders Experiences of Phase 1* London: Department of the Environment, Transport and the Regions www.regeneration.detr.gov.uk/ndc/phase1path

Department of the Environment, Transport and the Regions (1998a) *Modern Local Government: Guidance on Enhancing Public Participation, A Summary* London: Department of the Environment, Transport and the Regions

Department of the Environment, Transport and the Regions (1998b) *White Paper: Modern Local Government: In touch with the people* London: The Stationery Office

Department of the Environment (1977) *Policy for the Inner Cities* London: HMSO

Department of Health (2001a) *The NHS Plan: Investment and reform for NHS hospitals* London: Department of Health

Department of Health (2001b) *Intermediate Care HSC 20001/001/LAC (2001)1* London: Department of Health

Department of Health (2000a) *Health and Personal Social Services Statistics for England and Wales 1999* London: Department of Health

Department of Health (2000b) *Personal Social Services Current Expenditure: 1998-99* London: Department of Health

Department of Health (2000c) *Community Care Statistics 1999 Private Nursing Homes, Hospitals and Clinics* London: Department of Health

Department of Health (2000d) *For the Benefit of Patients: A Concordat with the Private and Voluntary Health Care Provider Sector* London: Department of Health

Department of Health (2000e) *The NHS Plan: A plan for investment, a plan for reform* London: The Stationery Office

Development Trust Association (2000) www.dta.org.uk

Donnison D (1984) 'The progressive potential of privatisation' in Le Grand J and Robinson P (eds) *Privatisation and the Welfare State* London: George Allen and Unwin

Edwards L (2001) *Why having a vote is not enough* New Democratic Spaces mimeo London: IPPR

Employment Select Committee (1999) *The Performance and Future Role of the Employment Service Seventh Report, Education and Employment Select Committee Vols I and II* London: The Stationery Office

Employment Select Committee (1998) *The New Deal, The New Deal Pathfinders* Eighth Report, Eighth Report, House of Commons London: The Stationery Office

Escott K and Whitfield D (1995) *The gender impact of CCT in local government* London: Equal Opportunities Commission

European Commission (1996) *Communication Services of General Interest in Europe* Brussels: European Commission

European Ombudsman (1997) *Annual Report 1997* Case 630/6.6.96/CJ/UK/IJH

Fabian Society (2000) *The Final Report of the Fabian Society's Commission on Taxation and Citizenship: Paying for Progress – A New Politics of Tax for Public Spending* London: Fabian Society

Finn D (2001) 'The Employment Service and PPPs' in Joseph E and Robinson P (eds) *Right up your street: Partnerships for local policy making and delivery* London: IPPR

Foley M (2001) 'The Changing Public-Private Balance' in Bloom A (ed) *Health Reform in Australia and New Zealand* Australia: Oxford University Press

Foster v British Gas (1990) 2 *Common Market Law Review* 833

Forder J, Hardy B, Knapp M R J, Wistow G and Kendall J (1996) *Broad Mixed Economy Mapping III* Report to the Department of Health

Freedland M (1998) 'Law, Public Services and Citizenship – new Domains, new regions?' in Freedland M and Sciarra S (eds) (1998) *Public Services and Citizenship in European Law: public and labour law perspectives* Oxford: Clarendon Press

Gaffney D, Shaoul J, and Pollock A (2000) *Funding London Underground: financial myths and economic realities* London: Listen to London 2000

Gaffney D, Pollock A, Price D and Shaoul J (1999) 'NHS Capital Expenditure and the Private Finance Initiative – expansion or contraction?' *British Medical Journal* 319 July 1999 pp48-57

Gamble A (2000) *Politics and Fate* Cambridge: Polity Press

General's Office: Government of Australia www.audit.vic.gov.au/sfo97/sfo9708

Gershon P (1999) *Review of Civil Procurement in Central Government* London: HM Treasury www.hm-treasury.gov.uk/docs/1999/pgfinalr.html

Glaister S, Scanlon R and Travers T (2000) *Getting partnership going: PPPs in transport* London: IPPR

Goldsmith (2001) R v Servite Houses and Wandsworth LBC, *ex parte* Goldsmith ACD 1-157

Goodin R (2000) 'Crumbling Pillars: Social Security Futures' *Political Quarterly* April-June 71/2

Grayling T (2001) *Should Railtrack be Publicly Owned?* Paper presented to Rail Renaissance Conference 21 February (mimeo)

Green D (2000) *Stakeholder Health Insurance* London: Institute for the Study of Civil Society

Greve C (2000) *Public-Private Partnerships as Alternatives to Contracting-Out? The Scandinavian Experience* Paper presented at the 61st Annual Conference of the American Society for Public Administration, USA www.polsci.ku.dk

Grout P A (1997) 'The Economics of the Private Finance Initiative' *Oxford Review of Economic Policy* 13.4

Hallgarten J and Watling R (2001) 'Zones of Contention' in Lissauer R and Robinson P (eds) *A Learning Process: PPPs in Education* London: IPPR

Ham C, Smith, J and Temple J (1998) *Hubs, Spokes & Policy Cycles, Paper for the King's Fund London Commission* London: King's Fund

Ham C (1996) 'Contestability: a middle path for health care' *British Medical Journal* 312:70-1

Hansmann H (1996) *The Ownership of Enterprise* Cambridge, Massachusetts and London: The Belknap Press of Harvard University

Harden I (1992) *The Contracting State* Buckingham: Open University Press

Harding A (1998) 'Public-Private Partnerships in the UK' in Pierre J (ed) *Partnerships in Urban Governance* Basingstoke: Macmillan Press

Harris Research Centre (1995) Poll cited in *The Independent* 12 June.

Hart O, Shleifer A and Vishny R W (1997) 'The Proper Scope of Government: theory and an Application to Prisons' *Quarterly Journal of Economics* 112

Hawksworth J (2000a) 'Implications of the public sector financial control framework for PPPs' Robinson *et al* (2000) *The Private Finance Initiative: Saviour, Villain or Irrelevance?* London: IPPR

Hawksworth J (2000b) 'Labour and Public Enterprise' *New Economy* 7.3

Hawksworth J and Holtham G (1998) 'A future for Public Enterprise' in Holtham G (ed) *Freedom with Responsibility* London: IPPR

Health Estates Facilities Management Association (2000) *Survey investigating estates and service strategies of English NHS Trusts* (unpublished)

Heffer S (2001)'We want less Public Services, Not More!' *Daily Mail* 10 January

Helm D (ed) (1989) *The Economic Borders of the State* Oxford: Clarendon Press

Highways Agency (2000) *A1 Darrington to Dishforth DBFO Project, Prequalification Document* London: Department for Environment, Transport and the Regions

Hilditch S (2001) 'Housing Investment in PPPs' in Joseph E and Robinson R (eds) *Right up your Street: partnerships for local policymaking and diversity* London: IPPR

Hirst P Q (1994) *Associative Democracy: New forms of Economic and Social Governance* Cambridge: Polity Press

HM Treasury (2001) *Holding to Account: The Review of Audit and Accountability for Central Government* (Report by Lord Sharman of Redlynch) London: HM Treasury www.treasury.gov.uk/pdf/2001/sharman_1302.pdf

HM Treasury (2000) *Public Private Partnerships* London: The Stationery Office

HM Treasury (1999a) *Colfox School, Dorset: A case study on the First DBFO School Project* London: Treasury Taskforce

HM Treasury (1999b) *Staff Transfers from Central Government: A Fair Deal for Staff Pensions* Annex to Cabinet Office (2000) *Staff Transfers in the Public Sector – Statement of Practice* London: The Stationery Office

HM Treasury (1999c) *Thresholds for the EC Procurement Directives, January 2000 to December 2001* www.hm-treasury.gov.uk/pub/html/docs/cup/ecpro/main.html

HM Treasury (1998) *Stability and Investment for the Long Term: Economic and Fiscal Strategy Report 1998* Cm 3978 London: The Stationery Office

HMSO (2000a) *Health and Social Care Bill* London: The Stationery Office

HMSO (2000b) *Local Government Act 2000* London: The Stationery Office

HMSO (2000c) *Freedom of Information Act 2000* London: The Stationery Office

HMSO (1999) *Local Government Act 1999* London: The Stationery Office

HMSO (1994) *De-regulation and Contracting-out Act 1994* London: The Stationery Office

HMSO (1970) *Local Authority (Goods and Services) Act 1970* London: The Stationery Office

Holland S (1975) *The Socialist Challenge* London: Quartet Books

Holtham G (ed) (1998) *Freedom with Responsibility* London: IPPR

Home Office (2000) *Departmental Report 1999-2000* London : Home Office

Houlder V (2000) 'Trading towards a common market' in *Financial Times – Understanding e-procurement* Winter 2000 www.ft.com/eprocurement/

House of Commons (2000) *Education and Employment Select Committee: Seventh Report: The Role of Private Sector Organisations in Public Education* London: The Stationary Office www.parliament.the-stationery-office.co.uk/pa/cm199900/cmselect/cmeduemp/118/11802.htm

Hunt M (1997) 'Constitutionalism and the Contractualisation of Government' in Taggart M (ed) *The Province of Administrative Law* Hart Publishing

Hutton W (2000) 'How we can get back on track' *The Observer* 22 November

ICM/Guardian (2001) poll cited in 'Better pay and due respect' by Travers T in *The Guardian* 20 March, 2001

Improvement and Development Agency/4Ps (2000) Joint evidence to the DETR/LGA sponsored Review of Local Government Commissioning and Procurement, December 2000

Improvement and Development Agency (IDeA) (2000) *So far so good...progress on delivering Best Value* IDeA www.idea.gov.uk/bestvalue

Improvement and Development Agency (IDeA) (2000a) *Procurement: Code of Practice* IDeA

Institute of Professionals, Managers and Specialists (2000) *Evidence to IPPR Call for Evidence*

Islington Education Commission (2000) *One Hundred Percent of Our Future – A Framework for Transforming Education in Islington* Statement to the Policy Committee

Kelly J and Whittlestone P (2000) 'Innovation for the Future of PFI' in Kelly G and Robinson P (eds) *A Healthy Partnership: The future of public private partnerships in the health service* London: IPPR

Kendall J (2001) 'Of knights, knaves and merchants: the case of residential care for older people in England in the late 1990s' *Social Policy and Administration* (forthcoming)

Kendall J, Matosevic I, Forder J, Knapp M, Hardy B and Ware P (2001) *The Motivations of Domiciliary Care Providers in England: New concepts, new findings* mimeo

Kettl D (1993) *Sharing Power: public governance and private markets* Washington DC: The Brookings Institution

King's Fund (2000) *Rehabilitation and intermediate care for older people* October Briefing Paper

Knapp M, Forder J, Kendall J and Pickard L (2001) 'The growth of independent sector provision in the UK' in Harper S (ed) *The Family in an Ageing Society* Oxford: Oxford University Press.

Laing and Buisson (2000a) *Laings Review of Private Healthcare* London: Laing and Buisson

Laing and Buisson (2000b) *Domiciliary Care Markets 2000* London: Laing and Buisson

Laing and Buisson (1999/2000) *Laing's Review of Private Healthcare* London: Laing and Buisson

Laing and Buisson (1999a) *Care of Elderly People Market Survey 1999* London: Laing and Buisson

Laing and Buisson (1999b) *Domiciliary Care Markets 1999* London: Laing and Buisson

Le Grand J (1998) 'Knights, Knaves and Pawns? Human Behaviour and Social Policy' *Journal of Social Policy* 26.2

Le Grand J (1982) *The Strategy of Equality: Redistribution and the Social Services* London: Allen and Unwin

Le Grand J and Bartlett W (eds) (1993) *Quasi-markets and Social Policy* Basingstoke: Macmillan Press

Le Grand J, Mays N and Mulligan J (eds) (1998) *Learning from the NHS Internal Market: A Review of the Evidence* London: King's Fund

Leeds City Council (2000) *Prospectus for a partner to enter into a Joint Venture Company to deliver education support and administrative services* Leeds City Council

Local Government Association (2000) *A model of local strategic partnerships: New Commitment to Regeneration* London: Local Government Association

Local Government Association (1999) *Take Your Partners: Report of the LGA Urban Commission Hearings into Partnership Working* London: Local Government Association www.lga.gov.uk/lga/capital/blg/partners.pdf

Local Government Management Board (1995) *CCT Information Service* London: Local Government Management Board

London Borough of Hackney (1999) *Woodberry Down Estates: Proposal for cross departmental asset management and service delivery* London: London Borough of Hackney

Lowndes V (2001) 'Local Partnerships and Participation' IPPR www.ippr.org.uk

Lowndes V *et al* (1998) *Enhancing Public Participation in Local Government: A Research Report* London: Department for Environment, Transport and the Regions

Mackintosh M (2000) 'Flexible Contracting? Economic Cultures and Implicit Contracts in Social Care' in *Journal of Social Policy* 29.1

Marquand D (2000) 'The New Statesman Essay: the Fall of Civic Culture' *The New Statesman* 13 November

Marshall T H (1950) *Citizenship and Social Class and other essays* Cambridge University Press

Martin J (1997) *Changing Accountability Relations: Politics, Consumers and the Market* Public Management Service, OECD

Martin S (2000) 'Implementing Best Value: Local Public Services in Transition' in *Public Administration* Vol 78 No 1

Matosevic T *et al* (forthcoming) *Independent Sector Domiciliary Care providers in 1999* mimeo

McGauran A (2001) 'Nothing is ruled out as PFI-style fast-track units are pondered' *The Health Service Journal* 1 March, 2001

Milburn A (1999) Speech at the IPPR Launch of the Commission on Public Private Partnerships 20 September, 1999

Moore J D (1996) 'Outsourcing firms ride changing tides' *Modern Healthcare* 26(36)

MORI (2000) *Attitudes Towards Public/Private Partnerships* Research Study Conducted for the General Healthcare Group (unpublished)

Mulgan G (1994) 'Democratic Dismissal: Competition and Contestability among the Quangos' in *Oxford Review of Economic Policy* 10.3

National Audit Office (2001a) *The Channel Tunnel Rail Link* HC 302 Session 2000/01 London: The Stationery Office

National Audit Office (2001b) *Education Action Zones: Meeting the Challenge – The Lessons Identified From Auditing the First 25 Zones* HC 130 Session 2000/01 London: The Stationery Office

National Audit Office (2000a) *The Cancellation of the Benefits Payment Card Project* HC 857 Session 1999-2000 London: The Stationery Office

National Audit Office (2000b) *The Financial Analysis for the London Underground Public Private Partnerships* HC 54 Session 2000-01 London: The Stationery Office

National Audit Office (2000c) *The Prison Service: the Refinancing of the Fazakerley PFI prison contract* HC 584 Session 1999-2000 London: The Stationery Office

National Audit Office (2000d) *Public-Private Partnership with Siemens Business Services* HC 493 Session 1999-2000: The Stationery Office

National Audit Office (1999a) *Dartford and Gravesham Hospital* HC 423 Session 1998-1999 London: The Stationery Office

National Audit Office (1999b) *The PFI Contract for the new Dartford and Gravesham Hospital* HC 423 Session 1998-99 London: The Stationery Office

National Audit Office (1999c) *Examining the Value for Money of Deals Under the Private Finance Initiative* HC 739 Session 998/99 London: The Stationery Office

National Audit Office (1989) *Hospital Building in England* HC 530 Session 1988-89 London: The Stationery Office

National Statistics (2001) *Social Trends* 31, UK edition 2001 London: The Stationery Office

Newdick C (2000) 'The NHS in Private Hands? Regulating Private Providers of NHS Services' *Law and Medicine: current legal issues* 3

Newman C (2001) 'Tube plans mocked as "woolly", Transport Kiley claims talks on the future of the underground have made little progress' in *Financial Times* 30 January

NHS Executive (1997) *NHS Priorities and Planning Guidance* EL (97) 39 Leeds: Department of Health

NHS Executive (2000) *Common Information Core in Department of Health Departmental Report 1999-2000* London: Department of Health

Nicholson C (2000) 'The PFI in Health' *New Economy* 7.3

Office for Standards in Education (OFSTED) (2001a) *Inspection of Islington Local Education Authority* London: Office for Standards in Education www.ofsted.gov.uk

Office for Standards in Education (OFSTED) (2001) *Education Action Zones: Commentary on the first six zone inspections* London: Office for Standards in Education

Office of Government Commerce (2000) *Delivering a Step Change: OGC's strategy to improve Government's Commercial Performance* London: Office of Government Commerce

Office of Government Commerce (2001) *Gateway Review: Executive Summary* www.ogc.gov.uk London: Office for Government Commerce

Office of Health Economics (1999) *Compendium of Health Statistics* London: Office of Health Economics

Office of National Statistics (1999) *Annual Abstract of Statistics 1999* London: The Stationery Office

Oliver D (2000) 'The Human Rights Act and the Frontiers of the State' in *Public Law* Autumn 2000

Osmon D (2000) 'The Future of the Tube' *New Economy* 7.1

Ouchi W (1980) 'Markets, bureaucracies, and clans' *Administrative Science Quarterly* 25

Palmer K (2000) *Contract issues in PPP/PFI* mimeo London: IPPR

Peck E and Bowers H (2000) 'Concordats in Intermediate Care' *Quality in Ageing* (forthcoming)

Performance and Innovation Unit (PIU) (2000) *Reaching Out: The Role of Central Government at Regional and Local Level* London: The Stationery Office

Pike A (2000) 'The private sector and PPPs' in Joseph E and Kelly G (eds) *Finding the Right Partner: diversity in public private partnerships* London: IPPR

Prescott J (2000) Speech by John Prescott MP to the IPPR Conference 'The New Partnership Agenda' 5 April 2000.

Preston J (2001) 'Bus service regulation and competition: international comparisons' in Grayling T (ed) *Any More Fares? Delivering better bus services* London: IPPR

Price D, Gaffney D and Pollock A (1999) *The Only Game in Town? A Report on the Cumberland Infirmary Carlisle PFI* UNISON Northern Region

PricewaterhouseCoopers (2000) *Building Performance: An empirical assessment of the relationship between schools capital investment and pupil performance* Research Report RR242 London: The Department for Education and Employment

Prison Service (2000) *Annual Report and Accounts 1999-2000* London: The Stationery Office

Prison Service News (2001) *Prison Service to run Manchester and Blakenhurst* 12 January www.hmprisonservice.gov.uk

Procurement Policy Unit (1998) *Procurement Policy Guidelines* www.ogc.gov.uk

Public Audit Forum (1999) *Implications for audit of the modernising government agenda* Public Audit Forum

Public Private Partnerships Programme (4ps) (2000) *Standardisation of Local Authority PFI Contracts, Draft Guidance for Consultation, in conjunction with the Treasury Task Force and Department for Environment, Transport and the Regions* www.4ps.co.uk

Radcliffe R (1998) 'Public vs Private Enterprise: Is there a third way?' in Holtham G (ed) *Freedom with Responsibility* London: IPPR

Rao N and Young K (1999) 'Revitalising Local Democracy' in National Centre for Social Research, British Social Attitudes *Who shares New Labour Values?* 16th Report 2000-01 edition Ashgate: Aldershot

Robinson P (2000) 'PFI and the Public Finances' in Robinson *et al* (2000) *The Private Finance Initiative: Saviour, Villain or Irrelevance?* London: IPPR

Robinson P and Rubin M (1999) *The Future of the Post Office* London: IPPR

Rustin M, Massey D and Hall S (eds) (1997) *The Next Ten Years for Blair's Britain* London: Lawrence and Wishart

Savas E S (2000) *Privatization and Public-Private Partnerships* New York: Chatham House Publishers

Servite (2001) R v Servite Houses and Wandsworth LBC *ex parte* Goldsmith ACD 1-157

Sharman N (2000a) *Managing Partnerships is Key to Modernising Local Government* Submission to IPPR CPPP Call for Evidence, London: IPPR

Smith A (2000) Speech to CPPP conference, 20 September www.ippr.org.uk

Social Exclusion Unit (1998) *Bringing Britain Together: a national strategy for neighbourhood renewal* Cm 4045 London: The Stationery Office

Social Exclusion Unit (2000) *National Strategy for Neighbourhood Renewal: a framework for consultation* London: Cabinet Office

Social Exclusion Unit (SEU) (2001) *A New Commitment to Neighbourhood Renewal: National Strategy Action Plan* London: Cabinet Office

Southwark Council (2000) *Southwark Education Public/Private Partnership Initiative Public Information Pack* London: Southwark Council

Steele J (1999) *Wasted Values: Harnessing the commitment of public managers* London: Public Management Foundation

Stewart J (1993) 'The Limitations of Government by Contract' in *Public Money and Management* 13

Stoker G (2000) *The Modernisers' Guide to Local Government* mimeo

Straw J (2000) Speech by Jack Straw MP to the IPPR on the Human Rights Act, 29 March 2000

Straw J (1998) Speech by Jack Straw MP to the Prison Officer's Association Conference, 19 May 1998

Sussex J (2001) *The Economics of the Private Finance Initiative in the NHS* London: Office of Health Economics

Szymanski S and Williams S (1993) 'Cheap rubbish? Competitive tendering and contracting out in refuse-collection 1981-88' in *Fiscal Studies* Vol 14 No 3 pp109-30

Taylor R (2000) 'Local Government and PPPs' in Joseph E and Kelly G (eds) *Finding the Right Partner: diversity in local public-private partnerships* London: IPPR

Thatcher M (2001) 'Blair hits e-government targets ahead of schedule' in *Public Finance* 19-25 January

The Industrial Society (2000) *The London Underground Public Private Partnership: An Independent Review* London: The Industrial Society

The Observer (2001) *Britain Uncovered* 18 March, 2001

Thompson N (2000) 'Investing in schools: the experience of the Private Finance Initiative in Brent in Lissauer R and Robinson P (eds) *A Learning Process: Public Private Partnerships in Education* London: IPPR

Thompson P (2000) 'Brixton breaks the mould' *Public Finance* 14 July

Timmins N (2000) 'Public spending: The British government is taking a longer view' in *Financial Times – Understanding e-procurement* supplement Winter 2000 www.ft.com/eprocurement/

Toynbee P and Walker D (2001) *Did Things Get Better?* London: Penguin

UNISON (2000) *Contracting out and the two-tier workforce* Report by the Best

Value Intelligence Unit, September 2000 *www.unison.org.uk/resources/index.htm*

Victorian Auditor General (1997) *Report of the Auditor-General on the Government's Annual Financial Statement, 1996-97* Melbourne: Victorian Auditor-General's Office/Government of Victoria

Vining A and Globerman S 'Contracting-out health care services: a conceptual framework' Health Policy 46 (1999)

Walzer M (1983) *Spheres of Justice: a Defense of Pluralism and Equality* New York: Basic Books

Westall A (2000) 'The third sector and PPPs' in Joseph E and Kelly G (eds) *Finding the Right Partner: diversity in public private partnerships* London: IPPR

Westall A (2001) 'The voluntary sector and PPPs' in Joseph E and Kelly G (eds) *Finding the Right Partner: diversity in local public-private partnerships* London: IPPR

Westall A and Foley J (2001) 'Local regeneration partnerships' in Joseph E and Robinson P (eds) *Right up your street: partnerships for local policy making and delivery* London: IPPR

Whitfield D (2001) *Public Services or Corporate Welfare: Rethinking the Nation State in the Global Economy* London: Pluto Press

Willetts D (1987) 'The role of the Prime Minister's Policy Unit' *Public Administration* 65

Williams J *et al* (2000) 'Patients and Procedures in short-stay independent hospitals in England and Wales 1997-1998' *Journal of Health Medicine* 22.1

Williamson O (1975) *Markets and Hierarchies: Analysis and Antitrust Implications* New York: Free Press

Williamson O (1985) *The economic institutions of capitalism: firms, markets, relational contracting* London: Collier Macmillan

World Health Organisation (1996) *Health Care Systems in Transition* Canada (preliminary version) Copenhagen: WHO Regional Office Central Europe

Commission publications

Since its launch in September 1999, the Commission has published a series of papers to highlight particular areas of the debate on PPPs:

Issue papers

The New Partnership Agenda by Gavin Kelly (April 2000) ISBN 1 86030 118 5

The paper considers the rationale underpinning the Commission and highlights the issues that need to be resolved if PPPs are to play a greater role in public services in the future.

Getting Partnership Going: PPPs in transport by Stephen Glaister, Rosemary Scanlon and Tony Travers (April 2000) ISBN I 86030 126 6

The paper analyses the role that PPPs can play in financing transport investment projects and argues that although the PFI is a useful financial tool for certain types of projects, for London Underground, it would not present the most cost-effective option.

A Healthy Partnership: the future of public private partnerships in the health service edited by Gavin Kelly and Peter Robinson (July 2000) ISBN 86030 129 0

This publication provides a close and expert analysis of the use and future potential of the PFI in health. The authors offer a set of innovative policy proposals which set out how the alleged shortcomings of PPPs within the acute and primary sector might be overcome. Contributors are Julian Le Grand, Seán Boyle, Anthony Harrison, John Kelly, Paul Whittlestone, Will Paxton and Rachel Lissauer.

Finding the right partner: diversity in local public private partnerships edited by Ella Joseph and Gavin Kelly (December 2000) ISBN I 86030 136 3

This publication shines a light on the questions of representation and involvement in local partnerships. Three leading commentators set out their vision of how the public, private and voluntary sectors need to adapt if partnerships are to fulfil their potential and how policy-makers can help to make this happen. Contributors are Alan Pike, Andrea Westall, Roger Taylor and Vikki Everett.

A learning process: public private partnerships in education edited by Rachel Lissauer and Peter Robinson (November 2000) ISBN I 86030 130 4

The publication looks at the possible role of the private sector in the management of schools, the evidence to date on the success of Education Action Zones and the experience of the PFI in schools. Contributors are Joe Hallgarten, Neil McIntosh, Noel Thompson, and Rob Watling.

Right up your street: partnerships for local policy making and delivery edited by Ella Joseph and Peter Robinson (March 2001) ISBN 86030 137 I

This publication looks at the potential of PPPs to contribute to local policy objectives. In particular the focus is on priority issues for deprived neighbourhoods:

providing employment services for jobseekers, regeneration and social housing. Contributors are Andrea Westall, Julie Foley, Steve Hilditch, Dan Finn and Keith Faulkner.

Working Papers

The Private Finance Initiative: Saviour, Villain or Irrelevance? By Peter Robinson, John Hawksworth, Jane Broadbent, Richard Laughlin and Colin Haslam (March 2000)

This is a collection of three papers on the PFI. All accept that PFI schemes have the potential to deliver value-for-money in certain circumstances, but argue that the public sector financial framework should provide a level playing field within which to make these judgements on a case by case basis.

Call for Evidence Consultation Paper on Public Private Partnerships (June 2000)

This consultation paper was received by over 600 organisations, in the private, public and voluntary sectors as part of the Commission's work to collate the views of a range of different stakeholders involved in the delivery of public services.

Summary of Responses to the Call for Evidence (November 2000)

This summarises the written submissions sent to the Commission, in response to the Call for Evidence Consultation paper sent out in June 2000.

Other publications

New Economy 7.3 (September 2000) (Blackwells publishers)

Featuring a contribution by the Chief Secretary to the Treasury, Andrew Smith MP, this volume of the IPPR's flagship journal is devoted to PPPs, focusing on a number of areas, including education, prisons and health.

Issue papers are available for **£7.50** from **Central Books** (020 8986 5488). Working papers can be obtained from the IPPR free of charge, or downloaded from the IPPR website (www.ippr.org).

Commission events

The Commission held a series of seminars and conferences to help inform its work. The main speakers at each event are listed below:

PPPs and the Future of the London Underground 13 January 2000 (Seminar)
> Stephen Glaister, Professor of Transport and Infrastructure, Imperial College, London
> Martin Callaghan, Director of PPPs, London Transport

Area-based Partnerships 13 March 2000 (Seminar)
> Barbara Ainger, Chief Executive, The Housing Finance Corporation
> Graham Moody, Graham Moody Associates

The New Partnership Agenda 5 April 2000 (Mini-conference)
> Rt Hon John Prescott MP, Deputy Prime Minister
> Rt Hon Andrew Smith MP, Chief Secretary to the Cabinet
> Kate Barker, Chief Economic Advisor, CBI and IPPR Commissioner
> Gavin Kelly, Secretary to the Commission on Public Private Partnerships

The Private Sector and the Public Service Ethos 20 April 2000 (Seminar)
> Jane Steele, Director of Research, Public Management Foundation
> John Swinney, Managing Director, JSS Pinnacle

Housing Partnerships 9 June 2000 (Seminar)
> Michael Oxley, Professor of Housing, Nottingham Trent University
> John Swinney, Managing Director, JSS Pinnacle

Employee Terms & Conditions 20 July 2000 (Seminar:supported by UNISON)
> Malcom Wing, National Secretary for Local Government, UNISON
> Robert Clarke, Managing Director, Babtie Group Ltd
> Peter Robinson, Senior Economist, IPPR

PPPs in Health 24 July 2000 (Mini-Conference)
> Rt Hon John Denham MP, Minister of State for Health
> Professor Julian Le Grand, Richard Titmuss Professor of Social Policy, LSE and IPPR Commissioner
> Dr Chai Patel, Chief Executive of Westminster Health Care
> Dr Jennifer Dixon, Director of Policy Review, King's Fund

PPPs in the Care of the Elderly 28 July (Seminar)
> Edward Peck, Director, Institute for Applied Health and Social Policy, King's College, London
> Matthew Taylor, Director, IPPR

Business Breakfast, Labour Party Conference 25 Sept 2000

    Shriti Vadera, Council of Economic Advisors, HM Treasury

    Chris Nicholson, Partner, KPMG and CPPP Commissioner

Improving the PFI/PPP process and Assessment of Value for Money (Seminar)

    Chris Waites, Tillinghurst Towers-Perrin

    Adrian Montague, Deputy Chairman, Partnerships UK

PPPs in Education 22 March 2001 (Seminar)

    David Normington, Director General of Schools, Department for Education and Employment

    Peter Robinson, Senior Economist, IPPR

PPPs and local partnerships 28 March 2001 (Seminar)

    Rt Hon Hilary Armstrong MP, Minister of State for Local Government and the Regions

    Nick Sharman, Deputy Chief Executive, London Borough of Islington

Written and oral evidence to the Commission

The Commission is very grateful for those persons and organisations who contributed to our work and informed our thinking. The following responded to the Call for Evidence, submitted written and oral evidence or answered queries:

Addleshaw Booth & Co
Barbara Ainger, The Housing Finance Corporation
Audit Commission
Barclays
Bartlett School of Graduate Studies
Malcolm Bates, Pearl Group and Author of The Bates Report
Ian Blair, Metropolitan Police Service
Vernon Bogdanor, Brasenose College, University of Oxford
Boots the Chemist
Anthony Bramley, HMP Lowdham Grange
Bridgewater Education Action Zone
BT
BUPA
Business Services Association
Patrick Byrne, Lodestone Patient Care
Martin Callaghan, London Transport
Campaign for State Education
Capita
Carillion
Manish Chande, Trillium
CIPFA Competitiveness Joint Committee
Civil Aviation Authority
Committee of Vice-Chancellors and Principals of the Universities of the UK
Community Care Providers Scotland
Community Foundation Network
Confederation of British Industry
Corporation of London
DentonWilde Sapte
Department of Health Studies, De Montfort University
Department of the Environment, Transport and the Regions
Department of Trade and Industry, AEA Technology Environment Unit
Jennifer Dixon, King's Fund
East Midlands Voluntary Sector Forum

EDS
English Partnerships
Environmental Services Association
Ernst & Young Project Finance
Vikki Everett, Newchurch & Company Ltd
Keith Faulkner, Manpower
Federation of Small Businesses
Geoff Filkin, New Local Government Network
Dan Finn, University of Portsmouth
General, Manufacturing and Boilermakers Union
Stephen Glaister, Imperial College, London
Glasgow Council
Glaxo Wellcome
Ian Harden, University of Sheffield
Harris EC
HBG PFI Projects
Judith Healy, European Observatory on Health Care Systems
Steve Hilditch, Paddington Consultancy
Hyder Business Services
Improvement and Development Agency
Initial Public Sector Personnel
Innisfree
Institute of Professionals, Managers and Specialists
Justin Keen, The King's Fund
David Kent, HM Prison Service
Kirklees Local Education Authority
KPMG
Leeds City Council
Libre Consulting
Liverpool City Council
Local Government Association
Local Government Information Unit
London Borough of Hackney
London Borough of Islington
Vivien Lowndes, De Montfort University
Kingsley Manning, Newchurch Consulting
David McDonnell, Director, HMP Wolds
Neil McIntosh, CfBT
Meara Management Consultancy
Millgroup, Norwich Union PPPs

MIND
Graham Moody, Graham Moody Associates
MSF
Herb Naphiet, UK Detention Services
Stephen Nathan, Prison Privatisation Report International
National Council for Voluntary Organisations
National Savings
National Union of Teachers
Nomura, Principal Finance Group
Paul Norbury, HMP Buckley Hall
Nottinghamshire County Council
Office of Government Commerce
Anhil Ohri, Regent's Park Healthcare Limited
Michael Oxley, Nottingham Trent University
Keith Palmer, NM Rothschilds & Sons
Partnerships UK
Chai Patel, Westminster Healthcare
Edward Peck, Institute for Applied Health and Social Policy
PolEcon Europe
Alyson Pollock, University College London
Primary Medical Property
Public and Commercial Services Union
Public Private Partnerships Programme (4Ps)
Quest Diagnostics
Rail and Maritime Union
Sir David Ramsbotham, HM Inspectorate of Prisons
Helen Randall, Nabarro Nathanson
Sue Richards, University of Birmingham
Kevin Rogers, HMP Doncaster
Royal College of Nursing
Royal Pharmaceutical Society
Sector Wide Europe
Serco Institute
Nick Sharman, London Borough of Islington
Simon Randall, Laurence Graham
Society of Chief Personnel Officers
Jane Steele, Public Management Foundation
Baroness Vivien Stern, International Centre for Prison Studies
Gary Sturgess, Serco plc
Swiss Re Life & Health

Taylor Woodrow
Roger Taylor, Newchurch & Company
Trades Union Congress
UNISON
University of Durham
University of Westminster
Chris Waites, Tillinghurst-Towers Perrin
Rob Watling, University of Leicester
Belinda Weir
Tim Wilson, WS Atkins
Xerox UK

Sources of information on Public Private Partnerships

Government Departments

Her Majesty's Treasury: www.hm-treasury.gov.uk

Department of the Environment, Transport and Regions: www.detr.gov.uk

Department of Health: www.doh.gov.uk

Department of Education and Employment: www.dfee.gov.uk

Department of Trade and Industry: www.dti.gov.uk

Home Office: www.homeoffice.gov.uk

Ministry of Defence: www.mod.gov.uk

House of Commons Select Committees

www.parliament.uk/commons/selcom/cmsel.htm

Government agencies

Her Majesty's Prison Service: www.hmprisonservice.gov.uk

Office of Government Commerce: www.ogc.gov.uk

Partnerships UK: www.partnershipsuk.org.uk

Audit bodies

Audit Commission: www.audit-commission.gov.uk

National Audit Office: www.nao.gov.uk

Northern Ireland Audit Office: www.niauditoffice.gov.uk

Public Audit Forum: www.public-audit-forum.gov.uk

Other

Improvement and Development Agency: www.idea.gov.uk

Local Government Association: www.lga.gov.uk

New Local Government Network: www.nlgn.org.uk

PFI Online: www.pfi-online.com

Public Management Foundation: www.pmfoundation.org.uk

Public Private Partnerships Programme (4Ps): www.4Ps.co.uk

The Source Public Management Journal: www.sourcepublishing.co.uk

Trades Union Congress (TUC): www.tuc.org.uk

UNISON: www.unison.gov.uk

The inclusion of any links in this publication does not imply that the IPPR or CPPP recommends or approves material on the linked page or material accessible from it. IPPR or the CPPP do not assume responsibility for information contained on those sites and disclaims all liability in respect of information contained on those sites.

Index